Colorado Rail
Annual No. 17

*Exquisitely restored Fort Collins Muncipal Railway
Birney 21 recreates a familiar scene of fifty years
earlier as it heads down Roosevelt Street in the
summer of 1985. (Al Kilminster photo)*

Colorado Rail Annual

A Journal of Railroad History
in the Rocky Mountain West

No. 17

Colorado Railroad Museum

Colorado Railroad Historical Foundation
P.O. Box 10
Golden, Colorado 80402

The Colorado Railroad Museum was established in 1958 to gather and preserve a tangible historic record of Colorado's fascinating railroad era. The Museum's invaluable collection of records, artifacts and equipment was begun in 1949, and the accumulation of important material is still continuing. The Museum is now operated by the non-profit Colorado Railroad Historical Foundation, Inc., in which your support and participation are cordially invited.

Trustees

Ronald C. Hill, *President*
Alexis McKinney, *Vice President*
Charles Albi
Roy E. Altenbach
Thomas E. Daniels
Michael Davis
Kenton H. Forrest
Cornelius W. Hauck
William C. Jones
Richard H. Kindig
Eldin C. Larsen
Edward Ruetz

Executive Director

Robert W. Richardson

Colorado Rail Annual No. 17

Editors
Charles Albi
William C. Jones

Consulting Editors:
A.D. Mastrogiuseppe
Robert W. Richardson

Published and distributed by
The Colorado Railroad Museum

Post Office Box 10, Golden, Colorado 80402

©Copyright 1987 by Colorado Railroad Museum. No part of this book may be reproduced without prior written authorization of the publisher, other than brief excerpts embodied in critical reviews.

ISBN 0-918654-17-3
Library of Congress Catalog Card No. 70-102682
Printed and Bound in the United States of America by
Johnson Publishing Company, Boulder, Colorado

Table of Contents page photos: The Denver-Kansas City **Rocket** *eastbound from Denver on November 25, 1937 (Otto Perry photo, Denver Public Library Western History Department); D&RGW Nos. 3613 and 1803 climbing Tennessee Pass at Mitchell with second No. 2, a cherry special, on May 21, 1949 (R.H. Kindig photo); Fort Collins Birneys 26, 21 and 23 on October 9, 1944 (George Chope photo, Museum collection).*

EDITORS' PREFACE

The content of previous Colorado Rail Annuals, with a few exceptions, has been concerned with narrow gauge railroading in the Rocky Mountains. In this volume we explore the histories of three subjects which up to now have been neglected, in spite of the extensive literature published in recent years about Colorado railroads. Several noted rail historians have provided us with manuscripts about the western extension of a well-remembered granger road, an account of the Rio Grande's first standard gauge crossing of the Continental Divide and—a first for our series of annuals—coverage of an electric street railway.

Mike Doty and Mel McFarland have written a detailed history of the Chicago Rock Island and Pacific in Colorado, from construction days 100 years ago, through the era of the famous *Rocky Mountain Rocket*, eventual abandonment in 1980 and current operation of successor companies. This narrative proves that Colorado railroading can be fascinating even without mountains.

Over 15 years ago, Bob Le Massena researched the story of the Rio Grande's route over Tennessee Pass, only to file his manuscript away while pursuing other writing projects. He has recently revised and updated his account of the most rugged portion of the Royal Gorge Route. We are most fortunate that several individuals, who are credited in Bob's acknowledgments, spontaneously and generously came forward with photographs and other material from their collections to make it possible for us to present the most complete coverage possible.

Ernie Peyton is the Boswell of the Fort Collins street-car system. His first account of its history was published 30 years ago and has long been out of print. Through the courtesy of Donald Duke, himself a publisher of many fine rail histories, we have been able to revise and expand the story of the famed Birneys on the happy occasion of the resumption of operation of car 21 by the Fort Collins Municipal Railway Society. Al Kilminster, one of the key figures in this project, has written an additional chapter to complete Ernie's original work.

Unlike most of the subjects of our prior annuals, all three lines covered in Annual 17 are, in one form or another, still operating entities.

Finally, although each author has acknowledged those who have assisted him individually, there are several additional people who have been of invaluable help to the editors in the preparation of the complete annual, and we would like to thank them here: Rick Cooley, Mike Danneman, Howard Fogg, Kenton Forrest, Martin Frick, Ed Fulcomer, Ross Grenard, Ronald C. Hill, Richard H. Kindig, John W. "Wally" Maxwell, Jr., James Ozment, Jerry Porter, Edward Ruetz, John Sherman, Jackson Thode, Chuck Weart and Tivis E. Wilkins. We also want to thank Jerry Johnson and Ron Blommel of Johnson Publishing Company who gave their time and attention to make sure that the many details of printing a book such as this one were handled properly.

We hope that you will enjoy reading this annual as much as we have enjoyed producing it.

Charles Albi
William C. Jones

TABLE OF CONTENTS

Maps of the Rock Island and Tennessee Pass in pocket at back of book.

*Shortly after 2 PM on a warm afternoon in the summer of 1941, the Denver section of the **Rocky Mountain Rocket** swings off the Union Pacific track onto its own rails at Limon, Colorado. The Colorado Springs train eases forward behind one of the unique AB6 units, and in a few minutes the two will be combined and speeding eastward to Chicago behind the shiny aluminum-striped red, maroon and silver diesels. (From an original acrylic painting by Mike Danneman, collection of Jerry Porter) Opposite is the large, flashing neon rooftop sign which advertised the **Rocket** in the 1300 block of Broadway in downtown Denver during the 1940s. (John W. Maxwell photo)*

ROCKETING TO THE ROCKIES

by Michael C. Doty
and
E.M. "Mel" McFarland

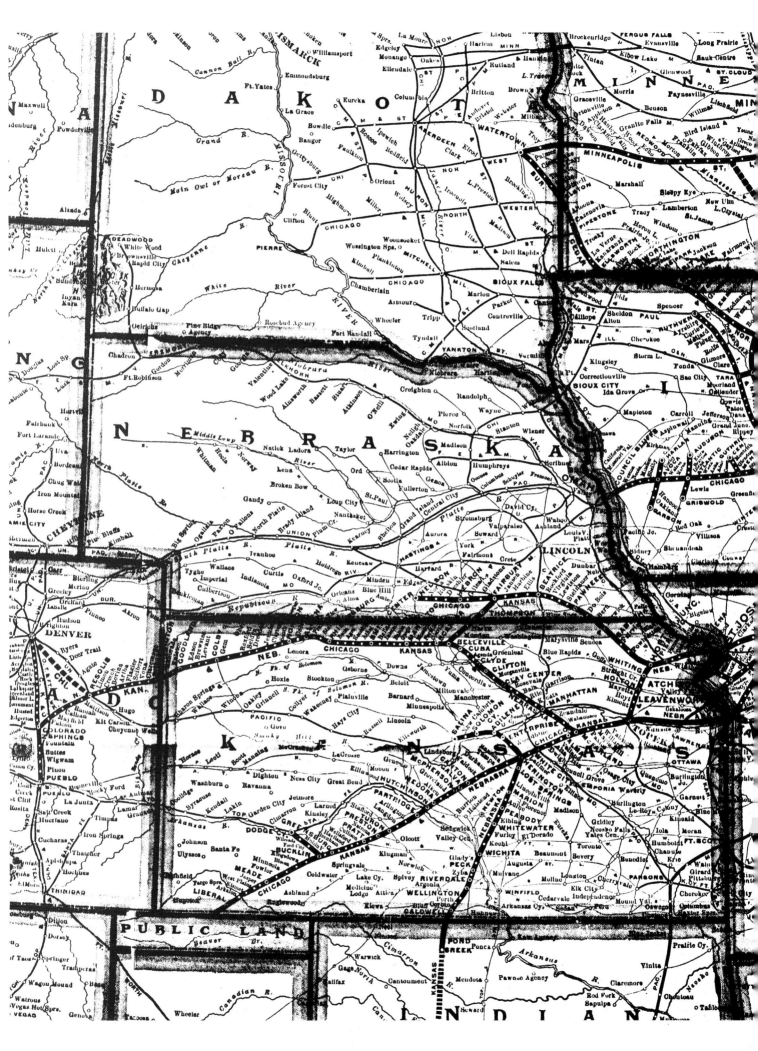

I. THE ROCK ISLAND IN COLORADO

In early 1882, plans were being drafted for a very ambitious extension of the Chicago, Rock Island and Pacific Railway Company. The considerations under study included surveying routes from the Mississippi River to the Rocky Mountains and California. The first action was placed in motion by the organization of a separate, but associated company, the Chicago, Kansas and Nebraska Railroad to construct lines into Nebraska, Colorado, New Mexico and Oklahoma (Indian Territory). The company was incorporated on December 30, 1885. The new railroad did no actual construction but it did order surveys and acquire rights-of-way and other properties. The majority of the activity was in Kansas and Nebraska, but the primary goal was actually the center of Colorado.

Colorado was largely narrow gauge country, and there were few links to the east. The Union Pacific's portion of the prosperous transcontinental railroad had barely scratched the northeast corner of the state. The Kansas Pacific had built into Denver in 1870 from central Kansas. The Atchison, Topeka and Santa Fe had a line into the southern portion of the state and had visions of building other lines throughout the area. General William J. Palmer, who had surveyed the west for the Kansas Pacific, was now building a narrow gauge empire. The General's Denver and Rio Grande, being built south from Denver, would provide a north-south link through Colorado to Mexico City. The Denver and Rio Grande was the first of the tiny narrow gauge roads in Colorado.

Numerous railroad schemes were being proposed in Colorado to tap the state's quickly developing mining industry; however, most would never see any form of construction. The links to the east were taking advantage of the situation and freight, in the form of narrow gauge equipment loaded on standard gauge cars, was becoming a regular occurrence.

Of prime interest to the Rock Island was the Colorado Midland, a standard gauge line proposing to build west into the heart of the mining districts, through narrow gauge territory. Where most of the railroads were avoiding building into the mountains, this one was boasting that it would go where there was no standard gauge. The Santa Fe was already closely monitoring the young company as another link to the west. The Colorado Midland was bolstered by the possible backing of railroads with direct connections to the industrial east. The Colorado Springs area was being promoted as a health resort, plus being the central location in the state. The Colorado

Midland could develop into a Rock Island link to the west coast.

The directors of the CRI&P were organizing companies in a very confusing pattern; among them was the Chicago, Rock Island and Colorado which was incorporated on January 30, 1886. The company, associated with the CK&N, shared most of the officers including the presicent, Ransom R. Cable, who was also president of the CRI&P. The CRI&C would eventually be consolidated with the CK&N. The route under study for the railroad was developing as the most direct route into the center of Colorado.

On March 17, 1886 in Topeka, Kansas, a charter was issued to the CK&N Railway for building numerous Kansas routes. The Nebraska charter was issued on March 31 to a separate CK&N corporation for construction in that state. Ransom R. Cable selected Marcus A. Low to set up and direct the CK&N corporations. Cable had seen Low's leadership and organizational ability as president of the St. Joseph and Iowa Railway, an earlier Rock Island subsidiary. The first headquarters of the CK&N was in Atchison, Kansas. Low consolidated the twin CK&N corporations on December 20, 1886.

A Kansas charter was issued on May 19, 1886 for a railroad across the northern counties toward Denver and Colorado Springs. On July 1, 1886 construction started on the massive building project. Horton, Kansas was the center of the activity, with lines going northwest and southwest. The northwestern line headed into Nebraska. At Fairbury, Nebraska a line would extend back into Kansas. At McFarland, Kansas, on the line which ran to the southwest from Horton, construction started to the northwest. The line would join the Fairbury line at Belleville, Kansas. A nearly straight line from Belleville to Denver had been surveyed; however, while grading of the CK&N was held up just beyond Norton, Kansas for the winter, plans were changed.

The southwestern line from Horton was being held at the Kansas-Indian Territory line. The construction was stalled until the fate of the area was settled. On March 2, 1888 the federal government granted the CK&N permission to build in the disputed area. H.A. Parker, chief engineer of the CK&N, and M.A. Low studied the situation in Northwest Kansas and Colorado, while the construction crews waited at Norton.

The spring arrived with a modified survey. Just west of Norton the CK&N would head southwest toward a newly proposed settlement called Goodland. The first buildings were being erected when the railroad grading crews passed through Goodland on March 3, 1888 going to Colorado. The builders would grade simultaneously east and west. Track laying crews traveled rapidly on the land prepared by the grading crews. The railroad really arrived in Goodland when the laying of ties and rail started. The pace of construction was such that the track layers arrived on July 3, 1888, after days of anticipation.

This map is from the November 18, 1888 Chicago Kansas & Nebraska public timetable, the first to be issued after completion of the line to Colorado just a couple of weeks earlier. Of particular interest is the proposed line parallel to the Union Pacific into Denver. Also note the fact that the crossing of the U.P. is shown erroneously at Resolis rather than Limon. (Museum collection)

In 1889 the ten-stall brick roundhouse at Goodland had just been completed. There were 45 locomotives assigned to the Colorado Division. Notice the CK&N boxcar being used as an office. (M.C. Parker collection)

The first train rolled into town on the morning of July 4, starting a day long celebration.

Goodland had already been selected as a division point on the railroad, while buildings and yards were being laid out as the track layers sped westward. The workers reached the old Kansas Pacific, now part of the Union Pacific, just north of its Lake siding. A few buildings had been built near the junction of the two lines, but in April 1889 the area was platted for the town of Limon Junction by the Union Pacific!

Eighteen miles east of Colorado Springs the CK&N grading crossed the Denver and New Orleans at Falcon. The D&NO was a standard gauge line that had been started in 1882 heading on a direct line from Denver to New Orleans. The company had changed its plans near Falcon and built southwestward toward Pueblo, rather than through the southeastern Colorado area. The D&NO had a couple of branch lines into a nearby coal field. The CK&N was pleased to find other mines in the area that had recently started shipping coal by wagon. M.A. Low himself contacted mine owners about the CK&N building its own service branches. One of these branches would run south crossing the D&NO at its Manitou Junction. The CK&N called this meeting with the D&NO Cable Junction in honor of the company president.

The grading crews reached the northern edge of Colorado Springs in September. Crossing under the Santa Fe's recently opened line to Denver, they followed a stream bed west to the Denver and Rio Grande's main line. West of the D&RG they platted Roswell City. The area east of the D&RG was laid out as a yard and shops called Roswell Junction, just Roswell for short. A main line track was built parallel to the dual gauge D&RG into Colorado Springs, two miles to the south. Initially a few irregular freight runs were made on the line between Goodland and Colorado Springs, but the first scheduled Rock Island passenger train arrived in Colorado Springs, starting daily service on November 4, 1888.

The CK&N immediately upon arrival in Colorado Springs leased its railroad to the CRI&P and it was absorbed into the parent company in 1891, following completion of the New Mexico sections. A trackage agreement with the D&RG on February 15, 1888 secured use of the Rio Grande's freight yards in Denver and Pueblo. Passenger service at the Denver and Pueblo union depots was included through the agreement with the D&RG. The Rio Grande would service Rock Island engines at its Burnham Shops in Denver and provide a freight office space in Pueblo. The Rock Island, in turn, would service D&RG engines and equipment at Roswell. The D&RG was converting over to a primarily standard gauge railroad, and this would help speed that change. The CRI&P would gain access to the Colorado Midland through its connection to the D&RG's Manitou Branch. A study for construction of a branch from Roswell to Colorado City was cancelled; however, some property was purchased near Roswell and along the western side of the D&RG into Colorado Springs.

The Union Pacific had a division point at Hugo, only ten miles east of Limon, which would not be relocated. The station at Lake became less important as the activity at Limon Junction increased. The UP was granted limited use of the CRI&P facilities and yards when the UP granted the Rock Island use of its line into Denver in April 1889. The CRI&P at that time stopped running trains between Colorado Springs and Denver over the D&RG on a regular basis.

The CK&N was not entirely through looking at Colorado though; a continuation of a branch off the line to

(continued on page 17)

A track gang is improving a fill about two miles west of Vona, Colorado in 1896. Foreman Ray Leapor is the tall man standing with his foot on the left rail. (Denver Public Library, Western History Department) Below is a stock certificate issued a few days before completion of the Colorado extension. (Author's collection)

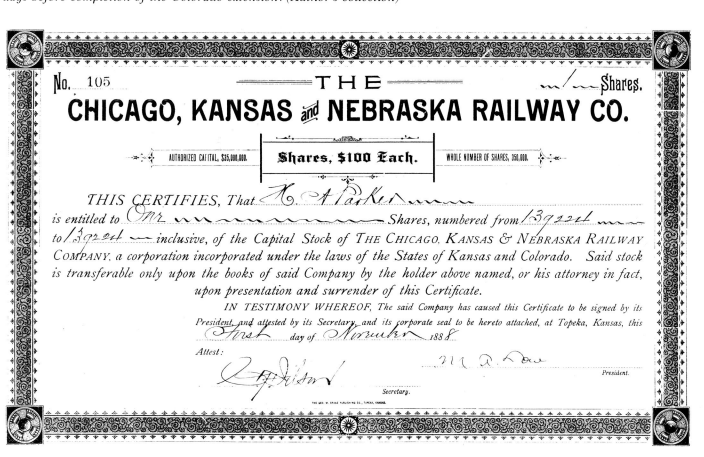

It is exactly 40 years since publication of Lucius Beebe's **Mixed Train Daily,** the first book to contain color reproductions of artwork by Howard Fogg. Therefore, it is especially appropriate to have Howard's fine portrait of Rock Island No. 5035 as the first of his paintings to appear on the jacket of a Colorado Rail Annual. It is reproduced with the kind permission of its owner, Ross B. Grenard.

Howard first saw a 5000 in the transportation exhibit of the 1933 Chicago World's Fair. He was very impresseed by it then, as a coal burner with a small tender, and it became even more impressive to him after being converted to oil and fitted with a large tender, as depicted here. He was not commissioned to do this painting but created it because of his fondness for these locomotives.

The painting was done in the late 1950's and depicts a mythical location somewhere near Limon in eastern Colorado, suggested by a dramatic photograph by Richard Steinheimer. It was exhibited with other Fogg works at a New York gallery in 1959, but none were sold. The art dealer advised Howard that "there just is no market for this sort of thing." Times have changed.

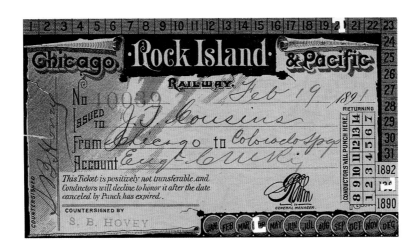

These passes are examples of many issued during the years of the Rock Island in Colorado. The 1891 pass was valid for one trip by a Colorado Midland engineer; the 1902 and later passes were good for annual travel by officials of several other Colorado lines. (Museum collection)

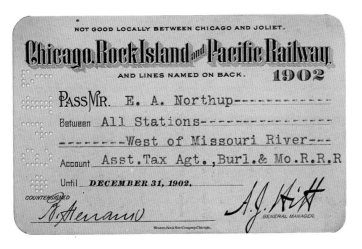

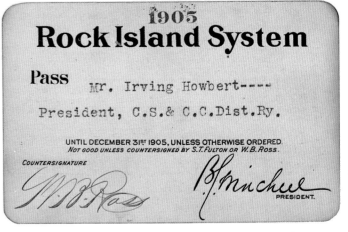

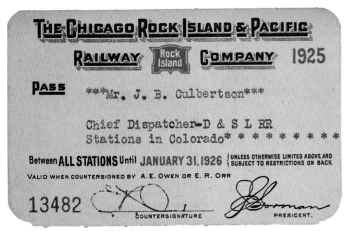

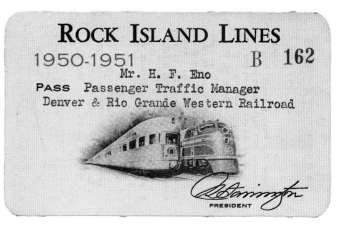

Reproduced here is the cover of an 1889 promotional brochure. At the upper left the artist has added a Yucca cactus (not native to the region) and a pair of prairie dogs to the otherwise featureless terrain along the route through eastern Colorado. Below that is shown the Ramona Hotel near Manitou Springs. Of the places named only Colorado Springs and Austin Bluffs, a near-by real estate promotion of the railroad, were on line. The others were on the Colorado Midland, except for Idaho Springs, west of Denver via the narrow gauge Colorado Central. (Denver Public Library, Western History Department)

New Mexico had been considered. The branch ran up to Dodge City, Kansas. The extension of that branch into Pueblo, Colorado paralleling the Santa Fe and northward to Cable Junction was held under study. The Missouri Pacific's constuction into Pueblo, as well as agreements with the Rio Grande, probably killed the proposal.

The Denver and New Orleans eventually, after several reorganizations, became part of the Colorado and Southern in 1899. The connection at Falcon became less important when the C&S shifted the bulk of its traffic onto the Santa Fe's line from Denver to Pueblo in 1901. The old D&NO main line was then used on a local service basis, mainly stock and coal. Passenger service was still available on the line, but in reduced form.

There were numerous reports of a Rock Island purchase of the Colorado Midland, even before the CRI&P arrived in Colorado Springs. The CM was taken over by the Santa Fe rather than the Rock Island in the 1890s when CM President J.J. Hagerman sold the bulk of his stock to the Santa Fe. The Santa Fe lost control in 1897. In 1901 a partnership between the C&S and the Rio Grande Western (a Palmer controlled railroad on the Utah end of the Denver and Rio Grande) purchased the Colorado Midland. The Rock Island's connection with the CM proved valuable for both railroads even after the CB&Q pulled some of the traffic that had been going to the Rock Island to the C&S and onto the CB&Q at Denver. The passenger interchange between the Rock Island and the Colorado Midland was never up to expectations due to the link with the Santa Fe, and later the Burlington. There were times when business between the CRI&P and CM was quite brisk, but in 1917 the Midland was up for sale and this time it was likely to be scrapped. The CM was sold to local investors who immediately set about rebuilding the once grand railroad. The condition of the CM caused problems when the United States Railroad Administration took control of the railroads in 1917. The CM was barred from all USRA traffic during World War I, which also hurt the western end of the Rock Island. A Rock Island inspection team toured the Colorado Midland in 1919 with thoughts of purchase of the dormant road. There were persistent rumors of the sale of the Midland to either the Rock Island or Santa Fe until the Midland was scrapped in 1921.

This is the first timetable, dated November 18, 1888, showing schedules over the new Rock Island lines to Denver, Colorado Springs and Pueblo. After this the CK&N name no longer appeared. The fastest Kansas City—Colorado Springs train, No. 115, took 23 hours 25 minutes, and the change from Central to Mountain time was made at Colorado Springs. Freight train schedules are also listed. (Museum collection)

BETWEEN KANSAS CITY, TOPEKA, CLAY CENTER, BELLEVILLE, PHILLIPSBURG, COLORADO SPRINGS, PUEBLO AND DENVER.

WESTWARD.

STATIONS.	Distance from Kansas City.	No. 111. Mail and Ex. Daily.	No. 115. Express Daily.	No. 221. Express Daily.		Elev'n above Sea In feet.
Union Passenger Station.						
KANSAS CITY, Mo......Lv.	.0	9.50 am	8.55 pm	11.15 am	....	....
NORTH TOPEKA, Kan...Ar.	67.2	11.50 am	11.05 pm	1.20 pm	....	....
TOPEKA, Kan........Ar.	68.2	12.00 m	11.15 pm	1.30 pm	....	892
TOPEKA..............Lv.	68.2	12.05 pm	11.20 pm	....	....	892
Sugar Works......... "	74.2	*12.18 pm	*11.32 pm	....	....	903
Valencia............ "	79.8	*12.29 pm	*11.44 pm	....	....	913
Willard............. "	83.6	*12.37 pm	*11.52 pm	....	....	927
Maple Hill.......... "	88.7	*12.47 pm	*12.02 am	No. 51.	....	972
Paxico.............. "	96.5	* 1.02 pm	*12.18 am	Freight	....	1006
McFARLAND.........Ar.	100.3	‡ 1.10 pm	12.25 am	Ex. Sun.	....	1035
CLAY CENTER LINE						
McFARLAND.........Lv.	100.3	1.30 pm	12.45 am	6.00 am	....	1035
Wabaunsee........... "	109.3	1.49 pm	* 1.04 am	6.45 am	....	1059
Zeandale............ "	114.1	2.00 pm	* 1.15 am	7.10 am	....	1007
MANHATTAN.......... "	121.5	2.16 pm	1.30 am	8.00 am	....	1027
Keats............... "	130.4	2.35 pm	* 1.49 am	8.50 am	....	1139
Riley............... "	139.0	2.54 pm	2.08 am	9.42 am	....	1289
Bala................ "	145.8	3.09 pm	* 2.22 am	10.30 am	....	1281
Rosevale............ "	151.9	3.22 pm	* 2.36 am	11.10 am	....	1195
CLAY CENTER........ "	157.7	3.36 pm	2.49 am	12.30 pm	....	1213
Morganville......... "	165.1	3.52 pm	3.05 am	1.18 pm	......	1248
CLIFTON............ "	173.3	4.10 pm	* 3.22 am	2.00 pm	....	1281
CLYDE.............. "	179.6	4.23 pm	3.30 am	2.50 pm	....	1310
Agenda.............. "	188.1	* 4.42 pm	* 3.55 am	3.37 pm	....	1424
CUBA............... "	194.5	4.57 pm	* 4.08 am	4.13 pm	....	1603
~~BELLEVILLE.......Ar.~~	~~204.4~~	~~5.20 pm~~	~~4.30 am~~	~~5.00 pm~~	....	1522
		No. 18.	No. 15.		No. 41. Freight Daily.	
BELLEVILLE........Lv.	204.4	5.30 pm	4.35 am	....	1.50 pm	1522
SCANDIA............ "	213.7	5.50 pm	4.56 am	....	2.40 pm	1438
Courtland........... "	219.6	6.03 pm	* 5.10 am	....	3.12 pm	1506
Formoso............. "	224.9	6.14 pm	* 5.22 am	....	3.40 pm	1521
Montrose............ "	230.0	* 6.25 pm	* 5.34 am	....	4.07 pm	1664
MANKATO............ "	237.1	6.41 pm	5.51 am	....	4.45 pm	1794
Otego............... "	245.1	6.58 pm	* 6.09 am	....	5.20 pm	1798
Ezbon............... "	249.8	7.08 pm	* 6.20 am	....	5.40 pm	1835
Lebanon............. "	256.5	7.23 pm	6.35 am	....	6.20 pm	1822
Bellaire...........Lv.	262.9	* 7.37 pm	* 6.50 am	....	6.50 pm	1872
SMITH CENTER...Ar.	269.1	‡ 7.50 pm	‡ 7.05 am	....	7.20 pm	1810
SMITH CENTER....Lv.	269.1	8.10 pm	7.25 am	....	7.20 pm	
Athol............... "	277.1	8.27 pm	* 7.43 am	....	9.05 pm	1792
Kensington.......... "	283.1	8.42 pm	7.57 am		9.32 pm	1779
Agra................ "	287.6	8.52 pm	8.08 am	No. 41.	9.52 pm	1862
Dana................ "	292.6	* 9.04 pm	8.20 am	Freight	10.18 pm	1870
PHILLIPSBURG....Ar.	298.8	9.20 pm	8.35 am	Ex. Sun.	10.45 pm	1945
PHILLIPSBURG....Lv.	298.8	9.25 pm	8.40 am	7.30 am	....	....
Stuttgart........... "	306.4	* 9.42 pm	* 8.57 am	8.09 am	....	2010
Prairie View........ "	313.3	* 9.57 pm	* 9.12 am	8.42 am	....	2182
ALMENA............. "	321.5	10.14 pm	9.29 am	9.29 am	....	2161
Calvert............. "	325.5	10.23 pm	9.38 am	9.56 am	....	2203
NORTON............. "	332.9	10.39 pm	9.55 am	11.00 am	....	2278
South Oronoque...... "	341.7	*10.57 pm	*10.13 am	11.51 am	....	2342
Clayton............. "	349.9	*11.13 pm	10.32 am	12.40 pm	....	2424
Jennings............ "	357.2	11.29 pm	10.48 am	1.40 pm	....	2498
Dresden............. "	365.6	*11.47 pm	11.06 am	2.37 pm	....	2737
Selden.............. "	375.1	*12.07 am	11.27 am	4.31 pm	....	2844
Rexford............. "	385.7	12.29 am	11.48 am	5.18 pm	....	2937
Gem................. "	394.7	*12.48 am	12.07 pm	6.00 pm	....	3099
COLBY.............. "	402.7	1.04 am	12.24 pm	7.08 pm	....	3145
Levant.............. "	410.8	* 1.22 am	12.42 pm	7.47 pm	....	3317
Brewster............ "	420.7	* 1.42 am	1.02 pm	8.35 pm	....	3421
Edson............... "	430.0	* 2.02 am	1.22 pm	9.20 pm	....	3578
GOODLAND.........Ar.	438.7	2.20 am	‡ 1.40 pm	10.00 pm	....	3693
COLORADO LINE						
GOODLAND.........Lv.	438.7	2.35 am	2.00 pm	5.00 am	....	....
Ruleton............. "	448.3	* 2.54 am	* 2.18 pm	5.38 am	....	3794
Kanorado............ "	456.2	* 3.09 am	* 2.32 pm	6.10 am	....	3912
Burlington.......... "	468.6	3.33 am	2.55 pm	7.00 am	....	4170
Bethune............. "	477.5	* 3.50 am	* 3.13 pm	8.06 am	....	4270
Claremont........... "	487.0	* 4.07 am	3.32 pm	8.56 am	....	4413
Vona................ "	491.3	* 4.21 am	* 3.47 pm	9.41 am	....	4605
Seibert............. "	501.2	4.35 am	4.00 pm	10.27 am	....	4711
Flagler............. "	512.2	* 4.57 am	4.23 pm	11.40 am	....	4930
Arriba.............. "	523.7	* 5.20 am	4.46 pm	12.28 pm	....	5240
Bovina.............. "	529.5	5.32 am	4.58 pm	12.54 pm	....	5381
Creech.............. "	535.7	* 5.43 am	* 5.10 pm	1.22 pm	....	5604
Limon............... "	545.8	6.03 am	5.33 pm	2.30 pm	....	5359
RESOLIS............ "	554.5	6.20 am	5.50 pm	3.30 pm	....	5579
Mattison............ "	564.7	* 6.39 am	6.10 pm	4.10 pm	....	5789
Ramah............... "	575.8	* 6.59 am	6.32 pm	4.55 pm	....	6094
Calhan.............. "	585.6	7.18 am	* 6.52 pm	5.35 pm	....	6509
Tip Top............. "	593.4	* 7.33 am	* 7.09 pm	6.08 pm	....	6890
Mayfield............ "	596.8	7.40 am	* 7.17 pm	6.22 pm	....	6789
Falcon.............. "	606.2	7.58 am	7.35 pm	7.00 pm	....	6831
Elsmere............. "	615.0	8.15 am	7.53 pm	7.53 pm	....	6407
Roswell............. "	622.1	8.30 am	8.10 pm	8.40 pm	....	6071
COL. SPRINGS......Ar.	624.5	‡ 8.40 am	‡ 8.20 pm	....	....	6002
Kelker.............. "	628.8	8.13 am	7.53 pm	....	....	....
Widefield........... "	633.2	8.22 am	8.02 am	....	....	....
Fountain............ "	637.9	8.31 am	8.11 pm	....	....	....
Buttes.............. "	643.7	8.42 am	8.22 pm	....	....	....
Wigwam.............. "	648.9	8.52 am	8.32 pm	....	....	....
Pinon............... "	655.0	9.03 am	8.44 pm	....	....	....
Cactus.............. "	661.4	9.15 am	8.55 pm	....	....	....
Dundee.............. "	666.7	9.25 am	9.05 pm	....	....	....
PUEBLO............Ar.	669.0	9.35 am	9.15 pm	....	....	4466
		No. 18.	No. 2[illegible].			
COL. SPRINGS......Lv.	.....	8.00 am	7.40 pm		....	....
Roswell...........Ar.	622.1	8.04 am	7.44 pm		....	....
Pikeview............ "	624.0	8.08 am	7.48 pm		....	....
Edgerton............ "	629.1	8.16 am	7.57 pm		....	....
Husted.............. "	632.8	8.22 am	8.03 pm		....	....
Borst............... "	636.5	8.29 am	8.10 pm		....	....
Monument............ "	638.8	8.33 am	8.15 pm		....	....
Palmer Lake......... "	642.5	8.39 am	8.21 pm		....	7238
Greenland........... "	647.7	8.48 am	8.30 pm		....	....
Larkspur............ "	651.6	8.55 am	8.37 pm		....	....
Glade............... "	656.2	9.03 am	8.45 pm		....	....
Douglas............. "	659.6	9.10 am	8.51 pm		....	....
Castle Rock......... "	662.1	9.16 am	8.55 pm		....	....
Plateau............. "	665.9	9.22 am	9.02 pm		....	....
Sedalia............. "	670.1	9.31 am	9.10 pm		....	....
Vista............... "	673.7	9.39 am	9.17 pm		....	....
Acequia............. "	677.4	9.46 am	9.25 pm		....	....
Littleton........... "	684.3	9.59 am	9.38 pm		....	....
Military Post....... "	686.3	10.02 am	9.42 pm		....	....
Petersburg.......... "	686.9	10.03 am	9.43 pm		....	....
Burnham............. "	692.6	10.15 am	9.55 pm		....	....
DENVER............Ar.	694.8	10.30 am	10.10 pm		....	5196

☞ Trains between Denver, Colorado Springs and Pueblo are run on Mountain time, being one hour slower than Central time.

EASTWARD.

STATIONS.	Distance from Denver.	No. 17. Mail and Ex. Daily.	No. 19. Exp. Daily.		
DENVER............Lv.	.0	4.45 pm	4.00 am		....
Burnham............. "	2.2	5.00 pm	4.15 am		....
Petersburg.......... "	7.9	5.12 pm	4.25 am		....
Military Post....... "	8.5	5.13 pm	4.26 am		....
Littleton........... "	10.5	5.18 pm	4.30 am		....
Acequia............. "	17.4	5.30 pm	4.42 am		....
Vista............... "	21.1	5.38 pm	4.48 am		....
Sedalia............. "	24.7	5.44 pm	4.55 am		....
Plateau............. "	28.9	5.50 pm	5.03 am		....
Castle Rock......... "	32.7	6.00 pm	5.11 am		....
Douglas............. "	35.2	6.04 pm	5.15 am		....
Glade............... "	38.6	6.11 pm	5.22 am		....
Lockspur............ "	43.2	6.21 pm	5.30 am		....
Greenland........... "	47.1	6.29 pm	5.39 am		....
Palmer Lake......... "	52.3	6.38 pm	5.50 am		....
Monument............ "	56.0	6.45 pm	5.57 am		....
Borst............... "	58.3	6.49 pm	6.01 am		....
Husted.............. "	62.0	6.55 pm	6.07 am		....
Edgerton............ "	65.7	7.01 pm	6.14 am		....
Pikeview............ "	70.8	7.09 pm	6.23 am		....
Roswell............. "	72.7	7.12 pm	6.26 am		....
COL. SPRINGS......Ar.	75.1	7.15 pm	6.30 am		....
		No. 14.	No. 16.		
PUEBLO............Lv.	.0	† 5.45 pm	† 5.00 am	....	....
Dundee.............. "	2.3	5.55 pm	5.10 am	....	....
~~Cactus.............. "~~	~~7.6~~	~~6.06 pm~~	~~5.21 am~~	....	....
Pinon............... "	14.0	6.18 pm	5.32 am	....	....
Wigwam.............. "	20.1	6.30 pm	5.44 am	....	....
Buttes.............. "	25.3	6.40 pm	5.53 am	....	....
Fountain............ "	31.1	6.50 pm	6.04 am		....
Widefield........... "	35.8	6.58 pm	6.13 am	No. 42.	....
Kelker.............. "	40.2	7.07 pm	6.22 pm	Freight.	....
COL. SPRINGS......Ar.	44.5	7.15 am	6.30 am	Ex. Sun.	....
COL. SPRINGS......Lv.	.....	8.35 pm	7.50 am	....	....
Roswell............. "	72.7	8.45 pm	8.00 am	4.00 am	....
COLORADO LINE					
Elsmere............. "	79.8	* 9.00 pm	8.15 am	4.33 am	....
Falcon.............. "	88.6	9.17 pm	8.33 am	5.13 am	....
Mayfield............ "	98.0	* 9.33 pm	8.52 am	5.55 am	....
Tip Top............. "	101.4	* 9.40 pm	* 8.58 am	6.12 am	....
Calhan.............. "	109.2	* 9.55 pm	9.14 am	7.18 am	....
Ramah............... "	119.0	*10.14 pm	9.33 am	8.03 am	....
Mattison............ "	130.1	*10.35 pm	9.55 am	8.55 am	....
RESOLIS............ "	140.3	10.54 pm	10.14 am	9.40 am	....
Limon............... "	149.0	11.10 pm	10.32 am	10.32 am	....
Creech.............. "	159.1	*11.32 pm	*10.55 am	11.30 am	....
Bovina.............. "	165.3	*11.44 pm	*11.07 am	11.59 am	....
Arriba.............. "	171.1	*11.55 pm	11.18 am	12.28 pm	....
Flagler............. "	182.6	*12.17 am	11.40 am	1.23 pm	....
Seibert............. "	193.6	12.38 am	12.02 pm	2.15 pm	....
Vona................ "	200.5	*12.51 am	12.15 pm	2.50 pm	....
Claremont........... "	207.8	* 1.05 am	12.29 pm	3.32 pm	....
Bethune............. "	217.3	* 1.23 am	*12.48 pm	4.28 pm	....
Burlington.......... "	226.2	1.40 am	1.05 pm	5.25 pm	....
Kanorado............ "	238.6	* 2.03 am	1.27 pm	6.17 pm	....
Ruleton............. "	246.5	* 2.18 am	1.42 pm	6.50 pm	....
GOODLAND.........Ar.	256.1	2.35 am	‡ 2.00 pm	7.30 pm	....
GOODLAND.........Lv.	256.1	2.40 am	2.20 pm	5.00 am	....
Edson............... "	264.8	* 2.57 am	2.38 pm	5.40 am	....
Brewster............ "	274.1	* 3.16 am	2.58 pm	6.24 am	....
Levant.............. "	284.0	* 3.37 am	3.18 pm	7.10 am	....
COLBY.............. "	292.1	3.53 am	3.34 pm	8.05 am	....
Gem................. "	300.1	* 4.10 am	3.51 pm	8.41 am	....
Rexford............. "	309.1	* 4.28 am	4.09 pm	9.22 am	....
Selden.............. "	319.7	* 4.51 am	4.31 pm	10.10 am	....
Dresden............. "	329.2	* 5.12 am	4.51 pm	11.06 am	....
Jennings............ "	337.6	5.28 am	5.08 pm	11.55 am	....
Clayton............. "	344.9	* 5.44 am	5.23 pm	12.40 pm	....
South Oronoque...... "	353.1	* 6.01 am	5.40 pm	1.30 pm	....
NORTON............. "	361.9	6.19 am	5.58 pm	2.45 pm	....
Calvert............. "	369.3	6.35 am	6.15 pm	3.32 pm	....
ALMENA............. "	373.3	6.43 am	6.25 pm	3.57 pm	....
Prairie View........ "	381.5	* 7.00 am	* 6.43 pm	4.48 pm	....
Stuttgart........... "	388.4	* 7.15 am	* 6.59 pm	5.30 pm	....
PHILLIPSBURG.....Ar.	396.0	7.30 am	7.15 pm	6.10 pm	....
PHILLIPSBURG.....Lv.	396.0	7.35 am	7.25 pm	3.10 am	....
Dana................ "	402.2	* 7.53 am	* 7.44 pm	3.38 am	....
Agra................ "	407.2	8.08 am	* 7.58 pm	4.00 am	....
Kensington.......... "	411.7	8.18 am	8.12 pm	4.22 am	....
Athol..............Lv.	417.7	* 8.32 am	8.27 pm	4.50 am	....
SMITH CENTER...Ar.	425.7	‡ 8.50 am	‡ 8.47 pm	5.26 am	....
SMITH CENTER...Lv.	425.7	9.10 am	9.07 pm	5.26 am	....
Bellaire............ "	431.9	* 9.25 am	* 9.22 pm	5.55 am	....
Lebanon............. "	438.3	9.39 am	9.37 pm	6.35 am	....
Ezbon............... "	445.0	9.54 am	* 9.52 pm	7.15 am	....
Otego............... "	449.7	10.05 am	*10.03 pm	7.40 am	....
MANKATO............ "	457.7	10.23 am	10.22 pm	8.22 am	....
Montrose............ "	464.8	*10.40 am	10.38 pm	9.00 am	....
Formoso............. "	469.9	10.52 am	*10.50 pm	9.27 am	
Courtland........... "	475.2	11.04 am	11.01 pm	9.55 am	No. 52.
SCANDIA............ "	481.1	11.18 am	11.15 pm	10.28 am	Freight.
BELLEVILLE.......Ar.	490.4	11.40 am	11.35 pm	11.15 am	Ex. Sun.
		No. 112.	No. 116.		
CLAY CENTER LINE					
BELLEVILLE........Lv.	490.4	11.50 am	11.45 pm	....	12.30 pm
CUBA............... "	500.3	12.12 pm	*12.07 am	....	1.26 pm
Agenda.............. "	506.7	*12.27 pm	*12.21 am	....	2.02 pm
CLYDE.............. "	515.2	12.46 pm	12.40 am	....	2.50 pm
CLIFTON............ "	521.5	1.00 pm	12.53 am	....	4.10 pm
Morganville......... "	529.7	1.18 pm	* 1.12 am	....	4.53 pm
CLAY CENTER........ "	537.1	1.35 pm	1.28 am	....	5.32 pm
Rosevale............ "	542.9	1.48 pm	* 1.41 am	....	6.05 pm
Bala................ "	549.0	2.02 pm	* 1.54 am	....	6.37 pm
Riley............... "	555.8	2.17 pm	2.08 am	....	7.10 pm
Keats............... "	564.4	2.35 pm	* 2.29 am	....	8.00 pm
MANHATTAN.......... "	573.3	2.55 pm	2.50 am	....	8.55 pm
Zeandale............ "	584.7	3.11 pm	* 3.08 am	....	9.30 pm
Wabaunsee........... "	585.5	3.22 pm	* 3.19 am	....	9.53 pm
McFARLAND.........Ar.	594.5	‡ 3.40 pm	3.40 am	....	10.35 pm
McFARLAND.........Lv.	494.5	4.00 pm	3.50 am	....	....
Paxico.............. "	598.3	* 4.08 pm	* 3.58 am	....	....
Maple Hill.......... "	606.1	* 4.24 pm	* 4.17 am	....	....
Willard............. "	611.2	* 4.34 pm	* 4.30 am	....	....
Valencia............ "	615.0	* 4.42 pm	* 4.38 am	....	....
Sugar Works......... "	620.6	* 4.53 pm	* 4.52 am	....	....
TOPEKA............Ar.	626.6	5.05 pm	5.05 am	....	....
		No. 112.	No. 116.	No. 222.	
TOPEKA............Lv.	626.6	5.10 pm	5.10 am	3.05 pm	No stops between Topeka and Kansas City.
NORTH TOPEKA......Lv.	627.6	5.20 pm	5.20 am	3.15 pm	
KANSAS CITY.......Ar.	694.8	7.20 pm	7.20 am	5.25 pm	

☞ Trains between Denver, Colorado Springs and Pueblo are run on Mountain time, being one hour slower than Central time.

The engineer and fireman of brand new 4-4-0 No. 527 pose in the Denver yard before departing with an eastbound freight train in 1900. (C.R. Fewlass photo, Denver Public Library, Western History Department)

In 1913 the C&S finally closed the old main line south of Falcon to Colorado Springs and Pueblo. The C&S then used the Rock Island's trackage from Elsmere to Cable Junction to serve its spurs near Manitou Junction. The production of the mines east of Colorado Springs was quite low at this time, and shipments were quite irregular. The Rock Island's mainline into Colorado Springs was occasionally used by the C&S but only on rare occasions. Falcon served as a terminus for nearly all trains from Denver. Passengers regularly transferred to Rock Island trains into Colorado Springs.

Nearly all the coal spurs had been removed by the end of the 1920s; however, a few close to Roswell did operate into the 1930s. In Pueblo, the activity on the Rock Island was down to one passenger round trip and a daily freight until the mid-1920s when those, too, were cut. The last Rock Island regular freight left Pueblo in 1928, but there were rumors of restarting service as late as 1958, when the last remaining service building was sold.

A flood on Memorial Day in 1935 destroyed a large section of Colorado Springs. Spring rains had saturated the ground until an afternoon cloudburst turned the placid Monument Creek into a raging river. Large sec-

tions of the Rio Grande and Santa Fe were destroyed. The Rock Island was severely damaged. The Roswell yards received a heavy blow as many older buildings vanished in the waters. The bridge east of the yards was swept off its abutments. The destruction continued south to the Colorado Springs depot, where yet another bridge was destroyed. The old Grier House received heavy water damage to the lower floor. Eastern and western Colorado Springs were connected by a single bridge after the flood.

The railroads quickly rebuilt, and the City of Colorado Springs initiated channelization of Monument Creek to prevent a repeat of the Memorial Day flood. In 1936, however, a similar storm caused flooding between Denver and Falcon. Large sections of the old D&NO railroad vanished. The old mainline was completely dismantled, what portions of it could be found, except for a few miles in southeast Denver. Portions of the Rock Island were flooded; however, repairs were not prohibitive, and trains were diverted over the Rio Grande into Denver. Trains northbound on the D&RGW from Colorado Springs were a rare event indeed after April 1889, but flooding such as in 1936, or winter storms might cause such diversions.

This 1914 Colorado Springs view shows the Rock Island's Grier Hotel, the large frame building to the right of the Denver & Rio Grande station. (Colorado College Library)

Steam was still used on trains 27 and 28 in 1948. P-40 Pacific 950 rolls across the plains somewhere east of Denver in October of that year. (Herbert O'Hanlon photo, G.C. Bassett collection)

The Rock Island held its own in Colorado Springs through the 1930s, but World War II brought increased military traffic. Unlike World War I, traffic volume increased due to activity on the line near Colorado Springs. Two major military bases were established at Colorado Springs. An Army post opened south of Colorado Springs and the Army Air Corps opened a post north of the Colorado Springs Airport. The old Elsmere siding changed from coal spur, to passing siding, to Airbase Spur connection in ten years. The old coal spur to Cable Junction had been torn up years before, but the rebuilding was easily done. One long pile trestle was the only complication. Soon heavyweight Pullman cars consigned to the Air Base or Camp Carson arrived over the Rock Island, as well as the other railroads in the area. Helper engines were required for the heavy trains eastbound for Goodland over the ridge at Tip Top.

In 1949, heavy winter storms over the plains caused diversion of Rock Island and Union Pacific traffic over more southerly routes. Spring floods in 1950 and 1951 in Nebraska and Kansas caused additional diversions. In times of these natural disasters the railroads cooperated. The extended diversions occasionally caused friction between the train crews, but fortunately none were long enough to cause serious violence.

Heavy rains in 1956 caused flooding in eastern Colorado that was reminiscent of 1936. The Rock Island received heavy bridge and grade damage. Riprap and old car bodies were added along the river bank from Resolis to Matheson and near Limon. The railroad was closed for nearly two weeks until the most serious wash-outs could be repaired.

Rains in June 1965 caused havoc on the Colorado Springs-Limon line. The railroad was washed out in 67 separate places in a 21-mile-long sretch between Calhan and Elsmere. Two bridges were destroyed, and two others were damaged. The Union Pacific's connection to Limon was particularly hard hit and was closed for well over a month. Rock Island trains that normally used that line were detoured over other UP tracks until the Colorado Springs-Limon section could be reopened.

The Colorado Springs line was reopened after eight days. Thirty-five section men worked fourteen-hour days. Five bridge crews, a total of 25 more men, worked around the clock. Eighty cars of ballast and ten cars of riprap and refuse were needed to put the line back in operation.

Bridge 5799, a thirty-foot steel span over a county road east of Peyton, was washed away and buried. The whole area was filled and the road was diverted over the grade. Several of the bridges had been rebuilt in 1936, 1956 and now again in 1965. Taking advantage of the situation, Rock Island crews lowered the track two and one-half feet under two overpasses just east of the Roswell Yard. The clearance was needed for piggyback and multi-level cars. Some 1250 feet of mainline was lowered.

Westbound trains were held at Goodland. After the lines were reopened, Denver passengers were either taken to Colorado Springs or taken by bus from Limon to Denver. The flooding caused problems on the D&RGW and the Santa Fe north of Colorado Springs. That area was reopened coincident with the reopening of the Colorado Springs-Limon section.

In 1970 children played with a switch under the Cascade Avenue bridge, one of those east of Roswell, causing a derailment. The railroad and the bridge were seriously damaged. Litigation over the situation, due to the weakened financial condition of the Rock Island, continued for nearly eight years.

Pushing through snow this doubleheaded freight led by an unidentified 2-8-0 derailed near Peyton with damage to both locomotives, some time during the 1930's. Low drifts in the region frequently caused numerous problems.

While blizzards were the bane of winter operation, flashfloods caused problems during the summer. A road foreman inspects damage to bridge 5499 on July 18, 1956. Below, bridge 5489 near Matheson had a long rip-rapped approach. This historic structure had been rebuilt from the old Rock River, Illinois bridge in 1902. (Cadillac & Lake City collection)

General Electric U25Bs pull an eastbound freight over the AT&SF/D&RGW "Joint Line" south of Castle Rock in June 1965 when the Union Pacific was repairing its flood damaged track normally used by the Rock Island east of Denver. After this time it would be increasingly rare to find such sets of CRI&P power with units of the same builder, model and paint scheme. (Otto Perry photo, Denver Public Library, Western History Department)

The end of the Rock Island was long and drawn out. It had variously been expected for nearly ten preceeding years. The closing took place at such a rate that when the final orders came, it still came as a surprise. The last run took place on Friday, March 28, 1980, when locomotives 4313, 4338 and 4326 arrived at Sandown at 8:30 P.M. The train had experienced difficulties with snow during its trip across eastern Colorado. The crew tied up at the Rio Grande's North Yard at 10:15 P.M., then dead headed back to their home terminal, with the diesels and caboose later returned to Council Bluffs, Iowa by the Union Pacific. The final trip to Colorado Springs had occurred in February.

Is was hard to believe that the Chicago, Rock Island and Pacific was indeed dead and that it was now refusing to be buried.

(Top) U25B 227 idles at Limon with ex-D&RGW 4202 during the grain rush in September 1974. Another GE, Detroit Edison 011 was one of the diesels leased by the Rock Island in the 1970s and is seen at Arriba in 1973. The former D&RGW units escaped repainting; No. 4200 is switching wheat at Flagler in the same year. (Paul Stradley photos)

Turning on the wye at Limon in June 1973, red and yellow GP40 No. 4708 and GP7 No. 1286 regularly worked west of Goodland although neither was equipped with dynamic brakes. FP7 No. 409, one of only ten such units delivered by EMD to the Rock Island in 1949 for both freight and passenger service, leads a train into the setting sun near Seibert in 1974. Below, an all-Rock Island consist is bound for Colorado Springs in the summer of 1977. Most of these turns from Limon were made at night, and the minimal tonnage is prophetic of the line's demise less than three years later. (Paul Stradley photos)

At Elsmere one of the last Rock Island trains into Colorado Springs departs as a caboose-hop with Pikes Peak in the distance of this early-1980 view. Below, one of the final loads into the Springs was this car of scrap bound for Pueblo. (Mel McFarland photos)

CHICAGO, ROCK ISLAND & PACIFIC

RAILWAY

➡ THE DIRECT ROUTE ⬅

From Chicago and Peoria to Rock Island, in ILILNOIS; Davenport, Des Moines and Council Bluffs, in IOWA; Minneapolis and St. Paul, in MINNESOTA; Watertown and Sioux Falls, in DAKOTA; St. Joseph and Kansas City, in MISSOURI; Omaha, Lincoln, Fairbury and Nelson, in NEBRASKA; Atchison, Topeka, Wichita and Dodge City, in KANSAS; Kingfisher, El Reno and Minco, in INDIAN TERRITORY; Denver, Colorado Springs and Pueblo, in COLORADO. THROUGH TOURIST SLEEPER EVERY WEEK, leaving Chicago Wednesdays at 6.00 P. M., for PACIFIC COAST POINTS, via Denver, Colorado.

➤ MAGNIFICENT ⬍

VESTIBULE EXPRESS TRAINS

❁ FROM CHICAGO ❁

TO THE		TO THE
Northwest		**Southwest**
and West.		**and South.**
DINING CARS.		*CHAIR CARS.*

The Great Health Resorts of the Rocky Mountains

MANITOU AND GLENWOOD SPRINGS,

Are reached by the ROCK ISLAND ROUTE TO DENVER.

TO THE TOP OF PIKE'S PEAK BY RAIL

Is accomplished by taking the GREAT ROCK ISLAND ROUTE to MANITOU, and then the Cog Road to the top.

For Tickets, Maps, Folders, or desired information, apply to any Coupon Ticket Office in the United States or Canada, or address

E. ST. JOHN,   **JOHN SEBASTIAN,**
Gen'l Manager, CHICAGO, ILL.   Gen'l Ticket & Pass. Ag't, CHICAGO, ILL.

I. L. LOOMIS,
New England Passenger Agent, 296 Washington St., Boston, Mass.

(Author's collection)

28

II. TRAIN OPERATIONS

Goodland had shipments ready when the first cars arrived in 1888. Freight was interchanged with the Union Pacific at Limon and Denver. In Denver there were connections with the Denver and Rio Grande, Colorado and Southern (narrow and standard gauge), the Denver and Salt Lake, and many others. At Colorado Springs there were the D&RG, C&S, Santa Fe, Colorado Midland, Colorado Springs and Cripple Creek District and, after the CM and CS&CCD were gone, the Midland Terminal. Shipments of decomposed granite were a valuable commodity for the MT starting in the 1920s, when the Rock Island started ordering increasingly larger amounts for ballast. Freight kept the Rock Island alive, but the passenger operations were the most memorable.

The first passenger trains into the Pikes Peak Region brought deluxe equipment and plush Pullman service. The introduction of the *Rocky Mountain Limited* in 1902 was hailed as a marvel. The train took 24 hours to travel from Chicago to Colorado Springs. The equipment was built for the train. Up until the *Rocky Mountain Limited* the equipment was regular CRI&P and Pullman cars, but with this train the trip to Colorado became special. The luxury of the train was highly advertised in regional and national literature. A slightly less opulent and less rapid *Colorado and California Express* followed the same route, but roughly 12 hours behind the *Limited*.

The luxury of the *Rocky Mountain Limited* was declining in the late 1930's even though the assigned equipment had been kept up to the latest standards. The *Colorado and California Express* had become the *Colorado Express* by the 1930s. In 1937 the Rock Island introduced the *Rocket* image, named after one of its early steam locomotives; it also gave the look and sound of a futuristic approach. In October the Kansas City-Denver *Rocket* started running tri-weekly, until February 1938, when the train was transferred to a Kansas City-Oklahoma City run. A connection to Chicago was made in Kansas City. The Colorado Springs passengers connected in Limon on gas-electric "Rocket Juniors" or when traffic was heavy, on an old heavyweight coach or two and a steam engine.

All aboard! A westbound Rock Island passenger train is ready to leave Goodland, Kansas in about 1906. Notice the recently installed electric lights along the platform and the stack of cream cans next to the small building at the left. (M.C. Parker collection)

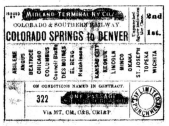

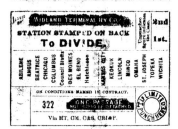

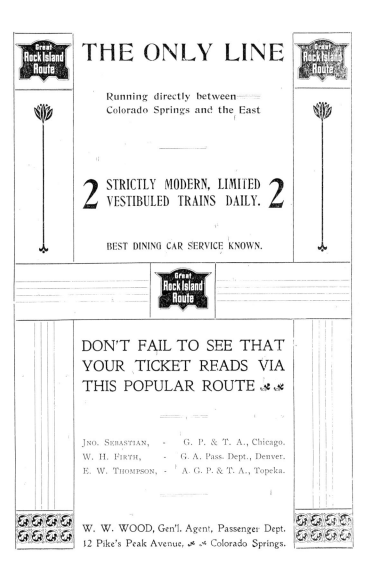

*Above is an advertisement placed in Colorado Springs newspapers to promote travel to the east, while below opposite is one appearing in Boston urging prospective travelers from New England to visit California via **The Big 5 Limited**. "Sunset's Golden Shore" certainly sounds more appealing than "Sunrise rock-bound coast!" (Author's collection) Above opposite is reproduced a letter from W.H. Firth, the CRI&P's general passenger agent in Denver, to the **Mining World**, politely declining to purchase advertising space in that trade publication. At left is an interline ticket issued by the Midland Terminal Ry. at Cripple Creek for passage via the MT to Divide, the Colorado Midland to Colorado Springs, the C&S to Denver, then east on the Rock Island. (Both, Museum collection)*

Denver, Colo.

Sept. 6 th., 1898.,

Mr. H?G.Myer,

      Solicitor, Mining, World,

Dear Sir;-

      Referring to yourfavor of September 2nd. I thank you very much for the kind advertising proposition, which I regret that existing arrangements will prohibit me from taking advantage of it.

Our advertising arrangements in Denver are confined very closely to the Daily papers of general news nature to the exclusion of all mediums usually grouped under the denomination of"Class". While I appreciate the circumstances under which your application is made, the stringency of the rule quoted, precludes me from entering into the contract with you at this time.

                  Yours truly,

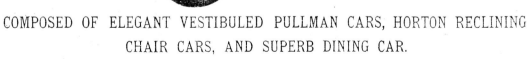

31

Heavy Mikado 2698 is beautifully backlighted by the morning sun as it works up the grade west of Bennett on the Union Pacific line to Denver, January 4, 1948. The undulating nature of the route through the high plains of eastern Colorado is quite evident here. (Otto Perry photo, Denver Public Library, Western History Department)

On October 18, 1936 the Colorado Springs section of the **Rocky Mountain Limited** *gathers speed eastbound out of Roswell, the Rock Island-founded community at the northern city limits of the Springs named after Roswell P. Flowers, a director of the railraod. During the 1930s this train operated on a 27-hour schedule to Chicago and was competitive in both running time and accommodations with the Burlington's* **Aristocrat** *and the Union Pacific's* **Columbine.** *(Otto Perry photo, California State Railroad Museum)*

Mountain type 4030, which itself had once powered the **Rocky Mountain Limited**, *pulls mixed train 26 to Limon, through Sable, just east of Denver, in February 1950. This train ran as the Omaha local east of Limon. Interestingly, the only other mainline mixed train in Colorado at the time was run by the Union Pacific over this same trackage enroute to Kansas. (Herbert O'Hanlon photo, G.C. Bassett collection)*

*On Armistice Day 1939 Electro-Motive E3 No. 624 glistened at the helm of the new seven-car **Rocky Mountain Rocket**, on display at Denver Union Station before entering service the next day. Otto Perry, always a faithful chronicler of such events, was there with his camera.*

November 12, 1939 marked the introduction of the *Rocky Mountain Rocket*. The fast diesel-powered train now ran daily between Chicago and Denver with a Colorado Springs link. Limon had long been the scene of a car shuffle with the Denver and Colorado Springs equipment, but soon a new twist was added. Electro-Motive custom built two AB units, a "B" (or cabless power unit) with a cab compartment. The 1000-horsepower unit also had a baggage compartment! The engines were delivered in May 1940 and were added to the *Rocky Mountain Rocket* specifically for the Colorado Springs section. The AB ran as a normal B unit out of Chicago, as the second or third engine depending upon the size of the train. At Limon #750 or 751 could lead the Colorado Springs, or occasionally the Denver section of the train, depending upon which was lightest. The strange little engines had their baggage sections removed and another power unit installed after a few years of service. There were two "sets" of equipment for the *Rocky Mountain Rocket*, and the two were enough to handle the train. Since the units were so unique there was no need for them anywhere else on the system. The two ended their years, highly modified, in Chicago commuter service, long after the last run of the *Rocky Mountain Rocket*.

36

*The first **Rocket** service in Colorado had been the tri-weekly three-car Denver-Kansas City **Rocket** which ran from October 18, 1937 until February 3, 1938. Otto captured the 606, one of the Rock Island's unique 1200-HP TA units, cutting through the early morning fog on the final departure from the Mile High City. The Colorado Springs connection was provided by a "Rocket Junior," 1927 St. Louis/EMC Railcar No. 9049 which had been given a Rocket paint scheme (top). The **Rocky Mountain Rocket** was still a formidable train in the early 1960s, when Otto found it ready to depart Limon eastbound. (Top, Colorado Springs Pioneers' Museum; other three photos, Denver Public Library, Western History Department)*

The mating of the Denver and Colorado Springs sections of the **Rocky Mountain Rocket** at Limon is shown in this series of views: The Colorado Springs AB unit is placed behind the lead E8 from Denver; then the Colorado Springs baggage-RPO goes ahead of the Denver baggage car; next the Colorado Springs cafe car is switched ahead of the Denver chair cars; finally the pullmans are coupled to the Denver observation car. Occasionally, this last car was included in the Colorado Springs section. Less than 15 minutes was allowed for all this shuffling before the 2:40 PM departure time. (Earl Cochran photos)

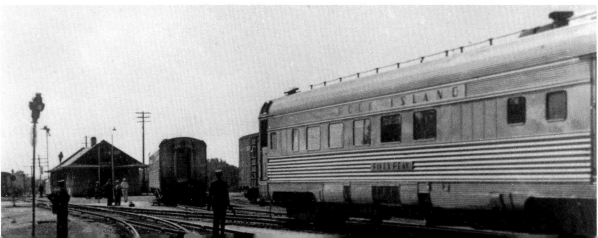

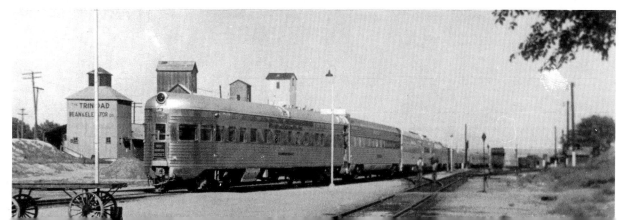

On July 7, 1940 the eastbound **Rocket** accelerates out of Limon with nine cars led by E6 No. 629 and AB No. 750. (Otto Perry photo, Denver Public Library, Western History Department) Below, E7 No. 636 with the Denver section is eastbound at Sable on the Union Pacific in May 1951. (Herbert O'Hanlon photo, G.C. Bassett collection).

On October 16, 1966 the last **Rocky Mountain Rocket** flashes through Agate and disappears down the U.P. rails toward Limon, bringing to an end 78 years of Chicago Rock Island & Pacific passenger service in the Centennial State. The occasion was almost unnoticed by the general public and railroad enthusiasts as well, and few were aware at the time that the Rock Island itself was already into the long decline toward its own demise only 14 years hence. (above, Lloyd Hendricks photos, Denver Public Library, Western History Department) After their **Rocket** service ended the unique AB units ran a few more years in Chicago commuter service—No. 751 is at Joliet, Illinois. (right, C.W. Burns photo)

41

R I SHOPS GOODLAND KAN

In 1910 the overall appearance of the Goodland roundhouse displays a very prosperous railroad. The newer
stalls provided additional capacity, while the shops on
the far side were able to do most of the repairs to the
locomotives assigned to the division. (M.C. Parker collection)

III. ROCK ISLAND FACILITIES

Division points were placed at Goodland, Kansas as well as Limon and Roswell. Limon and Goodland would be the real hubs of Rock Island activity during the expansion years. The steam era dictated that division points would require lots of manpower. The shops at Colorado Springs, even though matching Goodland and Limon in size, did not require the facilities once the steam era ended and declined much faster. The Denver and Pueblo terminals were not the responsibility of the Rock Island.

Depots and buildings along the line were originally of a fairly standard CK&N design, with individual modifications. Rock Island designated its depots as *east end* or *west end*, the significant difference being the location of the passenger waiting room. West end stations had the waiting rooms on the west end of the building. Curiously, the trains themselves had a *depot side*, and when the trains were cleaned at Roswell, the depot side of the exterior was cleaned first. Most of the depots were on the south side of the tracks, even though there were notable exceptions (Limon, Goodland and others).

In 1936 J.D. Farrington, new president of the Rock Island, initiated a modernization program which was highly visible across the railroad. New ties and rail, re-built bridges and buildings, rehabilitated shops, new road equipment and a complete cleaning of yards and right-of-way spread across the system. New depots replaced a few of the older depots, but most saw merely modernization. Nearly every building on the system was in need of major repairs.

In the years following World War II many of the buildings were again in need of repairs and another program was started to bring the Rock Island up to date. A few of the older buildings that had escaped major rebuilding in the 1930s saw modernization or removal. A rare sight was the few remaining CK&N structures in Kansas; none were left in Colorado.

The decline in passenger service in the 1960s saw the removal of many old buildings and reduced facilities. Ironically, freight service was declining with passenger traffic, and the end was near for many depots and sidings. In Kansas, depots remained for freight service by state law, but in Colorado many were sold and moved off the property or scrapped.

Station by station, from Goodland west, let us take a look at the Chicago Rock Island and Pacific and see just what effect the railroad had on the area it served.

GOODLAND

Sherman County, Kansas was a busy place in 1888. The Leavenworth and Denver Short Line, the Lincoln and Colorado Railway (part of the Union Pacific) as well as the CK&N were all surveying routes through the area. The Lincoln and Colorado was working west from Colby, but the CK&N and the L&C came out at opposite ends of revenue bond elections in Sherman County. The Rock Island bonds carried, but the L&C bonds failed. The L&C stopped at Colby.

The Goodland depot was a busy place at the turn of the century, and the lunchroom served train crews and passengers alike. A few men have gathered for the afternoon train to Colby, while the awnings help shade the upstairs division offices from the Kansas sun. (M.C. Parker collection.)

The two-and-one-half story Goodland depot was built in 1888. The large and comfortable building was a popular spot with the people of Goodland who regularly held gatherings in the railroad's meeting rooms. Westbound 364 is seen in 1889 with the mail train. On March 12, 1909 the depot burned to the ground (opposite). Fire-fighters from the town and the railroad fought the blaze, as we see from the top of a boxcar, but they could not save the structure. (both, M.C. Parker collection)

The railroad, and Goodland, wasted no time in seeing that this area became a popular spot on the railroad. The yards and shops were being laid out as the construction of the railroad steamed westward. A large depot and eating house, ten-stall roundhouse, water tank and coal trestle were under construction within days. The first passenger train arrived July 15, 1888 as a baggage car and two coaches with about a dozen passengers. On November 8 the first passenger train west from Goodland left on a seven hour run to Colorado Springs. New passenger equipment was ordered by the railroad for planned deluxe service between Chicago and Colorado Springs.

A two-and-one-half story "Queen Anne" style depot and hotel was built along the north side of the tracks, east of the shops and south of the business district. The building contained, in addition to the hotel, a dining room and lunch counter, as well as offices for the railroad. It was one of the largest buildings in the city. A separate laundry and baggage building was nearby. A green lawn and park separated the depot from the track and added to the passenger's impression of Goodland.

Goodland, a division point, was where crews changed. The majority of the road crews and the shop force had families and helped Goodland grow. The men and their families built homes, a boon to the economy of the young community. Special trains would stop at the station, including those of Theodore Roosevelt on his way to visits to Colorado in the late 1890s and early 1900s. President William Howard Taft stopped here enroute to Gunnison, Colorado in 1909. The hotel ballrooms were the site of many local cultural events, but that all nearly stopped on March 12, 1909.

The fire alarm sounded at 3 P.M. and was heard throughout the town. A group of company men along with local firemen fought the fire for hours. The flames would die down in one area and soar in another area. The building was engulfed in flames and smoke; the destruction was complete. After the fire only one brick chimney stood in the midst of the ashes. A small depot was erected on the site a year later, replacing a "box car ticket office."

A fire destroyed the railroad's coal trestle in 1892. A temporary trestle served until the replacement was built

In 1902 engineer E.S. Derby stands, oilcan in hand, with locomotive 13, the Goodland switch engine. The temporary coaling trestle replaced the original which had burned in 1892. New coal chutes were built in 1906. The temporary chutes can be seen to the left of the new wooden trestle, under construction below. (both, M.C. Parker collection)

in 1906. Fires were always a major problem in the days of coal fired steam locomotives. In the late 1930s steel towers replaced most of the wooden coal trestles on the division. The change to oil as fuel brought even more improvement from fire hazards.

The early ten-stall roundhouse was expanded to handle the more modern engines, doubling the capacity. A new car shop could handle the repair or rebuilding of any of the company's rolling stock. In the construction period on the CK&N the shops regularly built box cars, gondola cars and flat cars. The locomotive shop handled all light repairs and many heavy repairs on the engines. The shop crew continued to build an occasional freight car, as well as locomotive cab or tender frame.

Diesel freight service began on the Rock Island in 1944. A section of the old roundhouse had been removed in 1940 as fewer steam engines were assigned to the division. One diesel could replace several steam engines. The roundhouse and backshop crews were cut back, and eventually the entire roundhouse as well as the backshop were torn down. A modern depot of block construction replaced the older frame structure, which became a freight house and crew office. A small metal engine house could handle the minor repairs while major work was sent to Fairbury, Nebraska or Silvis, Illinois where there were large company shops.

The facilities were cut back to the minimum after the discontinuance of passenger trains. The condition of the buildings and services deteriorated greatly after 1970. The old passenger station, just east of the depot, became merely a shell of its former self when the freight office was moved into the depot. The turntable was kept in place, mainly used for turning the snowplow. In 1986 the old depot was finally removed rather than let stand derelict and add to the expense of taxation.

The fireproof all-steel coaling tower completed in 1936 was a much safer structure in many ways. Similar towers also were built at Limon and Roswell (Colorado Springs). In 1902 passenger locomotive 566 was all ready for a trip to Limon with conductor Jesse Thorson, Engineer A.L. Tapper and Fireman A.V. Crutchfield. The man in the cab is unidentified. The class E-15 4-4-0 had been built two years earlier and, except for an increased capacity tender, appears in "like new" condition. (both, M.C. Parker collection)

By 1940 five of the original roundhouse stalls had been torn down, but Goodland was still a busy location. A big R-67-B 5000-class 4-8-4 is on the turntable, while one of the Rock Island's unique semi-Vanderbilt "loaf of bread" tenders is under the gallows derrick in the foreground, perhaps being converted to a wedge snowplow. Note the "safety first" slogan on the roundhouse wall at right and, above the trees at the left, the rotary snowplow waiting for winter's arrival. The mainline to Colorado stretches to the horizon beyond.

By the late 1950's the entire roundhouse and backshops have been dismantled. A diesel house and office partially occupy the site of the old shop, with Rotary 95377 parked just beyond. The turntable was still used regularly to turn diesels.

A fence once surrounded the Goodland yards. No. 110 is working the yard south of the mainline—the little 0-6-0 had been built by the Rock Island in 1901 and served at this location most of its life, until 1933. It was scrapped two years later. (three photos, M.C. Parker collection)

CARUSO

Five miles west of Goodland this location served mainly as a maintenance section and passing siding. Early schemes for locating a town around the siding never developed.

RULETON

John H. Rule established the town of Rule on his homestead in mid-1880s, but the name was changed to Ruleton when the post office was started on April 23, 1887. The small community, which consisted largely of a store and the Rule homestead, served the farms in the area as a gathering spot. A new location for the town of Ruleton was platted once the railroad was surveyed. The store owned by A.L. Rich was moved into the new location. The railroad built a small depot, section house and stock pens. Stock pens were added a year later along the far end of the passing siding. An elevator was built soon after the railroad started regular freight service. A school and a few homes were built on the streets which were named after Kansas counties.

As in all of the towns along the railroad, farming and the trains held the economy of the townspeople. The towns grew in the good times and declined in the poor. The great depression had a marked effect on all of the railroad towns, but the dust bowl eras in the 1890s and again in the 1930s were more serious. The dust often covered the tracks causing delays and derailments. On occasion the snowplows were sent out to clear the line between Goodland and Limon.

(Top left) The second Goodland depot stands derelict in 1986, just prior to being torn down. The third and last depot is visible beyond. (Michael Doty photo) Second generation EMD 353 gets some minor servicing at the diesel house in the late 1970's (center), while wrecking crane 95023 waits for its next call. Assigned to the Western Division during the final 20 years of the Rock Island's life, this "big hook" got regular use as track conditions worsened. (Paul Stradley photos) On this page is the Ruleton, Kansas station—a standard Chicago Kansas and Nebraska "west end" depot— around the turn of the century. No train orders are indicated by the orderboard, and the agent, whose main concerns in life centered around the train schedules and the grain elevator down the track, can just be seen behind the cream cans on the wagon. (M.C. Parker collection)

ROCK ISLAND TRACK IN COLORADO

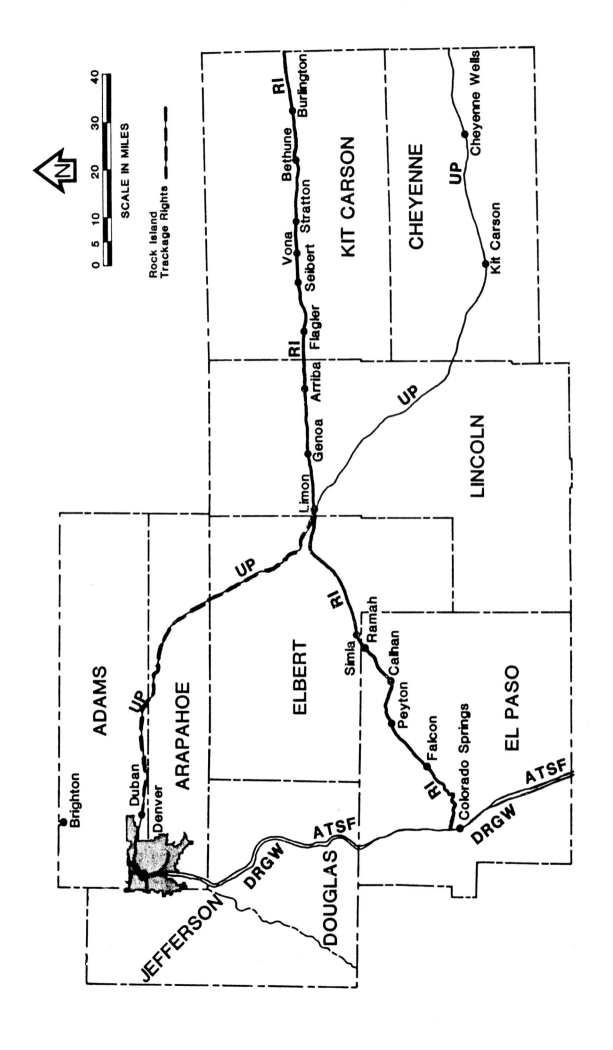

KANORADO

The railroad started Kanorado the day after it arrived in Goodland. The nearby town of Carlisle, founded in 1887, was gravely injured by the competition. Several of the businesses picked up their goods and moved to Kanorado. Some of the buildings were dragged into new locations with shelves stocked and ready for business. A grain elevator was built in 1890. The town of Carlisle hung on until the same year.

The railroad had a water tank, depot, section house and stockyards. Cars for the new elevator were cause for additional trackage. Two passenger trains a day stopped, bringing potential residents, and two others sped through without stopping. The railroad was the major employer in town for many years.

PECONIC

This was the first stop in Colorado, halfway to Burlington; a small town was planned around the passing siding. An elevator was built in 1890, but the town never developed. The trackage was expanded in June 1930 and has remained as a loading point since that time.

BURLINGTON

The Lowell Townsite Company built a few structures on its "Lowell" plat in 1887. The name Lowe was also used for a short time, but in 1888 the Rock Island located its townsite two miles west of Burlington. The "old" Burlington became a relative ghost town in a short time as the residents gradually migrated to the railroad's town. In 1889 the state established Kit Carson County and made Burlington the county seat.

The railroad's facilities included a water tank and windmill to pump the supply for the town and the railroad. Stockyards, section and mail buildings were built along the length of the siding. In 1890 a grain elevator greatly boosted the facilities.

WEST BURLINGTON

An industrial spur was built rather late in the Rock Island era. It served as a loading track for a variety of crops.

Kanorado, Kansas, almost on the state line, had another "west end" depot, so named because of the location of the waiting room at the west end of the building. This view looks southwest. (M.C. Parker collection) Left is the replacement depot at Burlington, a modern "west end" design but longer than others on the division. The map opposite indicates the Rock Island line in relation to the Union Pacific, Santa Fe and Rio Grande routes to Denver. (photo and map, Author's collection)

53

HUNGERFORD

A shortlived scheme for another farming community had enough merit that the railroad built a siding, but within a short time it was obvious that the plan was in error, and the siding sat vacant for a few years before it was removed. It was called Bethune Siding Number One for a few years when the company windmill for Bethune was located there. A coal house was the only other railroad structure in the area.

BETHUNE

The CK&N started by building a section house along the siding in 1888. A residential development was slow to catch on, but the first elevator in 1890 helped things along. A store opened in 1910, but the town was not platted until 1918. A post office was established that year in the new store. A stockyard was at the same time. The first depot was opened by the Rock Island in 1920. In 1926 the town was officially incorporated and opened its new school. A new water tank was built for the railroad in 1926, also improving the rather meager section facilities in town.

The depot was sold and hauled away to a farm a few miles away after the last *Rocky Mountain Rocket*. In 1985 it was moved from the farm to the new community being built as a museum in Burlington and restored to its operating appearance.

COLUMBIA

Platted, but not built, this planned community was between Bethune and Stratton in 1888. A siding was never built.

MUSKOKA

A few buildings were built around the siding at Muskoka, which was a mile and a half west of the spot where Columbia was planned. The siding was built, but it was little used, and remained for nearly a decade before it was abandoned.

STRATTON

A box car was assigned as the depot at Claremont in July 1888. The community was more ambitious than most along the line. Construction crews used the area as a center of operations. The location had good water and was in a good position between Limon and Goodland.

A two-story school was the highlight of the community in 1895. The railroad changed the name of the station due to postal department requests. The mail service continually confused Claremont, California with the Colorado town. The name Machias was tried, but the name Stratton was selected in 1906. It is heard that the name was selected in honor of Winfield Stratton, a prominent gold mine owner from Cripple Creek with a penchant for philanthropy.

A wye on the railroad was added to enable trains from either Goodland or Limon to turn while making the "local" runs to switch the elevators and stockyards along the line.

VONA

Platted in March 1889, it was reported to be named for the niece of Pearl King, the person who filed the plat. It was definitely a railroad town. It was one of the water stops on the climb westward. A freight depot was

The Bethune depot was moved to a farm after passenger service was discontinued in 1966 It has since been relocated to Burlington's historical collection of early buildings. (H.R. Huffer collection)

The block Vona depot retains the "V" bay window of the frame building and incorporates the more modern Rock Island image. (H.R. Huffer collection)

*On July 18, 1929 the **Rocky Mountain Limited** crossed a flood-damaged trestle near Stratton. The locomotive cleared, but the first baggage car derailed and the flooded stream washed away the bridge and two cars. Residents of Stratton and Vona attempted to rescue those in the submerged cars, but high water hindered their efforts. Eight of the ten dead, including two Pullman porters, were in the car **Cape Porpoise** at left. (Dora Erbert collection)*

established early but the passenger station was not added until a decade later. A number of farm related businesses were built around the elevator. A new larger elevator was added in 1915 along with a long spur. A lumber yard was short lived. The town was not officially incorporated until 1919.

Vona to Stratton was a problem area for the Rock Island. The normally dry Spring Creek would turn into a raging river after a heavy rain about once every five years. The original pile trestle washed out twice before 1900. In December 1920 a flash flood weakened the trestle and a large portion of the approach. A passenger train bound for Goodland was derailed and several lost their lives. A modern steel span proved to just as vulnerable as the old pile trestle.

SEIBERT

The railroad construction crews located this siding named after Henry Seibert, a stockholder and official of the Chicago Rock Island and Pacific. The nearby town of Hoyt, which had been founded only a year earlier when Dr. J.S. Hoyt had taken over an old stage station, was indignant. Dr. Hoyt had plotted a trail from central Nebraska to his new town, but once the railroad started building, many of the businesses and residents found Seibert to be more acceptable.

The depot was sold after the last *Rocket* and is now a gas station near the Interstate Highway.

The new Seibert depot had all the features of the later Rock Island frame depots: a simple hip roof, "V" bay window and dark yellow shingled sides. (H.D. Conner collection) The original structure, below, had been an "east end" depot built in 1888. (Denver Public Library, Western History Department)

KIPLING

A passing siding and section division, it also served as a check station for the trains stopped after or before the "Flagler Hole."

Halfway between Kipling and Flagler is a depression where the rolling plains make a drop to Sand Creek. This area is known as the "Flagler Hole." Slightly more than four miles in length, it is marked by a grade of just over one percent in both directions. Train speed and power were critical when passing through this area. The topography and need for caution probably were the reasons for the failure of the early community of Crystal Springs, another community close to Kipling but located at the bottom of "Flagler Hole."

Al Coin, a construction worker, was killed as a result of an accident during the building of the railroad. He was buried near the east end of the siding at Flagler, alongside the tracks. Railroad workers kept the grave well cared for and regularly decorated it with flowers. When highway construction endangered the site in the early 1970s, the grave was moved to the Flagler cemetery.

FLAGLER

Originally named Malowe, in honor of M.A. Lowe of the CK&N, the name fell into disfavor. Going from the sublime to the ridiculous it was called Bowser, for the general store owner's mutt for a short time. The name

was finally changed to Flagler to honor Henry M. Flagler. Flagler was a major investor and driving force in the Rock Island railroad. On his first occasion to travel over the Colorado line his train made a special stop, and the entire town turned out to meet him. It is said that he donated the money for the town's first library after the visit.

As was the case with most of the high plains communities, farming and later cattle were major businesses. Farming was not profitable until the development of mechanized farm equipment. In 1908 there was a general boom for many of the towns along the Rock Island, which was true for Flagler. In other towns the boom was a disaster; as people moved into the larger towns the marginal ones lost out. Grain shipments each year increased, and the number of elevators and storage bins doubled. A single carload of grain that had taken six to eight hours to load by hand was now taking less than half an hour.

The Flagler depot had its share of problems. The second floor was destroyed in a fire one night around the turn of the century. The curve at the depot was also of concern, since trains such as the *Rocky Mountain Limited* would build up speed for the "Flagler Hole." On more than one occasion cars derailed, but once the Limited left the rails, destroying the depot. The agent and the operators, sighting an approaching headlight, would casually wait on the south side of the tracks for the train to pass or stop. This tradition was maintained until the office at Flagler was closed.

At Flagler, station agents regularly waited across the track for trains to pass after a derailment destroyed the old CK&N-built depot. (H.D. Conner collection)

57

SAUGUS

Lacking good water, this small town died on the vine. A store hung on, but the residents moved to either Flagler or Arriba. A tiny depot lasted until after the start of World War I.

ARRIBA

The townsite at Arriba was selected in June 1888. The first rails were laid on the prepared ground through town on August 23. The mainline construction train working eastward hardly paused for any notice. The area was platted in September 1888. Charles A. Creel was a dedicated developer who took an interest in the area; however, he insisted on prohibition. Drinking and gambling would not be allowed in Arriba.

In 1904 C.C. Coleman purchased land east of Arriba and platted Frontier City. One of the first buildings was a saloon. In an attempt to control access to the new community, Creel cleared a strip of land between the rival settlements and declared it a "No Man's Land" with his home at the south end. He could easily monitor any activity across the strip.

In 1918 Frontier City was absorbed into Arriba, yet the vacant strip of land has virtually remained intact. The railroad station remained at Arriba, and the company did its best to stay out of the conflict, even though one of the main streets in Frontier City was Rock Island Avenue.

BOVINA

Bovine, a stop on the cattle trail north from Texas, was a short distance from the railroad's site for Bovina. The company platted the town in October 1888. The location was popular and steadily grew until it was larger than Genoa, Arriba or Limon. The railroad used the station as a primary water stop for trains climbing from Limon to Flagler. Cattle drives continued to pass through Bovina until about 1902 when the last one was recorded. Shipments of cattle were the business source for the railroad at Bovina until World War II. The town suffered through the Great Depression. The coming of the automobile helped keep Bovina on the map.

Modernization came slowly to most of the plains communities. Electricity arrived too late for Bovina, and many of the businesses had either closed or moved on

The order boards were up at Arriba, yet another CK&N west ender pictured in 1912. Aside from the grain elevators, these buildings were the most prominent in the small communities which dotted the eastern Colorado plains along the railroad. They were de facto civic centers as well, with the depot agent, waiting room and Western Union Telegraph connection with the world beyond the horizon. (H.D. Conner collection)

*Ten days before Christmas 1935, the eastbound **Rocky Mountain Limited** is wrapped in a cloud of fragrant soft coal smoke as it rolls along out of Limon at a sedate 45 mph behind 4-8-2 No. 4041, with the hogger keeping an eagle eye on the track ahead. These handsome passenger engines were known to Rock Island crews as "Forty-Hundreds." (Otto Perry photo, Denver Public Library, Western History Department)*

when a fire destroyed a major part of the town one hot spring day. The final blow came in the 1970s with the Interstate Highway. The roadway was of little benefit to most of the towns along the Rock Island, and for Bovina, it was the end. The spot is now merely an odd dot on some maps; even the railroad's siding has been gone for nearly three decades.

GENOA

The town of Genoa started off as a box car depot on the siding ten miles east of Limon. The siding was called Creech, after a Rock Island stockholder. In 1895 it was changed to Cable, but there was confusion with Cable Junction. Once more the name was changed, this time to Genoa.

On June 2, 1909 a petition was filed with the Colorado Railway Commission asking that the Rock Island be required to upgrade the depot, establish a day agent and place a crossing at the depot. The railroad complied with the order, and on the October 21 the road crossing and day operator portion of the order were complete. The new building was not in place as the depot until 1910,

when the box car depot was replaced.

The town was not incorporated until 1925. The main claim to fame for Genoa for many years was its scenic position; a tower provided a view into a wide area. The arrival of the Interstate 70 interchange changed all that. Today very few people stop to enjoy the view and museum.

In the last days of the Rock Island a blizzard crippled the eastern portion of Colorado. The deep cut west of town had always been a problem, but this storm proved the undoing of the push plow from Goodland. Striking the snow at nearly 60 miles an hour, it shot straight up and over. The railroad left the plow upside-down along the track. The Union Pacific cleared the balance of the line into Colorado Springs with a rotary plow. The derailed plow was finally recovered after the line was cleared of freight cars when the railroad was abandoned.

MUSTANG

This was a passing siding and helper station for the climb east out of Limon. For many years it had a small station at the east end.

59

LIMON

Construction on the Rock Island eastward and westward started at Limon in March 1888. Company equipment was brought in overland and on the Union Pacific Railroad. The informal name was Limon's Camp for the name of the construction camp foreman. The old Smoky Hill Trail from Kansas split into two routes near here. The northern trail headed northwestward, but the two converged at Denver. The CK&N survey followed the southern route for a few miles west.

W.S. Pershing, a land agent for the Union Pacific, moved from Hugo, division point southeast of Limon, to the camp and establish a settlement. The location served as a division point on the CK&N, but the UP only added sidings for its interchange. More than 300 regular employees worked at the Rock Island yards and shops.

The railroad built a Grier House Hotel and eating house across the tracks from the depot, which became a "union" depot under the agreements with the Union Pacific. A fire in the 1890s destroyed the first five-stall roundhouse. The replacement was lost in a similar fire in 1906. A larger 75-foot turntable replaced the short 60-foot table when the new roundhouse was finished. A pond and water treatment plant on the west end of the Big Sandy bridge were replaced in 1910. The plant also furnished fresh water for several stations along the line which had inadequate or poor water.

The yards saw continual upgrading and changes over the years. As traffic increased four new yard tracks were added in 1910. In 1926 the yards saw major changes when a new coal tower replaced the old coal chutes, a wye was built around the shops, and again yard tracks were added. Spurs to the elevators and warehouses were extended as they were needed. New oil facilities were added in 1938 and 1939 when the number of coal fired steam engines was cut back, and the number of new diesel locomotives increased.

A fire in 1930 heavily damaged the Grier House. The two railraods no longer used it as an eating house; dining cars had long since arrived on the trains, but shop men and travelers patronized the restaurant regularly. The hotel housed train crews, but those could stay in one of the nearby hotels like the Tompkins just north of the depot. In 1932 the old hotel and eating house was finally torn down.

Limon itself was not immune to the hazards of fire. On January 1, 1924 a block long section of businesses was destroyed. It took many years but most of them were replaced. Not to be forgotten by the town or the railroads was the spectacular fire on June 28, 1910 which destroyed the union depot, several freight cars and a small oil storage building. Reports from the period vary as to the cause of the fire, but quick work by the crew from the shops spared the loss of several passenger cars which were parked near the depot.

In the 1920s a strike caused hard feelings among the railroaders, and issues that were settled on the company level were never settled among many of the men.

During the Great Depression the Limon area limped along, as did all of the communities along the line. The

The Rock Island rostered more 4-8-4s than any other railroad in the United States and was surpassed internationally only by the Canadian National and the U.S.S.R. Several of the big "Fifty-Hundreds" were assigned to the Western Division for heavy trains into Denver. The 5031 is at Limon in October 1950. (Paul Stradley collection)

railroad cut back the yard, shop and road forces to a minimum. The impact of World War II was a complete reversal, and many of the men who had remained in the area were rehired. The shop crew was never back to what it had been in the late teens and early twenties. The road crews were hard pressed to keep up with the number of trains. A lull after the war lasted only a few months, when the late 1940s and early 1950s saw another rise in traffic, but this was never to be repeated. By the mid-1950s the yards and shops were only a ghost of their past. The roundhouse was torn down, replaced by a smaller diesel house, and even the water treatment plant with its large tanks was gone. In 1970 the thought that the depot might be removed and replaced by a much smaller building was considered. The Union Pacific brought in a metal building after the Rock Island was closed.

This 1914 panorama looking west from the top of the Limon watertower shows at the center the Grier House, with the second depot across the track. The Union Pacific mainline crosses from the left, curving off toward Denver beyond the depot, while the CRI&P Colorado Springs line crosses the Big Sandy River on a low pile trestle. Turning to the east, we see the roundhouse and yard across the top of the watertanks, with the wide open spaces beyond, Limon is indeed an oasis; in the 1980s a major wintertime activity is sheltering stranded motorists when Interstate 70 is closed by blizzards. (Limon Leader)

*The ritual of combining the eastbound and splitting the westbound Denver and Colorado Springs sections at Limon went on through the entire era of passenger service. The 1902 view above provides a good look at the original "east end" depot and the front of the Grier House. Below, no less than three locomotives are involved in the separation of the **Rocky Mountain Limited**; the Union Pacific diamond is in the foreground.*

The crew of a train from Colorado Springs, powered by a 1200 class 4-6-0, awaits the arrival of the Denver train while the manager of the Grier House awaits patrons in front of his hostelry. In another turn of the century view below, the Denver train has arrived first. (Four photos, Limon Library collection)

The story of this accident almost in front of the Limon depot has been lost. How such damage could have occured at the low speed within the yard limits stirs one's imagination. The date appears to be about 1920. (Limon Library collection)

Typical freight power used out of Limon is represented by these October 1939 shots of 2-8-0 No. 1927 (ALCO-Brooks 1907) on the ashpit and USRA light 2-8-2 No. 2317 (ALCO-Schenectady 1919) at the roundhouse. Many of the 2300-2319 series were assigned to the Western Division over the years, since they were considered a good fast freight engine on light and medium grades. It is interesting that the Union Pacific also used its light USRA 2480-2499 class from Denver to Limon and east on its line into Kansas. (R.B. Graham photos, G.C. Bassett collection)

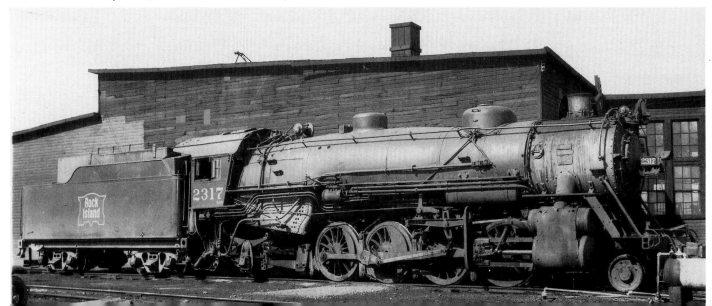

This aerial view of what remains today of the big roundhouse and smaller diesel house serves as a mute reminder of the glory days of The Great Rock Island Route. (Author's photo)

RESOLIS

In Elbert County, this town was laid out in 1888. The plat was filed on November 9, 1888 by C.F. Jilson, land developer for the CK&N. It was standard practice to locate towns along the line at an interval of eight to ten miles. Section crews worked sections divided by these communities. Resolis is roughly nine miles from Limon Junction. A box car was the first depot and post office. A coal house, tool houses for the section men and stock yards were located north of the town.

The population was never large, and in 1902 it had grown to only about sixty. It was located between the north and south branches of the Smoky Hill Trail. It was never on any main traffic route other than the railroad. The post office closed in 1914, but the population remained at about forty. The largest business in town, other than the railroad, was that of the general store. After 1920 the population decline reached a point where the station and other facilities were removed. The sidings were used for passing trains and occasional shipments of cattle.

The final blow came in when the siding was removed; however, a few years later due to increased demands

from shippers, a new Resolis was built four miles west of the old spot in April 1946. The siding was used regularly by maintenance crew work trains, due to the washout hazard on Big Sandy Creek just west of the location. The siding featured a stockyard and scales. In the late 1960s stock shipments by rail were so infrequent that even the new Resolis was removed.

MATHESON

This community was much older than many of the more recent railroad towns, but it had nearly vanished since the time when it was a stop on the Smoky Hill Trail. The railroad revived the community and created a problem by misspelling the name of the town. *Mattison* appeared on the timetables for almost 30 years before the correction in spelling was made. The railroad's depot, section house, tool houses and water tank were on the south edge of the platted town; however, the town gradually abandoned the original site and moved to higher ground after several floods destroyed some sections. The first grain elevator was built in 1914, and the business operated continuously until 1973 under a variety of owners.

*Since the custom-built AB diesels for this portion of its run were not delivered until 1940, the first trip of the Colorado Springs section of the **Rocky Mountain Rocket** on November 12, 1939 was headed by veteran 30-year-old Pacific 876. Why the interesting 40-foot arch-roofed mailcar with its projecting stovepipe was in the consist is a mystery, but its silver paint hardly disguises the contrast with the new streamlined stainless steel cars behind. (Otto Perry photo, Denver Public Library, Western History Department)*

There is a local tale of a train being washed away in a storm in August 1920 or 1921. It is said that the engine and several cars sank in the wet sand and were never recovered; however, a quite similar story is told on the nearby Union Pacific, which may be closer to the truth. The bell was purported to be the only item recovered from the Rock Island wreck, but there are no official accounts of the loss to be found.

The bridge east of Matheson, a fine old style steel structure, replaced an earlier pile trestle that was regularly washed out. In solving the problem, an old double track bridge over the Rock River in Illinois was dismantled and portions of it rebuilt into a single track structure which stands today as the Matheson bridge. Other spans from the bridge were used in several spots on the Rock Island such as over the Washita River in Oklahoma (scrapped 1940), Bridge 6100 (scrapped 1953), Bridge 5713 (scrapped 1969), Bridge 5868 (scrapped 1948) and Bridge 5489—all of which are thought to have been in the Texas-Oklahoma area.

In the early 1950s the old depot and large water tank were removed. A small station converted from a baggage building was moved in to be the freight office. In 1965 the small building was sold and moved away. In less than a year the last passenger train sped through town. The old smaller depot has been located on a farm south of town.

SIMLA

Bearing the same name as a city in India, Simla was founded in 1907. A saloon keeper in Ramah was "urged" to leave, and he started Simla, roughly half way between Matheson and Ramah. The raucus crowd must have followed him because Simla grew quickly. The railroad built a depot after using a box car for several years. The town became much more prosperous than Ramah. The railroad made continual upgradings until the peak in the 1940s. The grain and stock business were supported and sought out by the railroad in the early years. The elevator shipped grain through the 1970s. A center of commerce, the local lumber yard and oil company were very important customers. Small manufacturing concerns survived until the last freight service was halted.

The passenger station, which remained to serve the freight agent, was sold and moved north to Strasburg, on the Union Pacific. It serves as a comfortable home and has now been modernized and sheathed in red brick.

RAMAH

This name is reported to have been derived from a novel that the wife of the CK&N's chief surveyor was reading. The town is not directly on the site of an earlier camp called the O.Z. settlement which dated from Smoky

Simla was a shipping point on the Rock Island until the end and is still a busy location on the Cadillac & Lake City; however, the depot has been removed to a farm near Strasburg. (H.D. Conner collection) The Calhan station (below) is still standing. It has the typical roofline of the 1920-1930 replacements of the original CK&N structures. (H.R. Huffer collection)

Hill Trail days. The initials of the first postmaster became the name of the station.

The CK&N built a depot, section house, stockyards and scales. The growth of nearby Simla had a negative influence on Ramah, and by the 1960s there was little to show for the railroad's prosperity. The old water tank had been removed in 1937. The stockyards survived until 1946, after which stock was shipped from either Calhan or Simla. The siding was finally taken up in 1956-57.

CALHAN

A Mr. Calahan or Callahan, who was reportedly a conductor on the construction train, was given the honor of having his name used, or abused, as the name of this community. The town was settled largely by European and Russian immigrants who thought the area reminded them of their homelands. The railroads had advertised widely and eagerly transported the settlers to many communities in the West. An occasional prospective settler caused quite a stir when the spot he had selected from the advertising did not quite compare to the reality. Some of these immigrants moved around for years, but many stayed and made an effort to make the most of their selection.

Calhan's climate can be perfect for growing crops some years and quite different in others. The railroad had prob-

lems with the weather in the area: floods, droughts, rain, hail and blizzards. The CK&N build a depot, section house, bunk houses, tool houses, a baggage building, water tank, pump house and stockyards. The area boomed in the 1899-1903 era, and Calhan saw the building of a bank, stores and hotels. A lumber yard and grain elevator were built in 1907. Clay was mined at the "Paint Mines" and shipped over the railroad to Pueblo, where it was used in bricks.

In 1905 the Calhan Fair was a very informal event, but in 1910 it was expanded and was called the El Paso County Fair. This became an annual event, and the Rock

A truckdriver escaped death when the **Rocket** destroyed his water truck on a grade crossing near Calhan in June 1963. Only two passengers were hurt, and the others continued to Limon by bus. The train is framed by a section of broken rail, and the remains of the truck's tank are plastered to the front of the diesel. Crews of the flat-nosed 750 and 751 were fearful of such accidents—a similar occurrence once filled the locomotive cab with gravel. (Michael Doty collection)

Island ran special trains to Calhan from Colorado Springs and Limon between 1910 and 1925.

The area suffered from the Dust Bowl of the 1930s and the Great Depression, but made a substantial recovery by the 1940s. The decline of the railroad shipments was serious in Calhan, and the agent did the work of the former agents from Falcon to Matheson. The railroad maintained the station until the closing of the line, but it was primarily used as a section house. The agent's work was handled out of Colorado Springs starting in the late 1960s. The water tank had been gone since 1951, and the section crew used part of the depot from 1951 until 1966, when they took full use of it.

TIP TOP

Not actually a town, rather a geographic location, this was not only the highest spot between Limon and Colorado Springs but was the highest on the entire Rock Island railroad at 6875 feet. It was considered as a townsite during the survey period, but it was used mainly as a helper cut-off point. Occasionally an engine was added to a westbound at Limon, but the normal situation was for helpers to run from Roswell to Tip Top. The engine would then run in reverse to Roswell. The siding was removed in the 1950s, long after the last helper made this turn.

Peyton, Colorado in about 1905 was a thriving community. Only a couple of these buildings exist today, all others having been replaced by more modern structures. (Colorado Springs Library)

PEYTON

Peyton, originally called Mayfield, was a cluster of ranch buildings when the CK&N arrived. The name changed to Peyton to ease the confusion with Mayfield, California. The name of nearby Bijou Basin was considered, but the small enclave refused to relocate to Mayfield. The addition to the community honored local settler George Peyton. The railroad's depot, tool and coal house were built just south of the Peyton homestead. The Denver and New Orleans railroad, far to the north, was already adding to the development of the region. The area grew steadily, but in 1907 the addition of the Russell Gates store and elevator was seen as progressive. The store and elevator lasted until 1920, and the next

year a fire destroyed several of the businesses.

In 1935 flood waters damaged the roads as well as the railroad. Trains were diverted over the Rio Grande to Denver until repairs could be made. In 1956 and 1965 other floods caused problems in the area and major problems for the region.

In 1949 the mail contract was given to a small trucking line, and the Railway Post Office on the *Rocket* lost the contract to carry the mail for the communtiies between Limon and Colorado Springs after 60 years of service. The old depot, which had been built as a replacement of the old two-story CK&N station, was closed and sold to the Methodist Church in Calhan, where it was remodeled and added to the existing building.

FALCON

Granger, on the Denver and New Orleans, was about two miles north of the site selected by the CK&N near where it would cross under the D&NO mainline. The name Falcon was chosen as a reflection of the large number of the wild birds in the area. The town of Granger died quickly but the school survived several decades. Lavish advertising told glowing tales of beauty and water in the area. Falcon soon had homes, hotels and a newspaper in addition to the railroad structures. The D&NO had a siding and water tank at Granger; however, once the CK&N crews finished at Falcon, the D&NO built a small yard and interchange track. A wye was added several years later when trackage rights were obtained on the Rock Island. In 1920 the wye was relocated to handle larger locomotives. It remained in place until 1936.

With the loss of the Colorado and Southern (ex-D&NO) and the advent of trucks and buses, Falcon started to decline as a business and farming center; the depression guaranteed that. The railroad activity had declined when the area coal mines closed, but with the loss of the C&S the Rock Island business picked up a bit before declining later itself. The depot was closed in the 1940s and the exact disposition of the building is unknown, but recent excavations indicate that it may have been burned.

The D&NO's overpasses were west of town. A second overpass replaced the original structure, adding to the height and easing the curvature to the D&NO's yard. The Rock Island removed its bunkhouse in 1940 and the section house in 1947. The town was reduced to a few buildings alongside US 24 until the late 1960s when the area again started to grow, mainly as a suburban area of Colorado Springs.

SHIRLEY

The nearby Banning-Lewis Ranch shipped large quantities of stock here rather than ship from Falcon. A siding with pens was built in 1935 and expanded in 1938. The old station of Bierstadt on the D&NO had been used by the ranch for shipping until that line was finally abandoned. The siding became a spur in 1939, and it was removed in the 1960s.

A Colorado & Southern heavyweight open-platform car is spotted on the connecting track behind the "west end" depot at Falcon one afternoon about 1900 in this scene looking northeast. (Denver Public Library, Western History Department)

ELSMERE

This siding on the curve west of Shirley had a fine view of Pikes Peak. A community was laid out and failed. A coal branch toward Manitou Junction left from the west side of the hill, winding over Sand Creek. The area was busy in the era of the coal mines. The spur itself was removed in 1920, the section house was burned in 1923 and a car body replaced it. The little depot was chiefly used by the maintenance crews and in 1925 a large coal bunker was added with emergency coal for trains. The helpers often waited at Elsmere rather than return to Colorado Springs.

A portion of the old spur was rebuilt; however, the majority of the new spur into the air base was new. The new track into the flying field was built as a result of training activity started in 1942. A water tank was added at the same time. After the war the little depot, in dire need of major repairs, was removed. The line saw heavy traffic during World War II, but the military activity was minimal during the Korean War. A movie crew used the area around the spur, as well as portions of Camp (now Fort) Carson for a motion picture about the Korean War. The spur was removed in 1961 when the Air Force discontinued shipments by rail.

CABLE JUNCTION

At this point the Rock Island met the old D&NO at the end of the original branch from Elsmere. The two railroads served nearly 17 mines in the region, some jointly. The largest of the mines was the McFerran, just east of Manitou Junction (on the D&NO) and Cable Junction. The peak of activity was in the 1890s when the D&NO (Denver Texas and Gulf by that time) had operating rights from Falcon over the Rock Island. A few mines shipped some coal during World War I.

ROSWELL

The rail crew arrived on October 10, 1888, and the first train over the line other than a construction train, was on October 26. The original plat for Roswell City was west of the Denver and Rio Grande's mainline to Colorado Springs. A large yard was laid out which included a depot, 16-stall roundhouse, water tank, pump house, coal trestle with a 24-pocket coal chute, coal house, two oil houses, stockyard and coach repair shop. Numerous old car bodies were added over the years for sheds, offices and storage. Roswell City was annexed into Colorado City after a few years, and a new Roswell was built northeast across Monument Creek from Roswell yards.

Roswell was a center for the Rock Island families as the railroad employed nearly 200 men in the area, the majority with families. Stores, schools and, for a short time, a newspaper helped separate the community from Colorado Springs, In 1890-91 the Colorado Springs streetcar line was extended into Roswell. The line crossed the railroad at Tejon Street on a trestle. In 1905 a Rock Island train caught the bridge on fire, and it was all but destroyed. It took nearly a year for the two companies to settle, and the railroad rebuilt the structure in 1906. The community requested more service from the streetcar company, but by 1924 abandonment was being considered. The company offered Roswell all the community's tracks, a car, metered power and honor of its transfers if the community would buy that portion of the line. The citizens declined, and that was the first major section of the streetcar system to be dismantled.

The community, like Roswell City, was eventually annexed into Colorado Springs but long after the Rock Island atmosphere of the area had been lost. The shops were heavily damaged in the 1935 flood, but the damage to Roswell was minimal since it sat on higher ground. Large portions of the shops were not rebuilt after the

In 1896 "new" Roswell was only a cluster of buildings; the earlier Roswell City was out of view in the distance, but the dark line running above the roofs is the Denver & Rio Grande mainline. (M.C. Parker collection)

flood, and many families moved to other locations on the Rock Island. The shop force was again cut in 1939 with the decline of the steam and coaling facilities. By 1966, when the last *Rocket* left Colorado Springs, Roswell as a Rock Island family community was only a memory.

COLORADO SPRINGS

The superintendent's office was in the Grier Hotel which was built north of the stone Denver and Rio Grande depot. The hotel also provided an excellent dining room for the two railroads. The hotel's rooms were no rival to those of the nearby Antlers, but they were popular and reasonable for train crews and passengers waiting ovenight for a connection to Cripple Creek, for example. Near the depot was an ice house and storehouse, but the space on the east side of the track was limited. The Rock Island had additional tracks and buildings on the west side of the Rio Grande. Two warehouses were served by Rock Island spurs. In the 1950s a trailer-on-flat-car ramp was built where the old coach storage tracks had been. The hotel was closed in 1935 and torn down in the following year.

On May 8, 1938 this chaos resulted when 17 cars and a caboose on an eastbound freight rolled away from Falcon 16 miles back into the Roswell Yard. Fortunately, no one was injured—the caboose shown was one parked in the yards. Otto Perry was on the scene with his camera the next day. (Denver Public Library, Western History Department)

On a day in the 1920s train No. 7 has arrived in Colorado Springs behind No. 811, one of the Rock Island's first 4-6-2's, class P-28 built by ALCO-Brooks in 1903. (California State Railroad Museum) Chair car No. 2822, similar to the one behind the railway post office car, was parked behind the roundhouse at Roswell in October 1936. (Otto Perry, Denver Public Library, Western History Department)

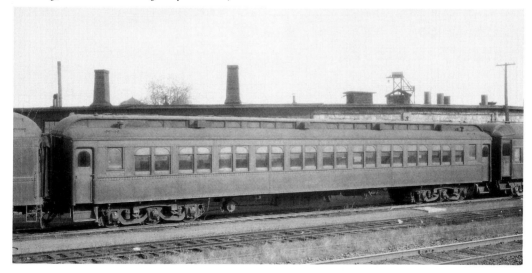

Thirty years later, the roundhouse was being used by a firm to store grain. The turntable had been removed and still serves as a bridge nearby. (Mel McFarland photo)

2-8-2 No. 2314 sits next to the Grier House in Colorado Springs on July 4, 1934 (Otto Perry photo, Denver Public Library, Western History Department) and in the D&RGW yard seven years later, by then converted to an oil burner and with a red Rock Island shield on its tender. (W. Krambeck photo, G.C. Bassett collection) Below, in 1936 the winter sky had obscured Pikes Peak when No. 906 waited for departure time with the **Rocky Mountain Limited** on a snowy day. The site of the recently demolished Grier is in the foreground. (Vern Fiddelke photo)

(Top) No. 1770 poses for Otto Perry under the large Rio Grande-Rock Island sign on the roof of the Colorado Springs station. This engine was sold to National Railways of Mexico in 1942. Very few 0-6-0 switchers were ever assigned to the Western Division. Otto found No. 226 at Roswell in April 1931. (both, Denver Public Library, Western History Department) The landmark Antlers Hotel can be seen beyond the smokebox of the 950, regularly assigned to the Colorado Springs mail train at the time of this 1939 photo. (R.B. Graham, G.C. Bassett collection)

With its distinctive red, maroon and silver squared-off diesels, the **Rocky Mountain Rocket** is one of the best remembered trains in Colorado. On January 10, 1943, Otto Perry took this excellent portrait of No. 750 accelerating eastward from Colorado Springs as the snowy 14110-foot summit of Pikes Peak sparkles beneath a clear winter sky. (Denver Public Library, Western History Department)

*The **Rocket** as it appeared in its last years is shown on these two pages: RPO-baggage 801, chair car **Colorado Springs**, cafe-lounge **Mesa Verde** and pullman **Air Force Academy**, which lasted long enough to be purchased by Amtrak. (four photos, Virl Davis)*

*The **Rocket** was scrubbed between trips at Roswell, always the "depot side" first, before being backed into the Colorado Springs station at 11 AM, ready for the trip to Chicago. (Pikes Peak Library District)*

*No. 751 awaits departure time at the Springs on August 23, 1943. On the rear end is an old heavy weight baggage car enroute to the Silvis, Illinois shops. (Joseph Schick photo, Western History Department, Denver Public Library) This billboard promoted the **Rocket** in Colorado Springs. Similar ones could be found across the system. Of interest is the additional notice about the Roswell Industrial District north of town, one of the last major Rock Island projects in Colorado. (Colorado Springs Public Library)*

Business car 100 in the unattractive blue, white and black paint scheme of the mid-1970s is on the private car spur just north of the Rio Grande station. (Michael Doty photo)

The new Roswell industrial area, located on the grounds of an old airport, was highly touted as in this publicity photograph, but it was a few years ahead of its time. GP7s 436 and 1259 are switching a 40-foot Union Pacific boxcar.

The main yard and shops in Colorado Springs were long gone, and Roswell consisted of only a few buildings by 1959. (Two photos, Stan Payne, Pikes Peak Library District)

PUEBLO

The CRI&P shared offices and yards with the D&RG in Pueblo, but soon it opened a separate ticket office. The designated trackage for the Rock Island was located in several sections of the yard, but the majority was located directly across from the Union Depot.

Pueblo, unfortunately, was memorable on a couple of occasions for the Rock Island. In April 1901 a Denver and Rio Grande passenger train crashed into a Rock Island passenger train at Eden, just north of town. The southbound Rock Island was trying to make it into the siding. The northbound D&RG had passed the south end of the siding and both trains were on the mainline. A waiting freight was on another siding, blocking the view of the two train crews. The crew of the waiting train attempted to flag the two others and even throw a switch ahead of the Rock Island train, and when the two hit both engineers had been alerted. The Rock Island train had stopped, but the D&RG train was still traveling at eight to ten miles an hour. The impact drove the engines back into their baggage cars. The crews were uninjured,

and there were no serious injuries among the passengers. The major discomfort was on the dining cars where dinners were thrown into laps.

In 1912, a Rock Island passenger train had just left the 8th Street Station on the Rio Grande when it struck a section of road which had been undermined by water in Fountain Creek. The locomotive, baggage car, combination baggage and smoking car and a coach dropped into the stream. Another coach was left balancing on the tracks.

The number of lives lost is unknown since the conductor on the *Chicago Express* was just starting to collect tickets. Complicating the situation, continued storms kept the water high, hampering the cleanup of the wreck and removal of the train. Bodies were recovered, along with baggage and personal items, as far as five miles downstream. Luggage was found for people who were not even known to be on the train.

It is interesting that the Rock Island could not take on passengers, or discharge them, between Colorado Springs and Pueblo. This was also true on the Union Pacific between Limon and Denver.

*Views of Rock Island trains in Pueblo are extremely rare. This postcard shows the Pueblo section of the **Limited** behind tenwheeler 1259, an 1898 Rock Island-built engine. (Mel McFarland collection)*

A new ALCO 1600-horsepower RS3 burbles past the Union Pacific depot at Agate on February 17, 1951. The new connection from Duban to D&RGW's North Yard in Denver had been opened on the first of the month, and several of these units had replaced the last Rock Island 2-8-2s and 4-8-4s in Colorado which had previously taken over from road diesels at Limon; North Yard had so steam facilities. (Otto Perry photo, Denver Public Library, Western History Department)

DENVER

In 1912 the Rock Island acquired one-sixth ownership of the Denver Union Depot Company. It was in its best interest after that time to direct more traffic into Denver than Colorado Springs. The Denver connection was most important to the freight operations. After 1918, when the Colorado Midland stopped providing a connection to western Colorado and Utah, Colorado Springs dropped in importance. The Denver and Rio Grande and the Denver and Salt Lake were the most important sources of revenue in Denver since all of the other lines had their own routes to the east. The Rock Island was most competitive with the Burlington and Santa Fe from Denver to Chicago.

Near the Union Pacific's Sandown siding just east of Denver, Duban was built in 1949-1950 as part of the new connection to the Denver and Rio Grande Western's new North Yard. Up to that time the Rock Island used only Union Pacific trackage except for the Denver and Rio Grande Western yard and roundhouse at Burnham. With the construction of North Yard, the use of a direct connection to the new Duban Yard sped traffic from the Rio Grande toward Chicago. The route across the north end of the city was vital to the Rock Island until the last train east from Denver. CRI&P track extended 4.0 miles northwest from Sandown to Belt, where connection was made with the D&RGW's Northwestern Terminal line to North Yard, 2.7 miles farther west.

Prior to the opening of the new Belt line, all CRI&P freights had continued into Denver on the U.P., then terminated at the Rio Grande's Burnham Yard. This doubleheader of 2-8-0 No. 2003 and 2-8-2 No. 2304 is inbound through the interlocking just north of Denver Union Station on October 1, 1939. (R.H. Kindig photo)

Big R-67-B 5059 enters Union Pacific's 38th Street Yard with a 41-car freight at 11:40 AM on December 14, 1941. (John W. Maxwell photo, Schick collection, Denver Public Library, Western History Department) Below, Pacific 950, with a four-car *Rocky Mountain Limited*, eases under the three-masted signal bridge at the northeast throat of Denver Union Station on May 27, 1939. Of note is the Union Pacific freight house to the left and the off-line lightweight coach just behind the baggage car. (R.H. Kindig photo)

In an era long before fiber-optic communications, No. 2307 passes beneath a lineman's nightmare of many-armed, double and quadruple pole overhead utility lines near downtown Denver in September 1939. (R.H. Kindig) The last passenger diesel purchased new by the Rock Island, 1952 vintage E8 No. 655 is just a few hundred yards from the end of its run at Denver Union Station with the **Rocket**, July 27, 1957. (G.C. Bassett collection)

Only on the Rock Island would one expect to find this combination: A six-unit diesel including four different models of first and second generation power of three builders (ALCO, EMD and GE) led by an ALCO FA unit re-engined by EMD! The location is Sandown Junction on April 7, 1968. (Ronald C. Hill) On January 14, 1970 (below) the 225 and 395, a GE/EMD set, roared eastward along the U.P. over the high plains of eastern Colorado, while on the other side of the long snowfence, the community of Strasburg basks in the short winter afternoon. (Lloyd Hendricks photo, Denver Public Library, Western History Department)

IV. CADILLAC AND LAKE CITY

Stepping back for a moment and tracing the Cadillac and Lake City from the start requires a departure from the Colorado-Kansas area. Prior to 1978 the C&LC (reporting marks CLK) had operated trackage in Michigan on an old branch line of Penn Central heritage. The C&LC had run until 1974 as a freight short line, operating passenger excursions on occasion. The 21 miles of ex-Pennsylvania Railroad had provided ten years of experience for the C&LC. In 1978 the railroad was approached by Gary Flander's Rail Car Corporation, with headquarters in Colorado Springs, with an offer of purchase. The C&LC then moved its office to Colorado but still held property in Michigan.

Rail Car was in the car rebuilding, repair and servicing business. On July 1, 1980 the dormant C&LC was reactivated to operate the Rock Island trackage in Denver. In January 1981, Howard Noble, who had been president and general manager of the road in Michigan, was put in charge of the Colorado operations. The C&LC was granted permission to operate the Colorado Springs trackage as well as trackage from Limon west to Simla and east to Goodland (later extended to Colby with BN rights into Goodland) on July 1, 1981. A bridge in eastern Colorado Springs was washed out preventing use of the line east from that point.

Roswell yards and the neighboring industrial trackage saw a volume of railroad cars like it had not seen in decades when Rail Car began using the area to rebuild coal train cars. A portion of its Pueblo operation was relocated inside the old wye at Roswell. At times, the old CRI&P rails held up to 350 coal hoppers.

The railroad was operating under an ICC approval, and it was working on a lease from the CRI&P trustees. The C&LC was using Rail Car-owned locomotives which had been purchased from a variety of sources, including the Burlington Northern and the Union Pacific. Power visible on the system included F7s from the BN and an ex-UP GP7 at Limon, ex-BN switchers at Denver and Roswell (including the rare NW5s). Service on the old line from Goodland to Limon slowly started to rebuild. The grain rush caused the little railroad to strain, but the service offered was more personal than the Rock Island had provided in years. The number of freight shipments began to rise.

In 1982 Rail Car and Cadillac and Lake City Railroad were split when certain agreements for the purchase by Rail Car were not met. The new Colorado and Eastern Railroad was formed by Rail Car to operate its equipment on the sections of the Rock Island that it would assume. A scramble between the two rail lines and the trustees created confusion. Rail Car withdrew its locomotives from Cadillac and Lake City. The trustees of the Rock Island gave the Colorado and Eastern rights to operate from Limon west and in Denver. The C&LC would operate Limon east.

Ex-Milwaukee Road 994 of the Cadillac and Lake City, with former D&RGW passenger cars, hauled 2400 people on a shuttle basis over the old Rock Island track from Colorado Springs to Calhan for the 1985 El Paso County Fair. None of this equipment is still on the property. (Michael Doty photo)

In 1983 the Cadillac and Lake City lost the trackage east of Limon to Mid-States Port Authority, a group composed of largely governmental bodies which had formed specifically to purchase large portions of the Rock Island and run it as a railroad. Kyle Railways was given a lease to operate the line through Kansas and into Limon, which it does under the name Kyle *Railroad*. For some time it was thought that MSPA would take over the line into Colorado Springs, but traffic on this section was thought to be insufficient. Colorado and Eastern had used the line mainly for car storage and had made minimal revenue runs over any of it.

The trustees were moving quickly to wrap up the ownership of all of the dormant and active leases on the railroad. The Colorado and Eastern was informed that its lease would be lost on all but three miles of the Colorado Springs route. Rail Car was shocked, since it had been led to believe that it would be able to purchase the line as it raised the funds.

The balance of the line east of Elsmere was again up for sale, to be scrapped. The governments of Elbert, Kiowa and El Paso Counties followed the lead of MSPA and set about to buy the line. The Denver and Rio Grande Western was given the Roswell area tracks and property and the mainline east to the point where the C&E trackage started at a washed out bridge. The trustees settled a debt with the D&RGW which had been incurred over long period of time by the Rock Island. Rail Car retained the Denver stockyards trackage, but the old Duban Yard was sold to a land developer.

In the scramble for tracks the C&LC was granted a lease on the line from Limon to Falcon from the new owners. The C&LC's last link to Michigan was lost in 1985 when the last 4.5 miles of the old operation were scrapped. The section of the railroad between Falcon and Elsmere was sold to a land developer, who has an operating agreement with the C&LC; however, the portion owned by the C&E remains in limbo.

The C&LC is operating as a freight and passenger carrier with up-to-date motive power and a variety of passenger equipment. The line is undergoing improvements and changes as revenues permit. The Kyle portion of the line has seen radical improvement. There are many modern locomotives in use as well as a variety of unusual older engines. Freight is the only business. The railroad has seen great rebuilding programs in the roadbed and track departments. A 1985-1987 project of re-ballasting and ties is nearly complete. New buildings are being planned and older ones removed. The old depot at Goodland is an example of an unused building's destruction.

A major blow to the railroad occurred in August 1986 when a string of loaded grain cars was sent rolling down the tracks toward Goodland by vandals. The cars hit a westbound train near the Spring Creek trestle between Stratton and Vona at about 3 A.M. The engine crew was killed, two engines destroyed and the pile of freight cars was nearly 100 feet tall! It took nearly two weeks to get operations back to normal.

On the C&LC the freight business co-exists with passenger business. Mixed trains are almost the order of the day. Excursions to the El Paso County Fair in 1985 and 1986 are reestablishing an old tradition. In September 1986 a special excursion was run to Limon to meet eastbound Union Pacific steam locomotive 8444 enroute to the 125th Anniversary of Kansas Statehood Celebration in Topeka. In October 1986 an excursion was run to Limon from Elsmere to mark the twentieth anniversary of the last trip east of the *Rocky Mountain Rocket*. Daily short excursions near Colorado Springs provide school children with their first train ride. The railroad is searching for additional passenger equipment and has recently acquired a snowplow. Shops and yards, as well as a museum, are planned for Falcon in the near future.

The Rock Island is gone, but the spirit of the *Rocky Mountain Limited* and the *Rocket* live on in the eastern plains of Colorado.

This ex-Rock Island railway post office car was purchased by the Rio Grande for use in maintenance-of way service. (Michael Doty photo)

Former Burlington Northern F units 716 and 752, which originally had been owned by the Spokane Portland & Seattle and Northern Pacific, are on their way to Colorado & Eastern trackage on the east side of Colorado Springs, hauling a string of "white lined" boxcars. This was the last time these engines ran under their own power; they later were heavily vandalized and finally sold. (Michael Doty photo)

*In 1986 it is not the **Rocky Mountain Rocket**, but a Cadillac and Lake City passenger special roaring across the snowy plains with a former Santa Fe CF7, New York Central observation car, **California Zephyr** coach and Burlington heavyweight commuter car continuing at least in part the spirit of one of Colorado's most fondly remembered railroads. (Mel McFarland photo)*

In Living Memory

Anniversary Celebration Features Planting of Trees to Those Who Aided in Making Rock Island History

THE Rock Island Railroad, as a part of its Seventieth Anniversary celebrations, October 10, will honor seventy of its deceased and former employes—one for every year of service of the company—by planting seventy memorial trees at as many different points on its lines.

These trees will be planted in honor of all classes of employes, from president down to section laborer.

Nearby each tree will be placed a concrete monument on which a bronze tablet is fastened, telling in whose honor the tree was planted. Some relative of the deceased employe will be appointed sponsor for each tree. Each tree will be planted with appropriate ceremonies in charge of a local committee of employes, appointed by the superintendent of the division on which the trees are planted.

The bronze plate inscription reads:

1852   ROCK ISLAND LINES   1922
Seventieth Anniversary
October Tenth
The memorial tree planted nearby
is Dedicated
By the Rock Island in affectionate
memory of
(NAME OF FORMER EMPLOYE)
Who by his industry, courage and loyalty through every vicissitude signally aided in the development of the Chicago, Rock Island & Pacific Railway into a great transportation system DEVOTED TO THE PUBLIC SERVICE.

In the case of each tree, a relative of the deceased employe in whose honor the tree is planted, will be appointed as "sponsor" for the tree to aid in its future care. Each sponsor will receive from President Gorman a personal commission appointing him or her official sponsor.

A total of ninety names were recommended to the Committee to be considered as worthy of being honored in the tree-planting ceremonies. These recommendations came from superintendents and other officers of the company. The list, together with the places recommended for the trees, follow:

Name and Former
Position—   Tree Planted at—

Elbridge G. Allen—Car Carpenter (father of Vice-President L. M. Allen)................Silvis, Ill.
Daniel Atwood—General Freight Agent......Kansas City, Mo.
C. R. Batchelder—Conductor (killed in service) Forest City, Ark.
Benj. B. Brayton—Superintendent..............Wilton, Iowa
Robt. C. Brinkley—President (C. O. & G.)......Brinkley, Ark.
Horace Broadbent—Engineer................Marseilles, Ill.
Thomas H. Brown—Right of Way Agent...Sioux Falls, S. D.
Patrick Burns—Section Foreman (father of Vice-President W. H. Burns).........Goodland, Kas.
R. R. Cable—President.......................Rock Island, Ill.
Wm. M. Cassidy—Crossing Flagman (killed in service)....
................................Washington Heights, Ill.
R. H. Chamberlin—Superintendent................Geneseo, Ill.
James Clifford—Section Foreman...............Minooka, Ill.
Charles Cobb—Engineer...................Hot Springs, Ark.
A. B. Copley—Assistant Manager..............Fairfield, Iowa
W. M. Conley—Engineer....................Hulbert, Ark.
Edward W. Dee—Conductor....................Enid, Okla.
Peter A. Dey—Chief Engineer (M. & M.)......Newton, Iowa
John Dickerman—Engineer....................Annawan, Ill.
Gen. G. M. Dodge—Chief Engineer.........Council Bluffs, Iowa
Patrick Egan—Conductor...................El Dorado, Ark.
Henry Farnam—Chief Engineer.................Bureau, Ill.
Rudolph Fink—Gen. Mgr. (C. O. & G.)........Lonoke, Ark.
John M. Finley—Engineer.....................Carlisle, Ark.
Roswell P. Flower—Director...................Joliet, Ill.
Chas. N. Gilmore—Superintendent..........Des Moines, Iowa
Wm. H. Givin—Superintendent............Cedar Falls, Iowa
John Givin—Superintendent..................Oskaloosa, Iowa
James Grant—President.....................Davenport, Iowa
George Greene—President (B. C. R. & M.)..Cedar Rapids, Iowa
David W. Hanks—Bridge Foreman (killed in service)....
....Limon, Colo.
Henry A. Hatfield—Section Foreman..........Belleville, Kas.
David Hartigan—Engineer...................McFarland, Kas.
Andrew J. Hitt—Freight Agent...........91st Street, Chicago
John Holmquist—Carpenter................Montezuma, Iowa
Patrick Howe—Roadmaster..................Estherville, Iowa
Sidney B. Hubbard—Conductor.................Burlington, Colo.
Chas. J. Ives—Superintendent (B. C. R. & N.).Burlington, Iowa
Alexander Jackson—Agricultural Agent...........Eldon, Mo.
James C. Jackson—Engineer..................Lincoln, Nebr.
John B. Jervis—President.................Rock Island Arsenal
William Jervis—Chief Engineer.................La Salle, Ill.
Everitte St. John—Gen. Passenger Agent...West Liberty, Iowa
W. L. St. John—General Superintendent.........Ottawa, Ill.
Charles W. Jones—Manager...............Mitchellville, Iowa
Abel Kimball—Superintendent....................Moline, Ill.
J. B. Kinney—Engineer.......................St. Joseph, Mo.
John A. Levins—Brakeman (killed in France)..Shawnee, Okla.
W. J. Logsdon—General Car Foreman........Chickasha, Okla.
M. A. Low—General Attorney..................Topeka, Kas.
C. M. Martin—Conductor......................Eldon, Iowa
Elbert W. Mason—Engineer.................Fairbury, Nebr.
Robert Mather—Vice-President.............Spirit Lake, Iowa

John C. McCabe—General Freight Agent......Ft. Worth, Tex.
Jewel McClosky—Engineer..................Muscatine, Iowa
John McGie—Superintendent...................El Reno, Okla.
C. B. McLaughlin—Agent.....................Indianola, Iowa
Wm. N. McLennan—Engineer (killed in service).Norton, Kas.
F. O. Melcher—Vice-President..............Little Rock, Ark.
George A. Merrill—Superintendent............Alexandria, La.
F. B. Mesick—General Freight Agent..............Pratt, Kas.
Dr. Wm. D. Middleton—Chief Surgeon........Iowa City, Iowa
Geo. W. Moltzen—Brakeman (killed in France) Mansfield, Ark.
H. U. Mudge—President.......................Denver, Colo.
Cornelius T. O'Brien—Engineer (killed in service)........
....Marengo, Iowa
Hilon A. Parker—Vice-President............Morgan Park, Ill.
Edward B. Peirce—General Solicitor.........Booneville, Ark.
W. G. Purdy—President.................Englewood (Chicago)
Chas. A. Ransom—Conductor..............Phillipsburg, Kas.
Hugh Riddle—President.......................Midlothian, Ill.
W. L. Robinson—Section Man....................Ruston, La.
T. H. Rogers—Engineer.......................Cambridge, Ill.
Henry F. Royce—General Superintendent........Tiskilwa, Ill.
John F. Tracy—President.........................Tracy, Ill.
Wm. M. Sage—Freight Traffic Manager..........Peoria, Ill.
John Sebastian—Vice-President and P. T. M..Colorado Springs
Winfield Scott Tinsman—General Manager........Trenton, Mo.
Robert Shields—Roadmaster...............Washington, Iowa
Joseph Sheffield—Engineer....................Sheffield, Ill.
Thomas H. Simmons—General Freight Agent.....Stuart, Iowa
Joseph B. Smalley—Superintendent...............Liberal, Kas.
E. Olin Soule—Traveling Passenger Agent....Iowa Falls, Iowa
W. H. Stillwell—Superintendent.................Manly, Iowa
Asa R. Swift, Superintendent of Telegraph.95th Street, Chicago
F. H. Tisdale—Engineer (killed in service)......Vinton, Iowa
Thomas B. Twombly—Master Mechanic......Dalhart, Texas
John T. Walker—Conductor (killed in service)..Cameron, Mo.
Paul E. Walker—Attorney.................Hutchinson, Kas.
F. P. Washburn—Conductor...................Nichols, Iowa
Wm. F. Werner—Carpenter (killed in service).Haileyville, Okla.
E. H. Whited—Ticket Agent..................Blue Island, Ill.
Henry Wood—President (C. O. & G.).......McAlester, Okla.

(Author's collection)

90

Rock Island to

✿Florida✿

From the Rocky Mountains to the Florida seacoast in luxurious ease.

Winter Tourist ratas in effect daily on and after December 1—very low.

Full particulars, with rates, by addressing

RockIsland System

W. W. WOOD, C.P.A.
2 Pike's Peak Ave.,
Colorad Springs, Colo.

G. W. MARTIN,
General Agent,
Denver.

This advertisement, complete with two typographical errors, appeared in Colorado Springs newspapers sometime prior to 1917. (Author's collection)

Otto Perry drove his own 1935 Ford V-8 black four-door sedan thousands of miles in pursuit of his railroad photography, so he no doubt was intrigued by this railfaring duplicate which he found parked near the station in Colorado Springs on May 9, 1938. (Denver Public Library, Western History Department)

BRIDGES   MILEPOSTS   SIDINGS   SPURS
GOODLAND, KANSAS TO COLORADO SPRINGS, COLORADO

STATION	ELEVATION	MILEPOST*	BRIDGE #	TYPE/DESCRIPTION	SIZE	YEAR BUILT	COMMENTS
GOODLAND	3689	423.8	4265	1-SPAN DECK PLATE GIRDER	42'6"		SOUTH FORK BEAVER CREEK
CARUSO	3708	426.5					
RULETON	3790	429.3					
		433.4					
KANORADO		435.4	4354	1-SPAN FIRE DECK PILE TRESTLE	16'3"		
		438.0	4380	1-SPAN DECK PLATE GIRDER	80' Span	1898	
		441.4					
PECONIC	4005	442.0	4420	3-SPAN DECK PLATE GIRDER	40' Spans		
		447.3	4495	2-SPAN FIRE DECK PILE TRESTLE			
BURLINGTON	4167	449.5					
HUNGERFORD	4243	453.7					
		459.1					
BETHUNE	4257	461.4	4614	5-SPAN FIRE DECK PILE TRESTLE			
		462.0					
		463.7	4637	2-SPAN DECK PLATE GIRDER	2-61' Spans	1897	LOST MAN CREEK
MUSKOKA		465.4					
		468.3					
		470.6	4706	3-SPAN DECK PLATE GIRDER			
STRATTON	4409	472.1					
		474.1	4741	11-SPAN FIRE PROOF DECK TRESTLE		1890	(See Note A) SPRING CREEK
		478.5	4785	4-SPAN PINE DECK TRESTLE	44'5"	1890	WHITE WATER CREEK (See Note B)
VONA	4500	479.3					
SEIBERT		486.3					
		488.5	4885	2-SPAN DECK PLATE GIRDER	2-60' Spans		SAND CREEK
KIPLING		492.8					
		493.2	4932	1-SPAN DECK TRUSS	124'7½"	1898	CONCRETE MASONRY
FLAGLER	4926	497.3					
		502.0	5020	1-SPAN DECK PLATE GIRDER	44' Span	1898	SUBGRADE CROSSING
SAUGUS		503.0					
		504.7	5047	1-SPAN DECK PLATE GIRDER	44' Span	1898	SUBGRADE CROSSING
		505.5	5055	1-SPAN DECK PLATE GIRDER	66' Span	1897	FILLED
		506.2	5062	3-SPAN BALLAST DECK PILE TRESTLE		1913	
ARRIBA	5245	508.8					
		514.6	5146	3-SPAN FIRE DECK PILE TRESTLE		1897	(See Note C)
BOVINA	5375	514.8					
GENOA	5599	520.7					
		524.0	5240	1-SPAN DECK PLATE GIRDER	40'		SUBGRADE CROSSING

*From St. Joseph, Missouri

Station	Sta. No.	M.P.	Br. No.	Structure	Length / Spans	Year	Remarks
LIMON	5359						
		528.1	5281	2-SPAN FIRE DECK PILE TRESTLE			
		529.3	5293	7-SPAN FIRE DECK PILE TRESTLE	104'9"		
		530.3	5303	2-SPAN FIRE DECK PILE TRESTLE		1895	FIREPROOF
		530.8	5308	5-SPAN DECK GIRDER	5-60' Spans	1907	BIG SANDY CREEK; (See Note D)
		532.0	5320	9-SPAN FIRE DECK PILE TRESTLE	135'3"		(See Note E)
		533.0	5330				U.S. HIGHWAY 24 OVERPASS
		535.8	5358	6-SPAN FIRE DECK PILE TRESTLE	88'5"	1897	(See Note E)
		536.2	5362	5-SPAN FIRE DECK PILE TRESTLE	73'5"	1899	(See Note F)
RESOLIS #1		539.5					(See Note G)
		539.8	5398	3-SPAN FIRE DECK PILE TRESTLE		1899	(See Note H)
		541.4	5414	2-SPAN DECK PLATE GIRDER	2-40' Spans	1903	
RESOLIS #2	5634	542.4			1500'		CATTLE LOADING SIDING
		543.1	5431	2-SPAN BALLAST DECK PILE TRESTLE	29'0"	1945	(See Note I)
		543.9	5439	23-SPAN FIRE DECK PILE TRESTLE		1899	(See Note J)
		546.1	5461	4-SPAN FIRE DECK TRESTLE	60'5"	1907	
		547.9	5479	3-SPAN FIRE DECK PILE TRESTLE			
		548.9	5489	2-SPAN THUR TRUSS	2-153'7" Span	1902	BIG SANDY CREEK (See Note K)
MATHESON	5787	549.6					
		549.9	5499	2-SPAN FIRE DECK PILE TRESTLE		1938	
		551.2	5512	3-SPAN BALLAST DECK PILE TRESTLE		1920	
		552.4	5524	2-SPAN FIRE DECK PILE TRESTLE	73'8"	1899	
		553.7	5537	4-SPAN PLATE DECK GIRDER	4-44' Spans	1901	CONCRETE MASONRY
		554.1	5541	3-SPAN FIRE DECK PILE TRESTLE	104'0"	1896	
		554.5	5545	5-SPAN FIRE DECK PILE TRESTLE	299'9"	1896	
		555.3	5553	19-SPAN FIRE DECK PILE TRESTLE			
SIMLA	5966	556.0					
		556.1	5561	4-SPAN FIRE DECK PILE TRESTLE			2-BRIDGES; RAIL REINFORCED
		556.3	5563	3-SPAN DECK PLATE GIRDER	2-20' Spans	1903	CONCRETE MASONRY
		558.0	5580	1-SPAN FIRE DECK PILE TRESTLE		1898	
		558.5	5585	6-SPAN FIRE DECK PILE TRESTLE	88'0"	1896	
		559.3	5593	3-SPAN FIRE DECK PILE TRESTLE		1907	
		560.2	5602	4-SPAN FIRE DECK PILE TRESTLE		1907	CONCRETE MASONRY 1940
RAMAH	6091	561.1					
		562.1	5621	4-SPAN FIRE DECK PILE TRESTLE		1907	FIRE PROOF; WILD CREEK
		562.4	5624	4-SPAN FIRE DECK PILE TRESTLE	58'5"	1907	CONCRETE MASONRY 1940
		563.0	5630	3-SPAN FIRE DECK PILE TRESTLE	58'5"	1903	
		563.7	5637	2-SPAN FIRE DECK PILE TRESTLE	73'1"	1907	WEST END EXTENDED 57' 11/57
		565.0	5650	5-SPAN FIRE DECK PILE TRESTLE	44'1"	1907	REPLACED BY 5-SPAN BDT 3/20
		565.3	5653	3-SPAN FIRE DECK PILE TRESTLE		1899	FILLED
		566.3	5663	7-SPAN FIRE DECK PILE TRESTLE	98'1"	1915	
		568.2			426'		SPUR TRACK REMOVED 3-16-28
		568.6	5686	5-SPAN FIRE DECK PILE TRESTLE	85'1"	1907	REPLACED BY 6-SPAN BALLAST DECK TRESTLE 1/62
		568.9	5689	8-SPAN FIRE DECK PILE TRESTLE	118'9"	1901	
		570.7	5707	7-SPAN FIRE DECK PILE TRESTLE		1899	FILLED

Station	No.	Milepost	Str. No.	Description	Length/Span	Year	Remarks
CALHAN	6505	570.8					
TIP-TOP	6875	578.4			1498'		SIDING REMOVED (See Note L)
		579.9	5799	1-SPAN DECK PLATE GIRDER	33' Span	1899	BRACKET CREEK. (See Note M)
		580.6	5806	1-SPAN DECK PLATE GIRDER	80' Span	1899	CONCRETE MASONRY
		581.4	5814	7-SPAN FIRE DECK PILE TRESTLE	108'3"	1899	
PEYTON	6785	582.0					
		582.7	5827	7-SPAN FIRE DECK PILE TRESTLE	108'3"	1899	
		584.1	5841	2-SPAN PLATE DECK GIRDER	2-80' Spans	1899	CONCRETE MASONRY
		586.1	5861	1-SPAN PLATE DECK GIRDER	66' Span	1899	BLACK SQUIRREL CREEK
		586.9	5869	5-SPAN FIRE DECK PILE TRESTLE		1988	
		587.5	5875	6-SPAN FIRE DECK PILE TRESTLE	91'9"	1899	
		588.3	5883	6-SPAN FIRE DECK PILE TRESTLE	94'2"	1899	
		589.1	5891	3-SPAN FIRE DECK PILE TRESTLE	46'6"	1899	
		589.2	5892	5-SPAN FIRE DECK PILE TRESTLE		1943	REPLACED BY 3-21' DECK PLATE GIRDERS
		589.4	5894	3-SPAN FIRE DECK PILE TRESTLE		1943	(See Note N)
		590.5	5905	5-SPAN FIRE DECK PILE TRESTLE		1899	
		591.1	5911	5-SPAN FIRE DECK PILE TRESTLE	70'6"	1988	SUBGRADE CROSSING
FALCON	6827	591.3					
		591.4	5914	4-SPAN FIRE DECK PILE TRESTLE		1917	(See Note O)
		591.6	5916	90' THRU TRUSS OVERHEAD CROSSING		1920	
		592.5	5925	2-SPAN FIRE DECK PILE TRESTLE			
		593.7	5937	7-SPAN BALLAST DECK PILE TRESTLE			
		593.9	5939	3-SPAN BALLAST DECK PILE TRESTLE			
SHIRLEY	6659	594.7					SIDING REMOVED
		596.8	5968	2-SPAN DECK PLATE GIRDER	928'	1986	GIRDERS REPAIRED 3-7-62
		597.4	5974	1-SPAN RAIL REINFORCED	2-60' Spans	1934	(See Note P)
		598.3	5983	2-SPAN FIRE DECK PILE TRESTLE	14'"		
		599.6			4.7 MILES	1894	SPUR TO McFARREN MINE 1894-1900
		599.8			3.5 MILES	1942	SPUR TO PETERSON AIR FORCE BASE
ELSMERE	6408	600.1					(See Note Q)
		600.2	6002	4-SPAN DECK PLATE GIRDER	4-60' Spans	1899	REDECKED 1915, CONCRETE MASONRY
		600.3	6003	4-SPAN BALLAST DECK PILE TRESTLE		1932	REMOVED BY C&E RY IN 1985
		601.0	6010	4-SPAN FIRE DECK PILE TRESTLE		1968	SIDING
		602.5			478'	1932	WASHED OUT IN 1980
		602.7	6027	7-SPAN BALLAST DECK PILE TRESTLE	551'	1960	SIDING
		603.8					
		605.5			1.1 MILES	1901	SPUR TO RAPSON COAL MINE 1901-1917
		605.7	6057	6-SPAN FIRE DECK PILE TRESTLE		1932	FILLED 8/63
		606.0	6060	4-SPAN FIRE DECK PILE TRESTLE			
		606.2			6 MILES	1950's	ROSWELL INDUSTRIAL TRACKAGE
		606.4	6064	PLATE DECK GIRDER			AT&SF OVERHEAD CROSSING
		606.5	6065				NEVADA AVENUE VIADUCT, (See Note R)
		606.6	6066				TEJON AVENUE VIADUCT, (See Note S)
		606.7	6067				CASCADE AVENUE VIADUCT, (See Note T)
		606.75			988'	1942	SPUR TO NAVY GAS AND SUPPLY CO

MASONRY PIER AND ABUTMENTS					
ROSWELL	6069	607.3			1960
		607.7			SPUR TO COLORADO SPRINGS WAREHOUSE
		607.8	6078	4-SPAN FIRE DECK PILE TRESTLE	FONTANERO STREET, (See Note U)
		608.0	6080	6-SPAN FIRE DECK PILE TRESTLE	FILLED BY THE D&RGW 1986
		608.4	6084	4-SPAN FIRE DECK PILE TRESTLE	UNITAH STREET, (See Note V)
		609.2	6092	4-SPAN FIRE DECK PILE TRESTLE	MONUMENT CREEK
		609.4	6094	4-SPAN DECK PLATE GIRDER	BIJOU STREET VIADUCT
COLORADO SPRINGS	5970	609.6			

NOTE #   COMMENTS

A   REPLACED BY 85'-DECK PLATE GIRDER BRIDGE DECEMBER 1930; ORIGINAL DESTROYED IN DERAILMENT

B   REPLACED BY DECK PLATE GIRDER WITH HEAVY-LOAD FIRE DECK BRACING 1934

C   REPLACED BY 42' FIRE DECK PILE TRESTLE IN 1918

D   CONCRETE MASONRY 1902; PAINTED "ROCK ISLAND LINES"

E   SUBGRADE CATTLE CROSSING; REPLACED BY 7-SPAN FIRE DECK PILE TRESTLE (97'11")

F   SUBGRADE CATTLE CROSSING; WASHED OUT IN AUGUST 1912 REPLACED BY 7-SPAN FIRE DECK PILE TRESTLE (97'10")

G   ORIGINALLY TWO BRIDGES; WHEN SIDING WAS REMOVED SECOND BRIDGE REMOVED

H   SUBGRADE CATTLE CROSSING; CONCRETE MASONRY; 2-BEAMS ADDED TO BRIDGE IN 1964

I   BALLAST DECK CHANGED TO OPEN DECK; EAST END EXTENDED BY THREE SPANS; STEEL PIERS ADDED 1954

J   REPLACED BY 4-SPAN FIRE DECK PILE TRESTLE (50') in NOVEMBER 1920

K   CONCRETE MASONRY 1902; ORIGINALLY A DOUBLE TRACK 8-SPAN THRU TRUSS BRIDGE LOCATED NEAR COLONA, ILLINOIS ACROSS THE ROCK RIVER. IT WAS BUILT BY THE AMERICN BRIDGE COMPANY "LASSIG WORKS" IN 1883. WHEN TAKEN APART, THE 8 SECTIONS WERE REUSED ACROSS THE ROCK ISLAND SYSTEM. FIVE OF THE SECTIONS WENT TO THE SOUTHERN DIVISION, ONE SECTION TO THE E&A LINE AND THE REMAINING TWO SECTIONS TO MATHESON, COLORADO. THESE TWO SECTIONS WERE REBUILT FROM DOUBLE TRACK TO SINGLE TRACK WIDTH AND PLACED OVER BIG SANDY CREEK.

L   CONCRETE MASONRY; WASHED OUT IN 1965 FLOOD; FILLED BY EL PASO COUNTY HIGHWAY DEPARTMENT; MURPHY ROAD

M   SUBGRADE CROSSING; HEAVY DAMAGE IN 1965 FLOOD, TEMPORARY REPAIRS WERE MADE BY INSTALLING 3 BENTS, PERMANENT REPAIRS WERE NEVER COMPLETED

N   ORIGINALLY BUILT IN 1892 ON THE DES MOINES VALLEY DIVISION AT MILEPOST 60.4 JUST EAST OF HARTFORD, IOWA. IT WAS RELOCATED AND REMODELED INTO ITS PRESENT FORM IN OCTOBER 1916.

O   ORIGINALLY TWO BRIDGES; WHEN THE SIDING WAS REMOVED ONE OF THE BRIDGES WAS DISMANTLED.

P   BUILT BY THE CADILLAC AND LAKE CITY FOR SAND AND GRAVEL UNLOADING.

Q   SIDING TO AIR BASE REMOVED 1963. LOCATED ALONG THIS SPUR WAS A 1-SPAN FIRE DECK PILE TRESTLE (NOT NUMBERED).

R   DURING THE 1965 FLOOD REPAIRS IN EASTERN COLORADO, THE TRACK UNDER NEVADA AND CASCADE AVENUES WAS LOWERED BY 2½' FOR CLEARANCE OF AUTO RACK CARS.

S   THIS WAS A STREETCAR OVERHEAD BRIDGE. STONE FROM THE ABUTMENTS STILL CAN BE SEEN ON THE NORTH SIDE OF THE TRACKS

T   SITE OF A DERAILMENT IN AUGUST 1970 CAUSED BY VANDALISM. CITY OF COLORADO SPRINGS SUED THE ROCK ISLAND TO REPLACE THE BRIDGE WHICH WAS DESTROYED IN THE DERAILMENT.

U   REBUILT BY THE STATE HIGHWAY DEPARTMENT IN 1961

V   REBUILT BY THE STATE HIGHWAY DEPARTMENT IN 1961.

Length of sidings in feet, location of water, fuel, interlocking plants, turning stations, scales and telephones.	SECOND CLASS			FIRST CLASS				Distance from Kansas City	Time-Table No. 171 JULY 14, 1940
	97 C.R.I.& P. Freight	333 Mixed	91 C.R.I.& P. Freight	37 Passenger	27 C.R.I.& P. Passenger	7 C.R.I.& P. Rocket Passenger	21 Passenger		STATIONS
	Daily	Daily	Daily	Daily	Saturday Sunday Monday	Daily	Daily		
3,983 WFTTP		1.35AM		12.32PM			6.08AM	535.5	DN-R HUGO Hu
5,745 P		1.53		12.40				541.7	BAGDAD — 6.2
1,505 WP		2.05		12.47			6.21	547.9	LAKE — 2.6
2,886 P		s 2.15		s12.53			6.25	550.5	(C. R. I. & P. Crossing) DN-R LIMON Mn — 0.1
	2.25PM		12.30PM		9.00AM	6.53AM		550.6	LIMON JUNCTION — 6.0
2,580 P	2.35	f 2.25	12.42	1.01	9.07	7.00	6.32	556.6	RIVER BEND — 6.6
2,580 TP	2.45	f 2.35	12.53	1.09	9.14	7.07	6.39	563.2	CEDAR POINT — 3.9
2,456 P	2.51	f 2.41	12.59	1.14	9.19	7.12		567.1	BUICK — 5.1
2,452 P	3.00	f 2.49	1.15	f 1.21	9.24	7.16	6.47	572.2	D AGATE Ax — 5.9
1,718 P	3.09	2.56	1.24	1.27	9.30	7.21		578.1	LOWLAND — 6.1
2,559 WFTTP	3.24	f 3.10	1.35	f 1.34	9.36	7.27	7.01	584.2	DN DEER TRAIL Dr — 5.9
2,529 P	3.34	3.18	1.44	1.43	9.42	7.33		590.1	PEORIA — 6.5
2,553 P	3.51	f 3.28	1.55	f 1.52	9.53	7.39	7.12	596.6	D BYERS By — 5.9
2,584 WP	4.10	f 3.38	2.07	f 2.00	10.01	7.45	7.18	602.5	D STRASBURG Sr — 6.4
2,433 P	4.24	f 3.50	2.19	f 2.07	10.07	7.51	7.24	608.9	D BENNETT Bt — 4.8
2,536 P	4.35	3.58	2.29	2.14	10.12	7.55		613.7	MANILA — 4.7
2,477 WP	4.45	f 4.05	2.36	f 2.20	10.17	7.59	7.33	618.4	WATKINS — 6.6
2,563 P	4.55	4.13	2.46	2.28	10.23	8.05	7.40	625.0	MESA — 3.1
P								628.1	MAGEE — 2.4
2,706 P	5.15	4.20	2.54	2.34	10.28	8.10	7.45	630.5	SABLE — 2.7
P								633.2	ROYDALE — 1.1
2,467 P	5.35	4.26	3.00	2.39	10.31	8.13	7.49	634.3	SANDOWN — 3.9
WFTTOP	A 5.50PM	A 4.45AM	A 3.10AM	A 2.44PM	A10.35AM	A 8.18AM	A 7.53AM	638.2	PULLMAN
									(102.7)
	(3.25) 25.6	(3.10) 32.4	(2.40) 32.8	(2.12) 46.9	(1.35) 55.3	(1.25) 61.8	(1.45) 58.7		.... Thru Time .... Average speed per hour

Westward trains are superior to trains of the same class in the opposite direction.—See Rule 72.

*This excerpt from a Union Pacific Colorado Division employees timetable includes Rock Island schedules over the line between Limon Junction and Pullman (Denver). (Museum collection) The unusual Otto Kuhler-styled ALCO DL109 was tried briefly on the **Rocky Mountain Rocket**, but long periods of high speed operation proved to be its downfall. No. 624 is seen here westbound west of Bennett on a day in 1940; from the angle of the sun it appears to be running late. (Herbert O'Hanlon photo, G.C. Bassett collection)*

DENVER SUBDIVISION — EASTWARD

Time-Table No. 171 — JULY 14, 1940

Length of sidings		Stations	Distance from Denver	FIRST CLASS 24 Passenger	FIRST CLASS 38 Passenger	FIRST CLASS 8 C.R.I.&P. Rocket Passenger	FIRST CLASS 28 C.R.I.&P. Passenger	FIRST CLASS 22 Passenger	SECOND CLASS 92 C.R.I.&P. Freight	SECOND CLASS 96 C.R.I.&P. Freight	SECOND CLASS 370 Mixed
8,983 WFTYP	DN-R	HUGO Hu	104.9	A 2.05AM	A10.56AM			A 6.55PM			A11.00PM
		6.2									
5,745 F		BAGDAD	98.7	1.53	10.48			6.46			10.46
		6.2									
1,505 WF		LAKE	92.5	1.47				6.40			f10.36
		2.6									
2,886 F	DN-R	(C.R.I.&P. Crossing) LIMON Mn	89.9	* 1.43	10.39			* 6.37			*10.29
		0.1									
		LIMON JUNCTION	89.8			A 2.25PM	A 4.40PM		A 6.50AM	A10.15AM	
		6.0									
2,580 F		RIVER BEND	83.8	1.33	10.32	2.17	4.32	6.29	6.32	9.45	f 9.59
		6.6									
2,530 TF		CEDAR POINT	77.2	1.25	10.25	2.10	4.25	6.22	6.20	9.32	f 9.49
		3.9									
2,456 F		BUICK	73.3	1.20		2.05	4.20	6.17	6.10	9.22	9.39
		5.1									
2,452 F	D	AGATE Ax	68.2	1.15	10.16	2.00	4.15	6.12	6.00	9.10	f 9.29
		5.9									
1,718 F		LOWLAND	62.3	1.10		1.55	4.09	6.07	5.48	8.58	9.11
		6.1									
2,559 WFTP	DN	DEER TRAIL Dr	56.2	1.04	10.05	1.50	4.03	6.01	5.37	8.45	* 9.00
		5.9									
2,529 F		PEORIA	50.3	12.56		1.43	3.57	5.55	5.27	8.25	8.41
		6.5									
2,553 F	D	BYERS By	43.8	12.50	9.53	1.38	3.51	5.49	5.18	8.12	f 8.31
		5.9									
2,584 WF	D	STRASBURG Sr	37.9	12.44	9.48	1.34	3.45	5.43	5.10	8.00	f 8.19
		6.4									
2,433 F	D	BENNETT Bt	31.5	12.37	9.42	1.29	3.39	5.37	5.00	7.47	f 8.00
		4.8									
2,536 F		MANILA	26.7	12.32		1.25	3.34	5.32	4.50	7.38	7.45
		4.7									
2,477 WF		WATKINS	22.0	12.28	9.33	1.21	3.29	5.28	4.40	7.30	f 7.37
		6.6									
2,563 F		MESA	15.4	12.21		1.16	3.22	5.21	4.30	7.18	7.25
		3.1									
F		MAGEE	12.3								
		2.4									
2,706 F		SABLE	9.9	12.15	9.22	1.12	3.16	5.15	4.20	7.08	7.15
		2.7									
F		ROYDALE	7.2								
		1.1									
2,467 F		SANDOWN	6.1	12.10		1.09	3.11	5.10	4.05	7.00	7.08
		3.9									
WFTTOP		PULLMAN	2.2	12.05AM	9.16AM	1.05PM	3.06PM	5.05PM	3.56AM	6.50PM	7.00PM
		(102.7)		Daily	Daily	Daily	Saturday Sunday Monday	Daily	Daily	Daily	Daily

.... Thru Time	(2.00)	(1.40)	(1.20)	(1.34)	(1.50)	(2.54)	(3.25)	(4.00)
.... Average speed per hour	51.4	61.6	65.7	55.9	56.0	30.2	25.6	25.7

Westward trains are superior to trains of the same class in the opposite direction.—See Rule 72.

Westward — Main Line — Eastward

SECOND CLASS	SECOND CLASS	FIRST CLASS	Capacity of Sidings	Capacity of Other Tracks	Station Numbers	SUBDIVISION 9 STATIONS	M.P. from St. Joseph	Signs	FIRST CLASS	SECOND CLASS	SECOND CLASS
59	81	7				Time Table No. 2 December 30, 1962			8	60	82
Freight	Freight	Psgr.							Psgr.	Freight	Freight
Daily	Daily	Daily							Daily	Daily	Daily
P.M. 10.25	P.M. 12.10	A.M. 4.54		Yard	2702	GD ....GOODLAND......●TO	423.8	RYd TWI	P.M. 3.18	A.M. 3.50	A.M. 6.40
						—5.5—					
10.31	12.20	5.00	51	12	2708	....CARUSO............P	429.3	....	3.10	3.28	6.28
						—4.1—					
10.36	12.26	5.03	50	20	2712	....RULETON..........P	433.4	....	3.07	3.24	6.23
						—8.0—					
10.44	12.36	5.09	87	71	2720	RA ...KANORADO, KAN....TO	441.4	....	3.01	3.14	6.13
						—5.9—					
10.50	12.44	5.14	50	9	2728	....PECONIC, COLO. .....P	447.3	....	2.56	3.07	6.05
						—6.4—					
10.57	12.53	q5.19	98	123	2732	BN....BURLINGTON......●TO	453.7	W	2.51	3.00	5.58
						—8.0—					
11.03	1.01	5.25	78	.....	2738	......HUNGERFORD.........P	459.7	....	2.43	2.53	5.51
						—2.5—					
		5.35 82	.....	35	2741	.......BETHUNE............	462.0	....			
						—10.1—					
11.16	1.15	5.35	83	52	2751	RT ...STRATTON.........TO	472.1	Y	2.33	2.38	5.35
						—7.2—					
11.24	1.24	5.41	50	23	2758	..........VONA.........P	479.3	....	2.27	2.30	5.18
						—7.0—					
11.32	1.33	5.47	51	32	2765	BT .....SEIBERT.........TO	486.3	....	2.21	2.22	5.09
						—11.0—					
11.44	1.46	5.56	90	34	2778	AG .....FLAGLER....●TO	497.3	....	2.12	2.07	4.53
						—11.5—					
11.59 P.M.	2.03 8	6.06	125	70	2787	BI.........ARRIBA...........TO	508.8	....	2.03	1.52	4.37
						—5.8—					
12.06 A.M.	2.15	6.11	50	17	2793	..........BOVINA............P	514.6	....		1.45	4.29
						—6.1—					
12.16	2.30	6.16	85	39	2799	GN .....GENOA......●TO	520.7	....	1.54	1.38	4.20
						—10.1—					
12.55 A.M.	3.10 P.M.	●6.30 A.M.	.....	Yard	2809	MN ....LIMON..........●TO	530.8	RYd FWY	1.45 P.M.	1.20 A.M.	4.00 A.M.
						107.0					

TRAINS EASTWARD ARE SUPERIOR TO TRAINS OF THE SAME CLASS WESTWARD.
FORM Y ORDERS AUTHORIZED.

No. 7 Burlington, conditional stop Monday through Saturday discharge from Lincoln and points east, receive for Denver and Colorado Springs, regular stop Sunday and Holidays.

No. 8 Receive for Lincoln and stop points east. Discharge from Denver and Colorado Springs.

Westward — Eastward

SECOND CLASS	SECOND CLASS	FIRST CLASS	Station Numbers	UNION PACIFIC JOINT TRACK	FIRST CLASS	SECOND CLASS	SECOND CLASS
81	59	7		Time Table No. 2 December 30, 1962	8	82	60
Freight	Freight	Psgr.			Psgr.	Freight	Freight
Daily	Daily	Daily			Daily	Daily	Daily
P.M. 3.25	A.M. 1.05	A.M. 6.45	2809	..........LIMON........... —83.8—	P.M. 1.24	A.M. 3.45	A.M. 1.15
5.35 5.45	4.00 A.M.	8.04	.....	..........SANDOWN......... —6.0—	12.11		11.00 P.M.
6.15 P.M.		8.25 A.M.	5000	..........DENVER......... 89.8	12.01 P.M.	1.30 A.M.	

See T. T. Rules 16a-b-c

Western Division

Westward — Main Line — Eastward

SECOND CLASS		FIRST CLASS		Capacity of Sidings	Capacity of Other Tracks	Station Numbers	SUBDIVISION 10 STATIONS Time Table No. 2 December 30, 1962	M. P. from St. Joseph	Signs	FIRST CLASS		SECOND CLASS	
85		7								8		86	
Freight		Psgr.								Psgr.		Freight	
Daily Except Sat.		Daily								Daily		Daily Except Sat.	
P.M. 4.00		A.M. 6.45	....	Yard	2809	MN.........LIMON.........#TO	530.8	RYd FWY		P.M. s1.28		A.M. 3.00	
			....	....	....	.........UP Crossing.......UX	530.8	....					
						——0.0——							
						——11.8——							
4.20		6.59	28	....	2818	.........RESOLIS.........P	542.6	....		1.14		2.10	
						——7.4——							
4.30		7.07	50	23	2828	.......MATHESON.........P	550.0	....		1.06		1.55	
						——6.3——							
4.40		7.14	38	28	2834	SM.........SIMLA.........TO	556.3	....		1.00		1.40	
						——4.8——							
4.50		7.20	24	21	2839	.........RAMAH.........P	561.1	....		12.55		1.25	
						——9.7——							
5.15		7.32	51	25	2849	GH.......CALHAN.........TO	570.8	....		12.45		1.04	
						——11.2——							
5.40		7.47	26	16	2861	.........PEYTON.........P	582.0	....		12.33		12.42 A.M.	
						——9.3——							
5.55		7.57	50	22	2870	.........FALCON.........P	591.3	....		12.23		12.22	
						——3.6——							
			....	14	2873	.........SHIRLEY.........P	594.9	....					
						——5.2——							
			....	43	2879	.........ELSMERE.........P	600.1	....					
						——7.2——							
7.30		8.15	57	Yard	2886	.........ROSWELL.........P	607.3	YdWTY		12.04		P.M. 11.30	
						——2.3——							
8.00 P.M.		s8.35 A.M.	....	Yard	2888	CS.......COLO. SPGS.......TO See T.T. Rule 16e.	609.6	RYdWY		12.01 P.M.		11.00 P.M.	
						78.8							

TRAINS EASTWARD ARE SUPERIOR TO TRAINS OF THE SAME CLASS WESTWARD, EXCEPT No. 7 IS SUPERIOR TO No. 8 AND No. 85. IS SUPERIOR TO No. 86

SECOND CLASS EXTRA TRAINS AND ENGINES MUST CLEAR THE TIME OF Nos. 7 and 8 NOT LESS THAN 15 MINUTES.

FORM Y ORDERS AUTHORIZED.

No. 86 may leave Colorado Springs without Clearance when train order office closed.

Westward — Sandown - North Yard — Eastward

Freight Trains (Information only)

		81	59	Capacity of Sidings	Capacity of Other Tracks		SUBDIVISION 9-A STATIONS Time Table No. 2 December 30, 1962	Distance from Sandown	Signs	82	60		
		Freight	Freight							Freight	Freight		
		Daily	Daily							Daily	Daily		
		P.M. 5.30 5.45	A.M. 4.00 4.10	105	Yard	.....	Rules 400 to 406 ....SANDOWN.........	......	Y	A.M. 2.15	P.M. 11.00		
							——4.0——						
		6.00	4.20				.........BELT.........	4.0	....	1.35	9.05		
		6.15 P.M.	4.30 A.M.				T. Table Rule 16d ..NORTH YARD-DENVER	6.7	RWEY	1.30 A.M.	9.00 P.M.		
							——6.7——						

Signal Indications M.P. 0.3 to M.P. 3-39

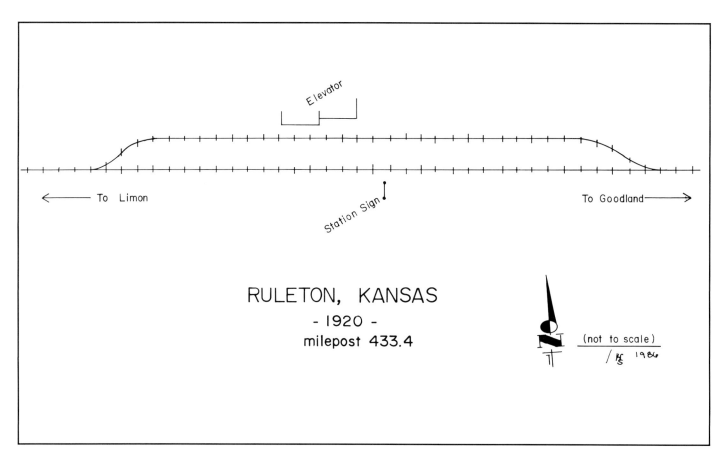

RULETON, KANSAS
- 1920 -
milepost 433.4

To Limon

Elevator

Station Sign

To Goodland

(not to scale)
/ Kf 1986

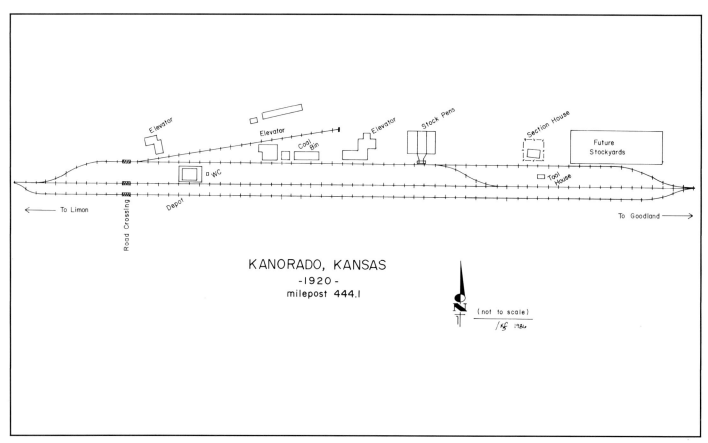

KANORADO, KANSAS
-1920-
milepost 444.1

To Limon

Road Crossing

Depot

Elevator

WC

Elevator

Coal Bin

Elevator

Stock Pens

Section House

Future Stockyards

Tool House

To Goodland

(not to scale)
/Kf 1986

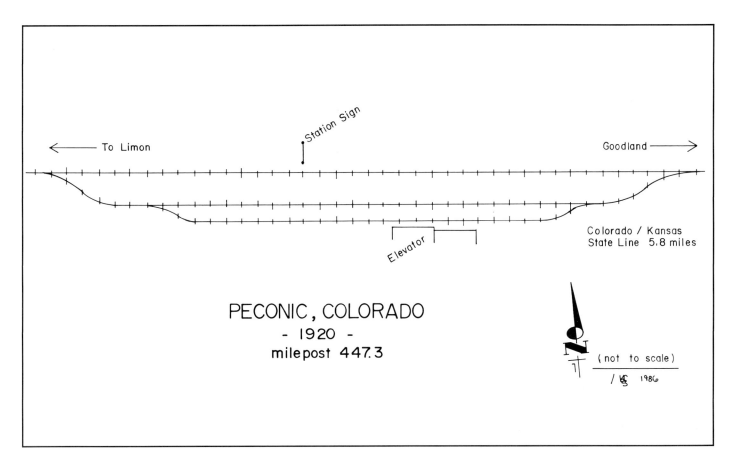

← To Limon

Station Sign

Goodland →

Elevator

Colorado / Kansas
State Line 5.8 miles

PECONIC, COLORADO
- 1920 -
milepost 447.3

N

(not to scale)
/ KS 1986

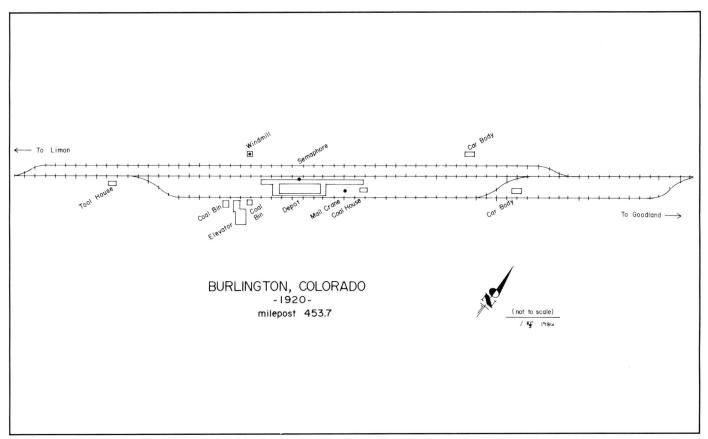

← To Limon

Windmill

Semaphore

Car Body

Tool House

Coal Bin

Coal Bin

Depot

Mail Crane

Coal House

Elevator

Car Body

To Goodland →

BURLINGTON, COLORADO
-1920-
milepost 453.7

N

(not to scale)
/ KS 1986

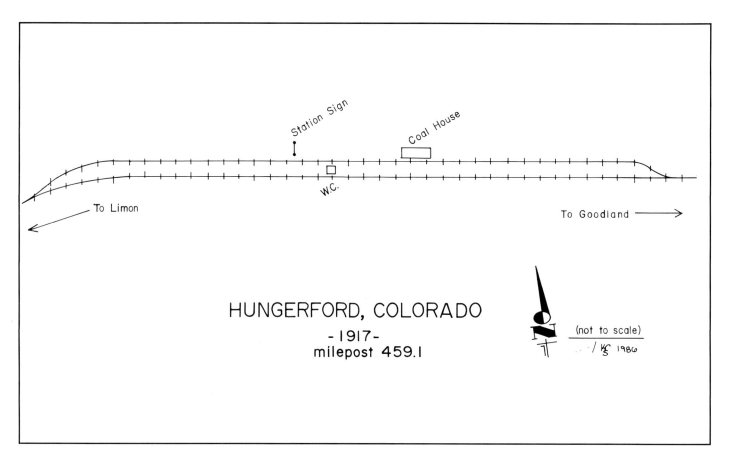

Station Sign

Coal House

W.C.

To Limon ←

To Goodland →

HUNGERFORD, COLORADO
-1917-
milepost 459.1

(not to scale)
/ kg 1986

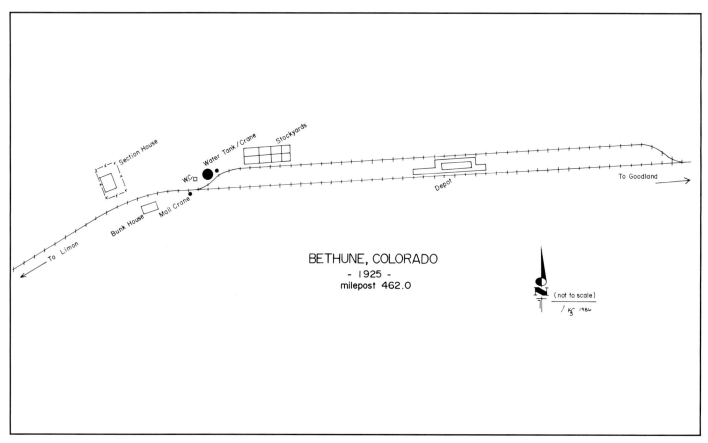

Section House

Water Tank/Crane

Stockyards

W.C.

Bunk House

Mail Crane

Depot

To Goodland →

To Limon

BETHUNE, COLORADO
- 1925 -
milepost 462.0

(not to scale)
/ kg 1986

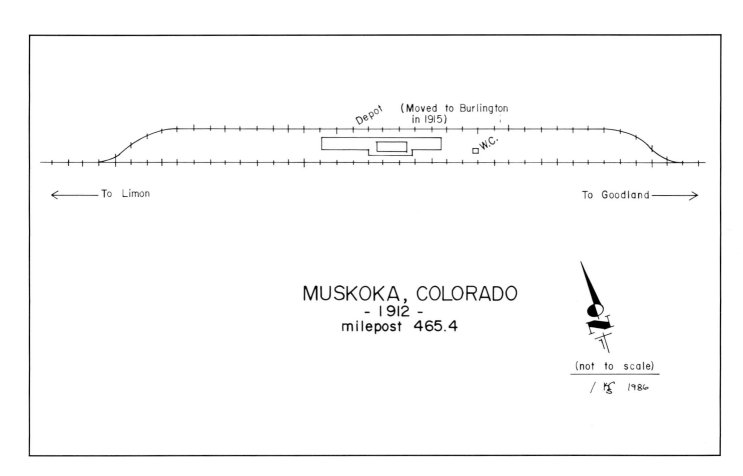

MUSKOKA, COLORADO
- 1912 -
milepost 465.4

(not to scale)

/ KS 1986

← To Limon

To Goodland →

Depot (Moved to Burlington in 1915)

W.C.

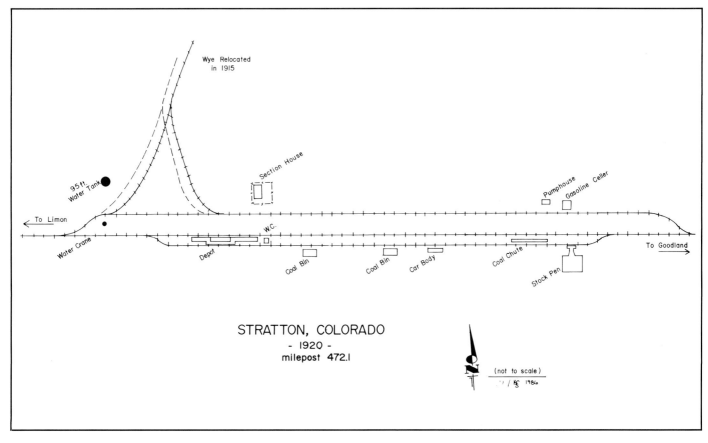

STRATTON, COLORADO
- 1920 -
milepost 472.1

(not to scale)

/ KS 1986

Wye Relocated in 1915

Section House

95 ft. Water Tank

← To Limon

Pumphouse

Gasoline Cellar

W.C.

Water Crane

Depot

Coal Bin

Coal Bin

Car Body

Coal Chute

Stock Pen

To Goodland →

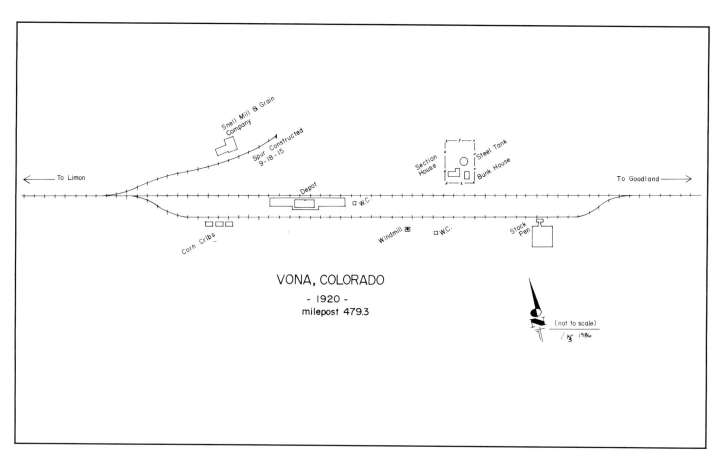

← To Limon

Snell Mill & Grain Company

Spur Constructed 9-18-15

Section House

Steel Tank

Bunk House

Depot

W.C.

To Goodland →

Corn Cribs

Windmill

W.C.

Stock Pen

VONA, COLORADO
- 1920 -
milepost 479.3

(not to scale)
KG 1986

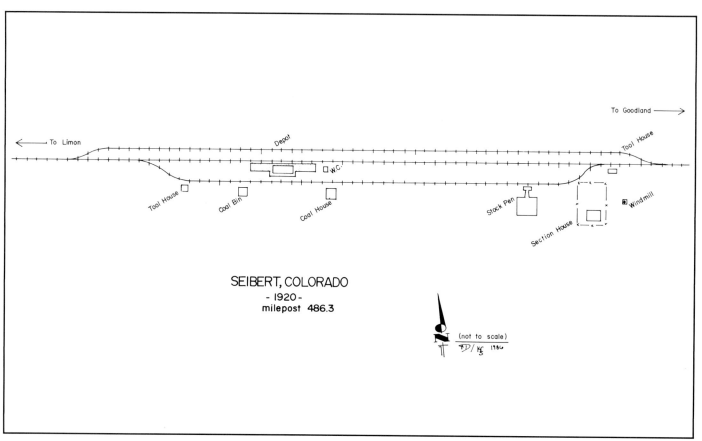

To Goodland →

← To Limon

Depot

Tool House

Tool House

W.C.

Coal Bin

Coal House

Stock Pen

Section House

Windmill

SEIBERT, COLORADO
- 1920 -
milepost 486.3

(not to scale)
FD/KG 1986

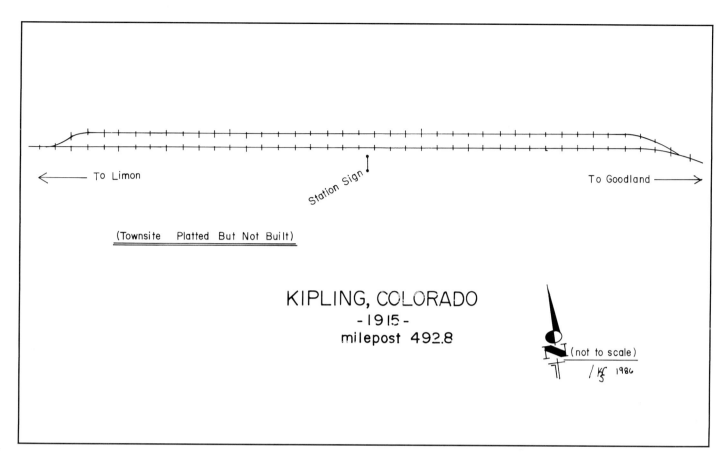

To Limon ←

Station Sign

To Goodland →

(Townsite   Platted But Not Built)

KIPLING, COLORADO
-1915-
milepost 492.8

N (not to scale)
/ KS 1986

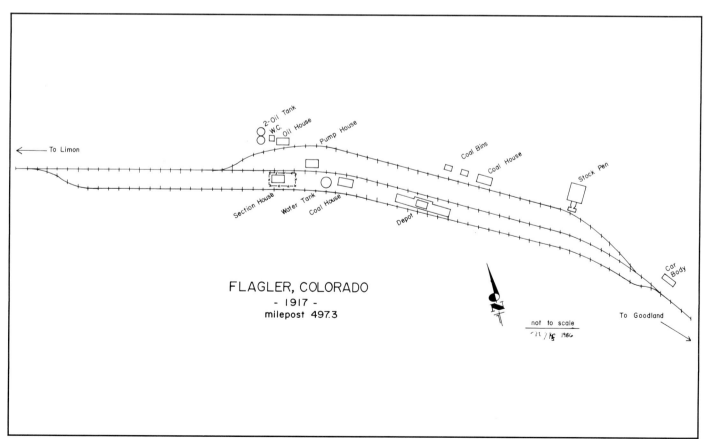

← To Limon

2-Oil Tank
W.C.
Oil House
Pump House
Coal Bins
Coal House
Stock Pen

Section House
Water Tank
Coal House
Depot
Car Body

To Goodland

FLAGLER, COLORADO
- 1917 -
milepost 497.3

not to scale
/ KS 1986

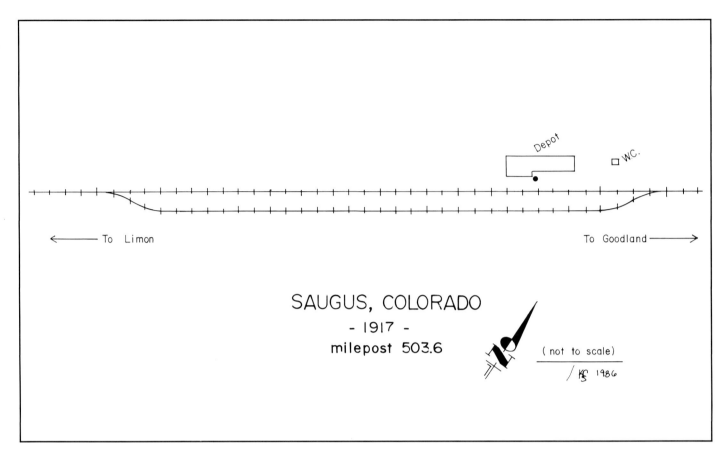

To Limon ←

To Goodland →

SAUGUS, COLORADO
- 1917 -
milepost 503.6

(not to scale)

KS 1986

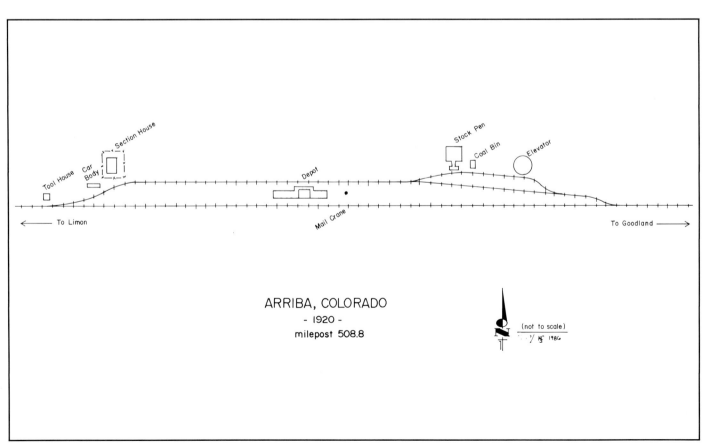

← To Limon

To Goodland →

ARRIBA, COLORADO
- 1920 -
milepost 508.8

(not to scale)

KS 1986

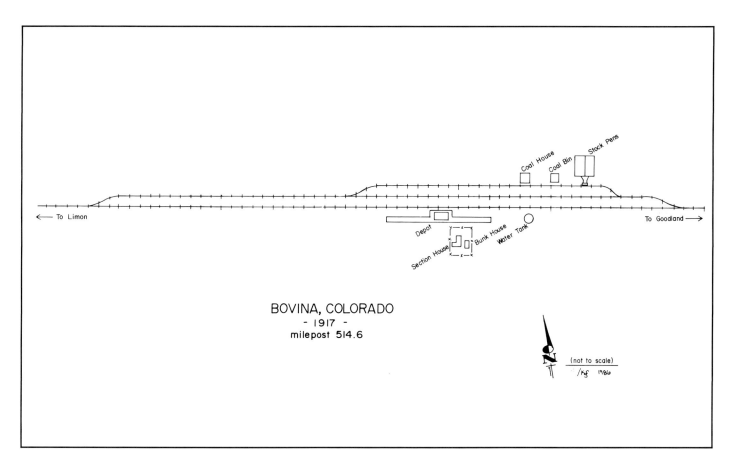

BOVINA, COLORADO
- 1917 -
milepost 514.6

N (not to scale)
/Kg 1986

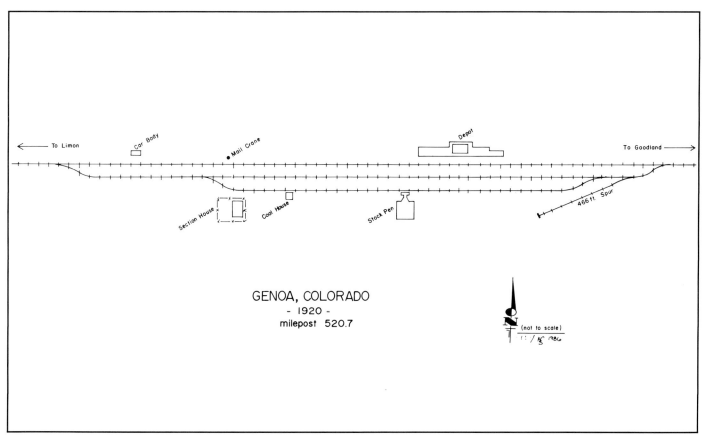

GENOA, COLORADO
- 1920 -
milepost 520.7

N (not to scale)
/Kg 1986

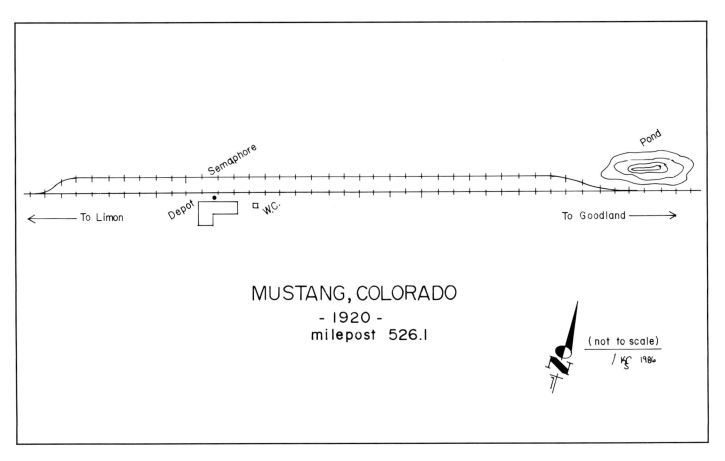

MUSTANG, COLORADO
- 1920 -
milepost 526.1

(not to scale)
/ KF 1986

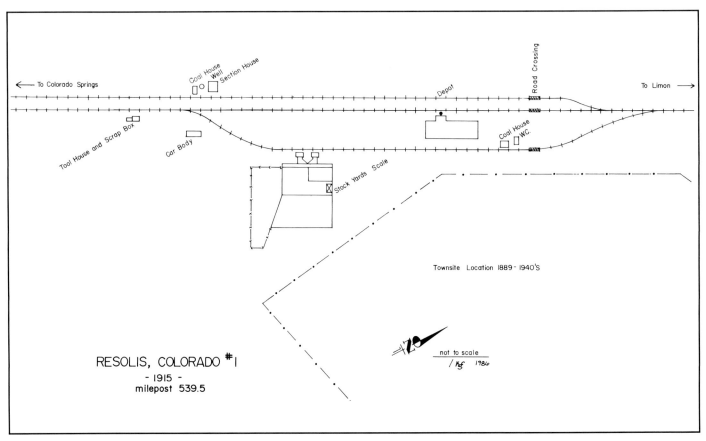

RESOLIS, COLORADO #1
- 1915 -
milepost 539.5

not to scale
/ KF 1986

108

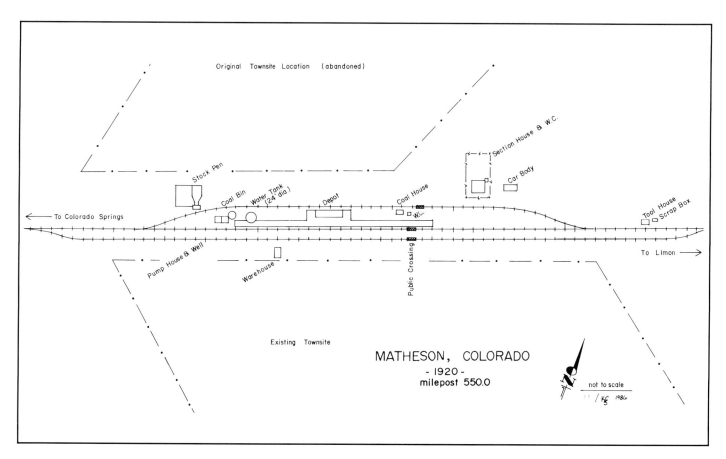

Original Townsite Location (abandoned)

Stock Pen

Coal Bin
Water Tank
(24' dia.)
Depot
Coal House
Section House & W.C.
Car Body

← To Colorado Springs
W.C.
Tool House
Scrap Box
To Limon →

Pump House & Well
Warehouse
Public Crossing

Existing Townsite

MATHESON, COLORADO
- 1920 -
milepost 550.0

not to scale
KŞ 1986

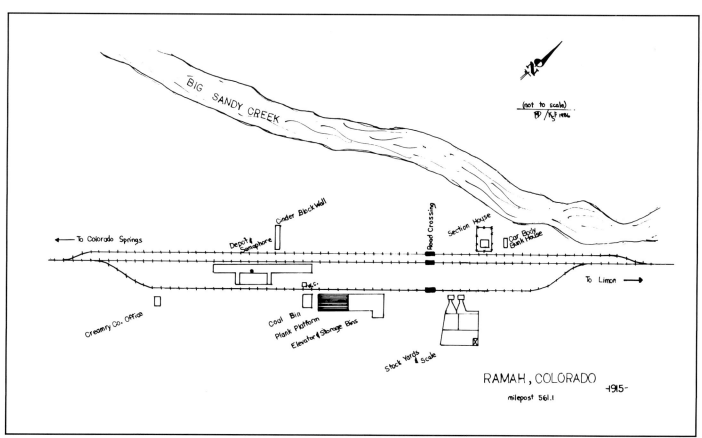

BIG SANDY CREEK

(not to scale)
BD/KŞ 1986

← To Colorado Springs

Depot &
Semaphore
Cinder Block Wall
Road Crossing
Section House
Car Body
Bunk House

To Limon →

Creamry Co. Office
W.C.
Coal Bin
Plank Platform
Elevator & Storage Bins
Stock Yards & Scale

RAMAH, COLORADO
-1915-
milepost 561.1

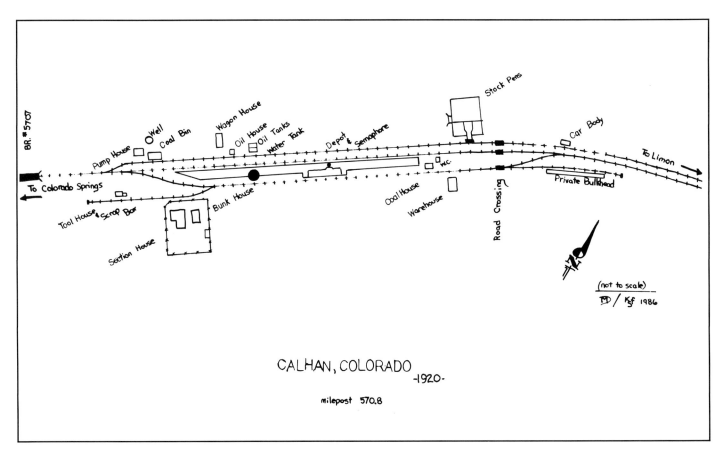

CALHAN, COLORADO
-1920-

milepost 570.8

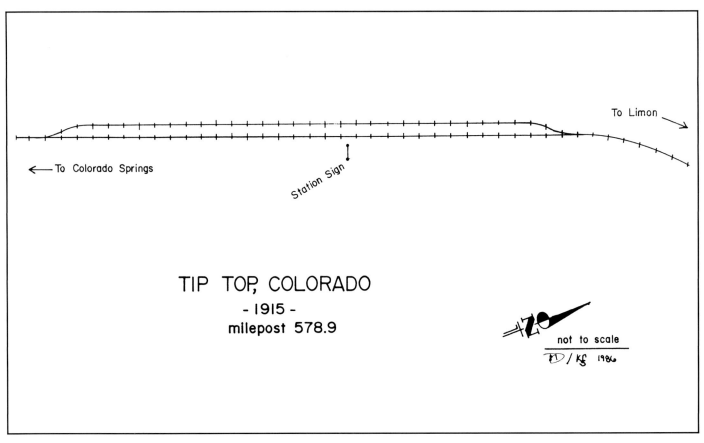

TIP TOP, COLORADO
- 1915 -
milepost 578.9

not to scale

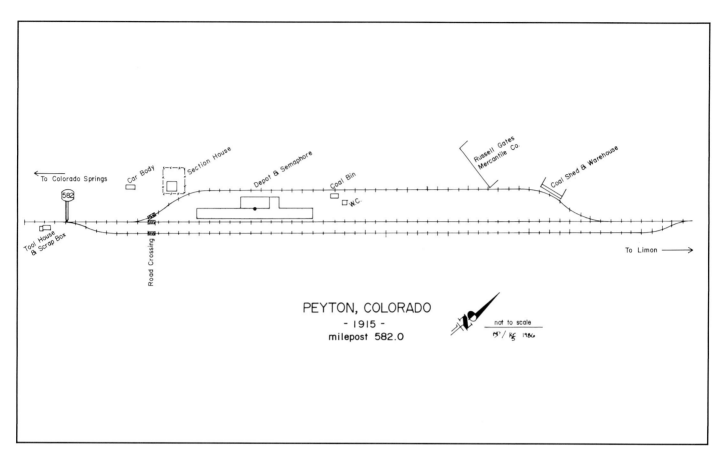

PEYTON, COLORADO
- 1915 -
milepost 582.0

not to scale

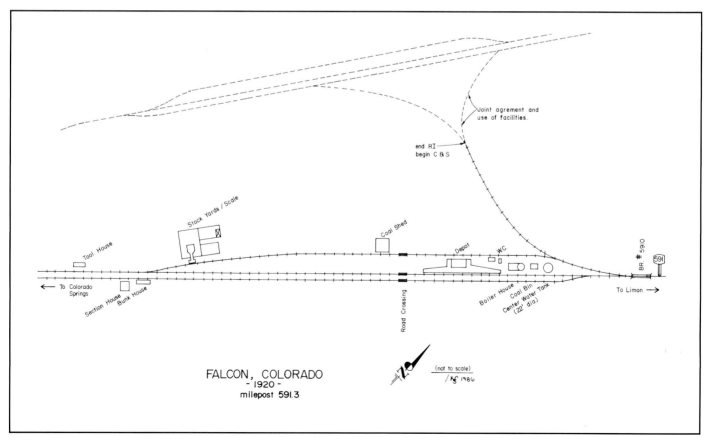

FALCON, COLORADO
- 1920 -
milepost 591.3

(not to scale)

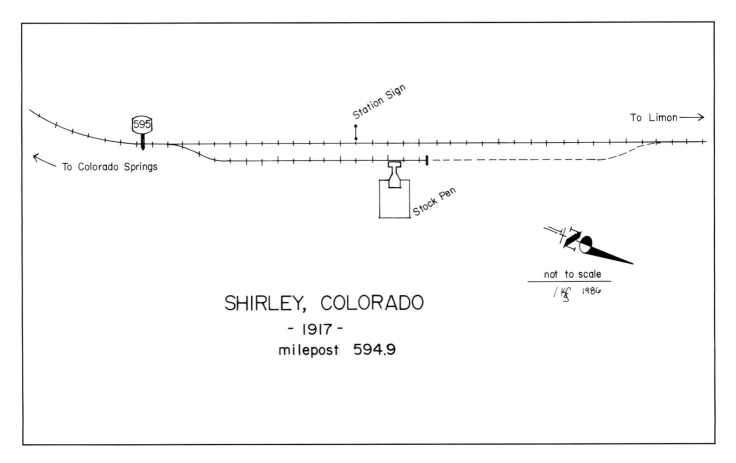

To Limon →

595

Station Sign

To Colorado Springs

Stock Pen

not to scale
/ kg 1986

SHIRLEY, COLORADO
- 1917 -
milepost 594.9

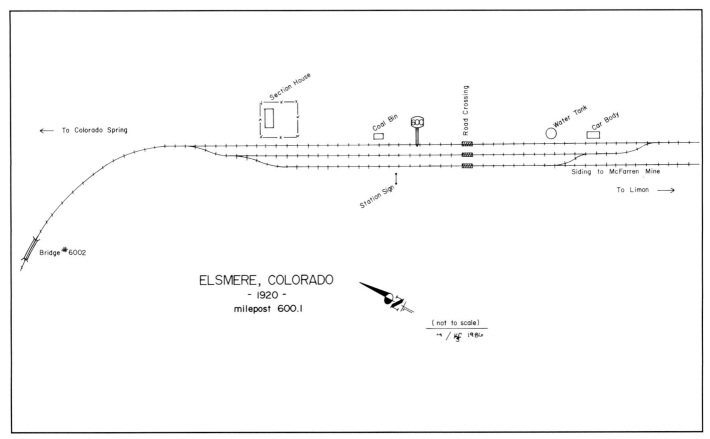

← To Colorado Spring

Section House

Coal Bin

500

Road Crossing

Water Tank

Car Body

Station Sign

Siding to McFarren Mine

To Limon →

Bridge #6002

ELSMERE, COLORADO
- 1920 -
milepost 600.1

(not to scale)
m / kg 1986

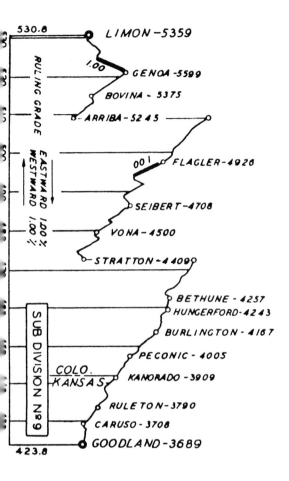

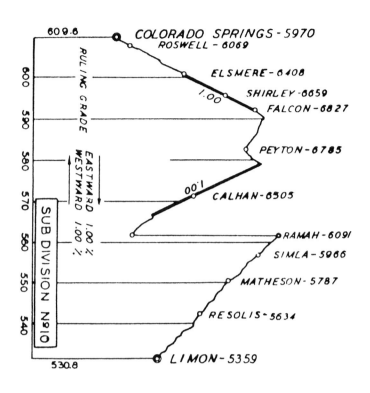

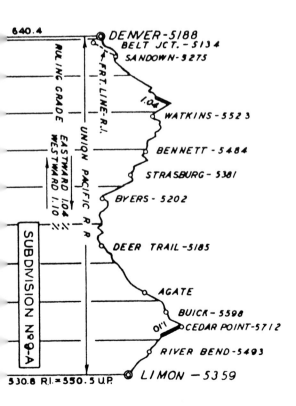

These profile charts are from Western Division Timetable No. 2, December 30, 1962 and illustrate that on the high plains of eastern Colorado the Rock Island was far from a flat prairie railroad. Note that the Union Pacific Limon-Denver trackage is shown as CRI&P subdivision 9-A. (Charles Albi collection)

The 1956 Christmas card sent to its friends and patrons by the Rock Island featured this Howard Fogg rendition of Rotary 95377 clearing the drifts east of Colorado Springs ahead of a 1200 series GP7 and its cozy wooden caboose. (Museum collection) The oil-burning plow, built by Lima-Hamilton in 1950, was stationed at Goodland, where it is pictured below in April 1965, less than a year before its retirement. (Chuck Weart collection)

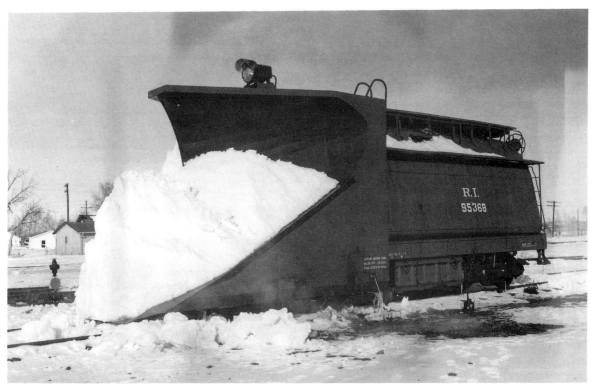

The Rock Island converted several of its unique semi-Vanderbilt steam locomotive tenders into wedge plows; the 95368 is at Limon in the winter of 1962. (Otto C. Perry photo, Denver Public Library, Western History Department) Below, No. 95583 was used in March 1977 in an attempt to open the line west of Goodland. Later in the day, while ramming a hard-packed drift at 40 M.P.H. one mile west of Genoa, this plow was flipped on its back and the two diesel units derailed. (Chuck Weart photo)

After the 1977 storm in eastern Colorado another Lima-Hamilton rotary plow—Union Pacific 900076—was called upon to clear the CRI&P between Limon and Colorado Springs. In a scene reminiscent of those taken seven decades before on the Moffat Road high in the Rocky Mountains, the big plow clears a deep drift east of Peyton on the first day of spring. (John W. "Wally" Maxwell, Jr. photo) Below, the Rock's 4512 and 4332 power the U.P. outfit on toward the base of Pikes Peak. (Chuck Weart photo)

Blasting snow and black oil smoke into the blue Colorado sky, Union Pacific 900076 charges past the boarded-up station at Calhan. This is an historic moment—the last use of a steam powered rotary snowplow on a Class I North American railroad—and Chuck Weart was on hand to record this scene for future generations to witness some of the drama of one of these powerful machines in action.

APRIL, 1941
CORRECTED TO APRIL 27, 1941

APRIL, 1941
CORRECTED TO APRIL 27, 1941

Rock Island

Rock Island

TIME TABLES

TIME TABLES

Fast Through **FREIGHT SERVICE**

Route of the **ROCKETS**

How to go..

ROCKY MOUNTAIN ROCKET
At the Foot of Famous Pikes Peak

From Chicago to the snowcapped peaks, sunny valleys and deep canyons of the Colorado Rockies, it is just a pleasant over-night ride on the Rocky Mountain Rocket.

Operating over the only route with separate direct lines and independent through service from Chicago to both Denver and Colorado Springs. The train divides at Limon. Coach and sleeping car facilities are available to both Denver and Colorado Springs. These fine trains are streamlined, roller bearing equipped, and powered by Diesel electric locomotives. They operate smoothly at a cruising speed in excess of 90 miles per hour.

The reclining seat chair cars are available to patrons traveling at coach fares. Chairs are adjustable and conducive to restful sleeping. The cushions, scientifically contoured and luxuriously padded, give maximum comfort. Pillows are available from the attendant. There are large and well-lighted smoking and rest rooms for both men and women. Latest type drinking fountains assure a constant supply of cool drinking water.

The sleeping cars have private rooms and sectional space.

There is the roomette, a completely enclosed private room for one person, the double bedroom with its wide comfortable sofa, and the new compartment. All rooms have private toilet facilities, mirrored cabinets and ample luggage space.

The sections are composed of a lower and upper berth, each of which may be occupied by one or two persons.

The observation car is the social center of the train. Twenty-five chairs are companionably grouped and attractively upholstered and invite complete relaxation. There is a writing desk and buffet lounge with an attendant who caters to refreshment desires.

In the dining car one will find roomy comfort, luxurious atmosphere, and dining car meals that satisfy the most jaded appetite.

The club diner built primarily for the convenience of coach patrons is open to Pullman patrons if they so desire. It supplements the full meal service available in the regular diner. This car also provides a lounge and beverage service, as well as full meal service between Limon and Colorado Springs.

All-Expense Tours — While the Rock Island operates no all-expense tours, yet, many and varied are those available through the various travel bureaus that ticket their patrons on the Rocky Mountain Rocket. These one unit price package tours include train fare, meals, hotel and sightseeing. Descriptive folders may be secured from your nearest Rock Island Representative.

**Reclining Seat
Chair Car**

**Observation
Parlor Lounge**

The Club Diner

**Double Bedroom
en suite**

The "Route of the Rockets" took second place to no other carrier in offering colorful advertising matter. On the opposite page is reproduced a timetable cover of 1941, while above is a glowing description of the Rocket taken from a 1949 brochure "Scenic Colorado—Vacation Land Supreme." Note that the publicity people in their typical style have placed the streamliner on a double track mainline which appears to be located on the Midland Terminal at Woodland Park! (both, Charles Albi collection)

Chicago, Rock Island & Pacific Railway.
TELEGRAPH DEPARTMENT.

Time Sent.		Time Rec'd.
M.		M.

This blank to be used only in Telegraph Service.   All messages should be written in ink.   Messages filed for transmission when TRAIN MAIL would have served the purpose, must be referred to Supt. of Telegraph (after being sent) attached to Form 63.   Messages should be worded as briefly as consistent with their perfect understanding.

Approved: **E. ST. JOHN**, Gen'l Manager.   A. R. SWIFT, Supt. of Telegraph.

June 28, 1895

To The Gold Link Brokerage Co
Denver Colo

Gents
Please find enclosed $2 00/xx money order No. 2089, to make payment (monthly) on my 100 shares of Orphan Boy Stock,
Respy
E. W. Cooper
Herrington
Kans

Nearly eight decades after a Rock Island official in Herrington, Kansas had purchased stock on an installment plan in Colorado's Orphan Boy Mine, a solid trainload of new automobiles rolled from U.P.'s Kansas Pacific line onto CRI&P track at Sandown Junction just east of Denver. The railroad had indeed contributed to the economy of the Centennial State over a long span of its history and in a wide variety of ways. (Above, Museum collection; below, Lloyd Hendricks photo, Denver Public Library, Western History Department)

ACKNOWLEDGMENTS

The Rock Island Railroad is a fairly fresh trail to follow, but is rather frustrating due to the lack of historical preservation in the eastern Colorado region. Railroad publicists flocked to the grand mountain regions of Colorado and treated the plains as part of Kansas. The interest in local history along the Rock Island has been slow moving, but there is an active spirit along the line and perhaps this project will help keep it rolling.

A few historians on the Rock Island route helped guide us and keep us "honest": most graciously Marion C. Parker of Goodland, Kansas, a crewmember on the last *Rocket*, has been unmatched in his guidance and assistance. Glen Wilson, Robert French, Woody Ralston and Mr. & Mrs. C.W. Willcox, all with personal ties to the railroad, aided with family and first hand experiences.

Photographs of the Rock Island are difficult to find, and in private collections, Gordon Bassett led the way. Art Gibson, Alvie Harris, Paul Brown, Mary Owen, Earl Cochran and Dora Erbert gave valuable contributions. Augie Mastrogiuseppi of the Denver Public Library Western History Department provided access to the Otto C. Perry and Joseph Schick collections. Mary Davis of the Pikes Peak Library District guided us through the mass of *Gazette Telegraph* photographs. Newspapers along the line were contacted and the *Limon Leader*, and *Burlington Record* stand out in their cooperative spirit.

Howard Noble, Paul Brown and William Riester of the Cadillac and Lake City have proved invaluable in helping the project by searching out old Rock Island material from company files and assisting in preparation of an accurate history of the C&LC. The Colorado Midland Chapter of the National Railway Historical Society maintains a Rock Island collection which has been searched for letters and records. The El Paso, Elbert, Kiowa, Lincoln and Sherman County Assessors' offices have been most cooperative in providing access to railroad material, as has the Colorado State Archives. Ted Shonts of the El Paso County Assessor's office has remained alert for material. The Rock Island Technical Society provided assistance as a forum for the format of this manuscript. Flagler's collection is nearly large enough for a book in itself, and Paul Stradley granted access to the entire collection for our research and use. The hospitality of the people in eastern Colorado is unmatched. The McArthurs at the "Old Town" in Burlington continue to work to preserve the entire history of the area, including that of the railroad. (In 1986 the old Midland Terminal Railway Post Office car which the Rock Island had used at Burlington was destroyed by fire—another artifact lost, but others remain.)

In wrapping up this manuscript, Kimberly Filip assisted by drawing numerous station maps. Our friends have heard the stories more often than they care to mention, but as friends and wives are prone to do, they supported us and we thank them. We will continue our interest in The Rock and the Cadillac and Lake City.

On a sunny winter afternoon in February 1980 one of the last Rock Island trains from Colorado Springs to Limon passes quietly through the tiny community of Falcon, the old junction with the long-gone Denver & New Orleans, where the sidetrack was now almost lost in the dry prairie vegetation. (Mel McFarland photo)

BIBLIOGRAPHY

Books and Articles:

Forrest, Kenton and Charles Albi, *Denver's Railroads*, Colorado Railroad Museum, Golden 1981 (revised edition, 1986).

Hayes, William Edward, *Iron Road to Empire*, Simmons-Boardman Publishing, New York, 1953.

Shaffer, Ray, *A Guide to Place Names on the Colorado Prairie*, Pruett Publishing, Boulder, 1978.

Stagner, Lloyd E., *Rock Island Motive Power, 1933-1955*, Pruett Publishing, Boulder, 1980.

Stagner, Lloyd E., "In 4-8-4's, If Not In Finances, Rock Island Excelled," *Trains*, March 1981.

Wilkins, Tivis E., *Colorado Railroads*, Pruett Publishing, Boulder, 1974.

Newspapers and Periodicals:

Burlington Record

Gazette Telegraph (Colorado Springs)

   The Limon Leader

   The Rocky Mountain News (Denver)

Iron Horse News (Colorado Railroad Museum, Golden), October 1966, April 1977 and April 1980.

The Rocket (Rock Island Lines magazine), various issues—primarily October 1952, October 1958, November 1969 and December 1969.

Two former Burlington Northern diesels, ALCO C425 No. 4262 (originally Spokane Portland & Seattle) and EMD GP7 No. 1551 (originally Great Northern), lead a 40-car Kyle Railroad freight out of Goodland on July 23, 1983, when the track was still owned by the Rock Island trustee. The automatic block signals had been taken out of service. ("Chip" Sherman photo) Thirty-five years earlier (opposite) an old caboose had rattled along at the end of a westbound freight near Watkins, Colorado. Around the Rock Island emblem on No. 17995's side is the inscription "Safety-Courtesy-Service." (Herbert O'Hanlon photo, G.C. Bassett collection)

It is September 1949, the finale of all-steam operations over Tennessee Pass In this familiar panorama at West Mitchell the 3613 doubleheads with the 1503 upgrade toward the summit tunnel, 2½ miles distant. The original narrow gauge roadbed can just be discerned above the articulated's boiler. (Robert A. LeMassena photo)

TENNESSEE PASS

by
Robert A. Le Massena

On a clear, cold wintry morning an eastbound doubleheaded passenger train has just stopped at the Tennessee Pass depot after having passed through the tunnel below the summit. This World War I era scene shows the structure after it had received some modifications. After enduring the harsh climate of Tennessee Pass for 70 years, the historic station was closed in November 1958 because it no longer served any useful purpose. (Bill Brown painting, A.D. Mastrogiuseppe collection)

I. THE EARLY YEARS

Quite apart from being the highest railroad crossing of the Continental Divide in North America, Tennessee Pass* possesses intriguing historical distinctions. Probably the most significant aspect of its history is that General William Jackson Palmer had no intention of building the mainline of his Denver & Rio Grande Railway over the pass; however, the Articles of Incorporation did provide for a branchline—the Western Colorado Railway—which would follow the Grand River into western Colorado, thence into Utah. Originally, D&RG rails were directed toward Mexico City, via Santa Fê, New Mexico, and El Paso, Texas, until some unfortunate generalship caused the loss of New Mexico's gateway, Raton Pass, to the Atchison Topeka & Santa Fê railroad in the late 1870s. After essaying a detour over La Veta Pass, and retrieving the Arkansas River (Royal Gorge) right-of-way from his rival, the AT&SF, General Palmer terminated his narrow gauge enterprise at Trinidad, and, like the prospectors, penetrated the unknown Rocky Mountain wilderness in search of gold and silver traffic to fill his freight and passenger cars. At least this type of business would produce immediate revenue, a characteristic not inherent in the future mercantile commerce of old Mexico, which at that time had only one railroad, the Mexicano, connecting Mexico City with the port of Veracruz on the Gulf of Mexico.

By 1880, after ten years of railroad construction, Palmer had pushed his tiny track into the far mountains of southwestern Colorado, as well as up the Arkansas River to Leadville. At this point the General was 277 miles out of his Denver terminus, yet only 80 air-line miles distant, and his railroad was headed northward instead of southward. On November 15 track was laid atop Fremont Pass at 11,329 feet above the sea, and on the 15th of December the rails reached the 10,015 foot summit of Cumbres Pass. Marshall Pass, at 10,858 feet, was traversed on May 10, 1881, and on the 17th of August tracks had attained the 10,433-foot crest of Tennessee Pass. Excepting Cumbres Pass, all were Continental Divide crossings; and the first and last were for branches from the mainline. To surmount Tennessee Pass the rails climbed only 11 miles from Malta, the junction with the line to Leadville, on a two percent gradient and a couple of miles of four percent through Cranes Park. On the northern side the right-of-way sloped downward through Mitchell Park into Eagle Park, then down the canyon of the Eagle River to Rock Creek, 30 miles from Malta. The average gradient was two percent, but in some places it was three percent.

During the 1880s D&RG rails infiltrated all of Colorado's southwestern mountain country, so eager was the railroad to participate in the lucrative prosperity of a precious metal boom. While individuals became incredibly wealthy, Palmer's railroad was busily and rapidly going broke; its extensions were costing more than its income. What it needed was a respite to allow consolidation of its frantic expansion, but it was denied the opportunity. Two other railroads and a fabulous silver strike prevented any chance for the D&RG to manage its system in a normal fashion.

Palmer himself was involved with two other projects: a railroad from Mexico City to Manzanillo, a Pacific Ocean port, and an extension of the D&RGW (Denver & Rio Grande Western Railway, a separate company) into Utah. The Mexican railroad, after laying some trackage, fizzled in 1883, and Palmer resigned his position with the D&RG so that he could devote his entire effort to the D&RGW. He had acquired three short railroads in Utah, he had connected them with new track, he had added an extension from Salt Lake City to Ogden, and he had directed his construction gangs to lay track eastward toward Grand Junction in Colorado, where D&RG track terminated. Palmer engaged D&RG forces to build westward from Grand Junction, and on March 30, 1883, the rails were joined at Desert Switch out in the Utah desert. From its incorporation in 1881, the D&RGW had fabricated a 346-mile mainline connecting the D&RG with the Union Pacific and Central Pacific systems at Ogden, all in less than two years.

During 1884 and 1885 there were no additions to D&RG trackage, but Aspen's rich silver ores and the consequent construction of the *standard gauge* Colorado Midland railroad, from Colorado Springs directly through the mountains to Aspen, forced the D&RG into immediate action. Commencing at Rock Creek in the summer of 1887, it laid narrow gauge rails on standard gauge ties down the precipitous twisting canyon of the Eagle River to its confluence with the Grand River, thence down the Grand's rocky canyon to Glenwood Springs and upstream along the Roaring Fork River to Aspen. Arriving there on November 1, two months ahead of the Colorado Midland whose route penetrated the Continental Divide west of Leadville in a tunnel 1100 feet higher than Tennessee Pass, the D&RG found that its rail distance to Denver was 122 miles longer than that over the CM. Aware that the Colorado Midland was contemplating an extension to Salt Lake City, the D&RG added 27 miles of narrow gauge track from Glenwood Springs to Rifle Creek in 1889 and was dismayed to learn that the D&RGW had been reorganized as the Rio Grande Western, which was already changing its track to standard

---

*Enroute to California, John C. Fremont and his party traversed the pass in 1845, but it was not named until the 1860s, when a group of prospectors from Tennessee crossed the Continental Divide at that location between Tennessee Creek and the Eagle River.

(continued on page 130)

This scene looks northward across Eagle Park toward Pando from the original narrow gauge line; the new standard gauge line was located on the rocky wall at the left. This photo presents an enigma. The track reached this spot in September 1881; yet the locomotive, which was built in March 1880, appears to have just been delivered to the D&RG. This site can be reached today via a road built on the abandoned railroad grade. Pando is a Spanish word meaning slow, deep water. (William H. Jackson photo, Denver Public Library Western History Department)

gauge, starting at Ogden. Having no choice but to convert its own track also, the D&RG added a third rail from Pueblo to Leadville in 1890. Then, it built a new narrow gauge line through a tunnel beneath Tennessee Pass, connecting with the existing track at Pando, the upstream end of Eagle River Canyon. From Pando to Rifle Creek one rail was removed to change the gauge, but beyond Rifle Creek a new standard-gauge railroad was constructed into Grand Junction. Named Rio Grande Junction, it was owned equally by the D&RG and CM railroads.

The new line diverged from the original one eight miles beyond Malta, at an elevation of 10,080 feet, and maintained the 1.4% Arkansas Valley gradient until the steep terrain prevented further progress. At that point a half-mile tunnel was bored through the ridge, 200 feet below the summit of the pass. On the northern side the track sloped downward on a three percent gradient and joined the narrow gauge track at Mitchell's, elevation 9880 feet. Below Mitchell's the original right-of-way had encircled the eastern edge of Eagle Park before plunging into upper Eagle River Canyon. The new alignment, still holding the three percent gradient, was located high on the western rocky wall of the park, requiring considerable rock removal and the drilling of a 242-foot tunnel through a projecting eminence. At Pando, midpoint of the steep northern side grade, was a two mile stretch of track whose gradient ranged from level to 1.7%. Here downgrade trains could stop to cool wheels and brakeshoes, and uphill trains could halt to replenish the engines' water supply. North of Pando the gradient was just under three percent as far as Red Cliff, where it eased somewhat to 2.5%. The alignment in the narrow canyon was a continuous succession of curves for eight miles, with several of 10-16 degrees. Between Malta and Red Cliff the new track was 23 miles long, the original one 27 miles. The bottom of the hill, where the gradient became less than 1.5%, was at Minturn, five miles west of Rock Creek and named after D&RG Vice-President Thomas Minturn. There the helper engine facilities were augmented by a ten-stall roundhouse and a new 62-foot turntable.

Although work on the Tennessee Pass tunnel commenced in December 1889, it was evident that its completion would determine when standard gauge trains could begin running. Meanwhile, because the D&RG probably did not want to disrupt the lucrative freight traffic to and from Aspen, it retained the narrow-gauge track until the last possible moment. Hence, the new line through the tunnel and as far as Pando was built narrow gauge. Track through the tunnel was completed on October 29, 1890, and 2-8-0 No.246 made the initial trip (southward) through it. On the 31st 4-4-0 No.86 pulled two cars assigned to Division Superintendent

Robert N. Ridgway northward through the bore. This could very well have been the last narrow-gauge train operated through the tunnel, as well as the last one on the old line over Tennessee Pass. Wasting no time, track gangs began to change the track, using heavier rails, and by November 23 the conversion had been accomplished sufficiently for operation of the first standard gauge trains. What evidence there is suggests that the conversion progressed from Malta toward Rifle Creek and Aspen.

Changing the track gauge required the establishment of a new station—Tennessee Pass—and the construction of facilities for handling helper locomotives based at Minturn. All of those structures were located close to the south portal of the tunnel and were installed in 1890. The two-story depot building, 24x33 feet, was on the east side of the track; the 16x24 foot water tank was placed between the depot and tunnel adit. Across the tracks was a 62-foot turntable housed in a corrugated iron shed, as was the 20x120-foot engine house.

Prior to the change of gauge two passenger trains had crossed Tennessee Pass each way daily. The *Glenwood Express*, which had departed Denver at 7:30 PM, arrived at 8:35 AM, and at 10:42 AM a mixed train from Leadville arrived, then departed at 11:10. In the opposite direction the mixed train paused from 2:15 to 2:40 PM, and at 6:07 PM the *Denver Express* arrived. These consists were replaced by two pairs of standard gauge trains named *California Fast Mail/California & Eastern Fast Mail*, and *Pacific Coast Limited/Atlantic Coast Limited*, all operated between Denver and Ogden. By 1901 four passenger and four freight trains were scheduled to pass through the tunnel every day, in both directions. In 1887 a passenger train needed one hour 35 minutes to climb the eastward grade to Tennessee Pass; the downgrade pace westward was cautious, one hour 42 minutes. A mixed consist took close to an hour longer each way.

The enormous surge of freight and passenger traffic following the inauguration of the new standard gauge route via Tennessee Pass caused the D&RG to order 130 new locomotives from the Baldwin Locomotive Works between 1887 and 1891. These were 33 Class 106 4-6-0s numbered 506-538, 75 Class 113 2-8-0s numbered 555-629, and 22 Class 100 2-6-0s numbered 805-826, intended for passenger, freight and switching service, respectively. On the northern (steeper) side of the pass two road service engines were used on each train leaving Minturn, but a 1901 operating timetable shows that the 2-6-0s also were used as helpers. During the next decade the railroad acquired heavier 4-6-0s and 2-8-0s, but they were not utilized beyond Salida. No wonder that Rio Grande crews envied the abilities of Colorado Midland 2-8-0s, equivalent to Classes 159 and 175, whenever they were detoured because of snow blockades on Hagerman Pass.

Photographer William H. Jackson's special train was posed in the upper end of the Eagle River's rocky canyon for this portrait. (Denver Public Library Western History Department)

At the turn of the century the Denver & Rio Grande experienced an upheaval which was to affect every aspect of its corporate structure and activity. The Gould family had obtained control of the Rio Grande Western and the Missouri Pacific, and through the latter was able to control the D&RG, thus forming a system stretching from St. Louis to Ogden. Even more trains rolled over D&RG track, and to accommodate them, more trackage was needed on the steep northern side of Tennessee Pass. Between 1903 and 1910 a second track was added in segments: Minturn to Rex (four miles in 1903), Rex to Red Cliff (four miles in 1907), Red Cliff to Pando (five miles in 1909), Pando to Deen Tunnel (three miles in 1910). There was no room for a second track on the eastern wall of Eagle Canyon between Rex and Red Cliff; the roadbed for that track was carved out of the canyon's sheer western wall, a location which required three tunnels at Rock Creek (408 feet) and Belden (66 feet and 275 feet), all between Mileposts 296 and 297. One minor advantage was achieved, however; the maximum gradient was reduced fromn 3.3% to 3.0%. Larger locomotives also began to appear on the pass—103 2-8-0s in five groups of increasing weight between 1900 and 1908, and 44 4-6-0s in three groups between 1902 and 1909. These were the last of those wheel arrangements built for the D&RG; henceforth, locomotives were to increase dramatically in their weights and tractive efforts.

In early 1899 a blizzard blocked the Colorado Midland's track over the mountains, causing it to operate over the D&RG for two and a half months; and in 1910 the Rio Grande ran over CM trackage for three weeks while a cave-in was cleared from the Tennessee Pass tunnel. Also in 1910 the D&RG's extension to the Pacific Coast—the Western Pacific Railway—was opened for end-to-end passenger service which made connections at Salt Lake City with D&RG trains named *Western Pacific & San Francisco Express* and *Rio Grande-Chicago Special*. Unfortunately, insufficient traffic caused their demise after one season in 1911, a fate shared with the Denver-Salt Lake City deluxe *Scenic Limited* in 1906.

If passenger service did not attain anticipated levels of business, freight traffic demonstrated an acute need for more powerful locomotives, a situation which brought five new wheel arrangements to the railroad in just seven years. This episode of motive power development commenced in 1910, when the D&RG borrowed one of the Denver North-Western & Pacific's new 0-6+6-0 Mallets for trial trips on Tennessee Pass. The results were so successful that eight 2-6+6-2s were purchased from the American Locomotive Co. Half were assigned to the northern slope of Tennessee Pass; the others worked on the western side of Soldier Summit in Utah. Fourteen

2-8-2s came from Baldwin Locomotive Works in 1912, but they remained on the mainline between Salida and Denver. In 1913 Baldwin delivered six 4-6-2s, which were operated in passenger service over Tennessee Pass, but of much greater importance was the arrival of sixteen 2-8+8-2 Mallets from American. Initially they were utilized as the road engine on freight trains between Denver and Grand Junction, but their small drivers and enormous cylinders soon disclosed that they were better suited to the two to 2.4% grade on the eastern side of Soldier Summit, the 2.5 to three percent grades of La Veta Pass and the three percent grade of Tennessee Pass. The final group in 1916 consisted of ten 2-10-2s from American's factory; five worked on Tennessee Pass as helpers, the other five hauled freight trains between Denver and Salida. Despite their great tractive effort, which exceeded that of the 2-6+6-2s by 35%, their larger drivers (63 inches vs 57 inches for 2-8-0s and both kinds of Mallets) and longer rigid wheelbase were not compatible with the D&RG's sinuous track which was notable for the profusion and sharpness of its curvature. They must have caused so much trouble with derailments and spread or overturned rails that only a single photograph of one of them at work between Pueblo and Grand Junction has been found.

At the end of 1917 the United States Railroad Administration took over operational control of the D&RG because of the nation's entry in World War I, an event which was to affect Tennessee Pass traffic in a highly unusual manner. First, the USRA, in a typically misinformed decision, diverted almost all railroad traffic between Colorado Springs and Grand Junction to the Colorado Midland, without regard for its light track and steep grades, just because it possessed the shorter route. Despite an heroic effort lasting four months the CM became so choked with nearly motionless trains that in May the USRA re-routed all traffic over the D&RG. After having seen almost no trains during that period, Tennessee Pass suddenly found itself embarrassed with more trains than it could handle comfortably. Meanwhile, the Rio Grande had requested a court-administered receivership, which meant that no more locomotives could be purchased to relieve the congestion. Hence, some otherwise idle CM locomotives were leased for service between Minturn and Grand Junction, thus allowing the D&RG to assign more of its own power to the Minturn-Salida segment. Federal control ended in 1920, leaving the railroad in an advanced state of deterioration, and the Colorado Midland on the verge of imminent abandonment. A year later the D&RG was reorganized as the Denver & Rio Grande Western Railroad, but within another year the railroad was back under a new receivership.

This photo depicts the end-of-track at Rock Creek in 1882. It is difficult to believe that the mining operations in this remote location justified the construction of the original narrow gauge line from Malta, over Tennessee Pass and through the precipitous canyon of the Eagle River, to this point. Also, it is equally difficult to visualize today's mainline here. (Nathan Boyce photo, Museum collection)

The conversion of the narrow gauge track to standard gauge between Pando (junction of the old and new narrow gauge lines) and Rock Creek (end of old narrow gauge track) was different from that beyond Rock Creek, as is illustrated in this photo. The new standard gauge rail was laid 10¼ inches outside the eastern (right) narrow gauge rail. This location made the centerline of the old and new track coincide. The other new standard gauge rail was laid 36 inches from the first one, thus providing a temporary narrow gauge track, which allowed the removal of the old narrow gauge rails without interupting traffic. Finally, the second standard gauge rail would be moved outward to its proper standard gauge position. (Alfred Brisbois photo, Viktor Laszlo collection)

This pair of scenes shows the ore loading facilities at Belden, only 0.7 miles from the end-of-track at Rock Creek. Both cable and rail trams transported ore mined from the cliffs high above the rails. (Nathan Boyce photo, Museum collection; right, Colorado Historical Society)

135

(opposite) These are pages from the Construction Engineer Beerbower's "Force Book" which tell about starting work on the tunnel in November and December 1889.

R.M. Ridgway, on the left, the D&RG's Fourth Division superintendent, was observing the work at the south end of the tunnel when this photo was taken in the summer of 1890. Work on the tunnel was prosecuted at six faces simultaneously: north portal, south portal, and in each direction from two vertical shafts. This was the scene at the bottom of the northern shaft. (Jackson Thode collection)

Tennessee Pass Tunnel
Diary, Nov. 3rd 1889
to

— Sunday Nov. 3rd —
Construction, party in charge
W. A. Beerbower Asst. Eng. arrived
at Tennessee Pass. weather clear,
Snow covering ground to depth of
1 foot.

(W. A. Beerbower Asst. Eng
  David Leche — Inst. man &c
  W. T. McComb Chainman
  A. S. Anderson, Axman)

— Monday, Nov. 4th —
Weather clear and cold, Retraced
Alignment from Sta. 159+68⁴ to
Sta. 171+63²

Tuesday, Nov. 5th
Snowing. Checked alignment
from Sta. 171+63² to 192+98. checked
Apex angle at tangent produced to Sta.
191+49³

—Wednesday, Nov. 6th —
weather = clear and cold.
Checked Alignment from Sta 192+
98 to Sta. 210+18.

Thursday, Dec 5th
Weather - Snow falling all day.
"All hands" at work fixing camp

Friday, Dec. 6th
Weather - Fair.
Completed fixing up camp.
P.M. first ground broken for Tunnel
(N. Appr.) at Sta. 188+50. Force = 9 Laborers and
½ Foreman.

Saturday, Dec. 7th
Weather. Fair
At office work.
Force at N. End of Tunnel 20 Laborers
   "   "   "   "   1 Foreman

Sunday. Dec 8th
Weather, cloudy. slight snow P.M.
Calculating C. S. Areas, N. End Tunnel
Force at N. End of Tunnel = 40 Laborers - 2 Foremen
Ground broken for Shaft at Sta.
169+50
Force S. of summit in Shaft = 2 men 1 Foreman

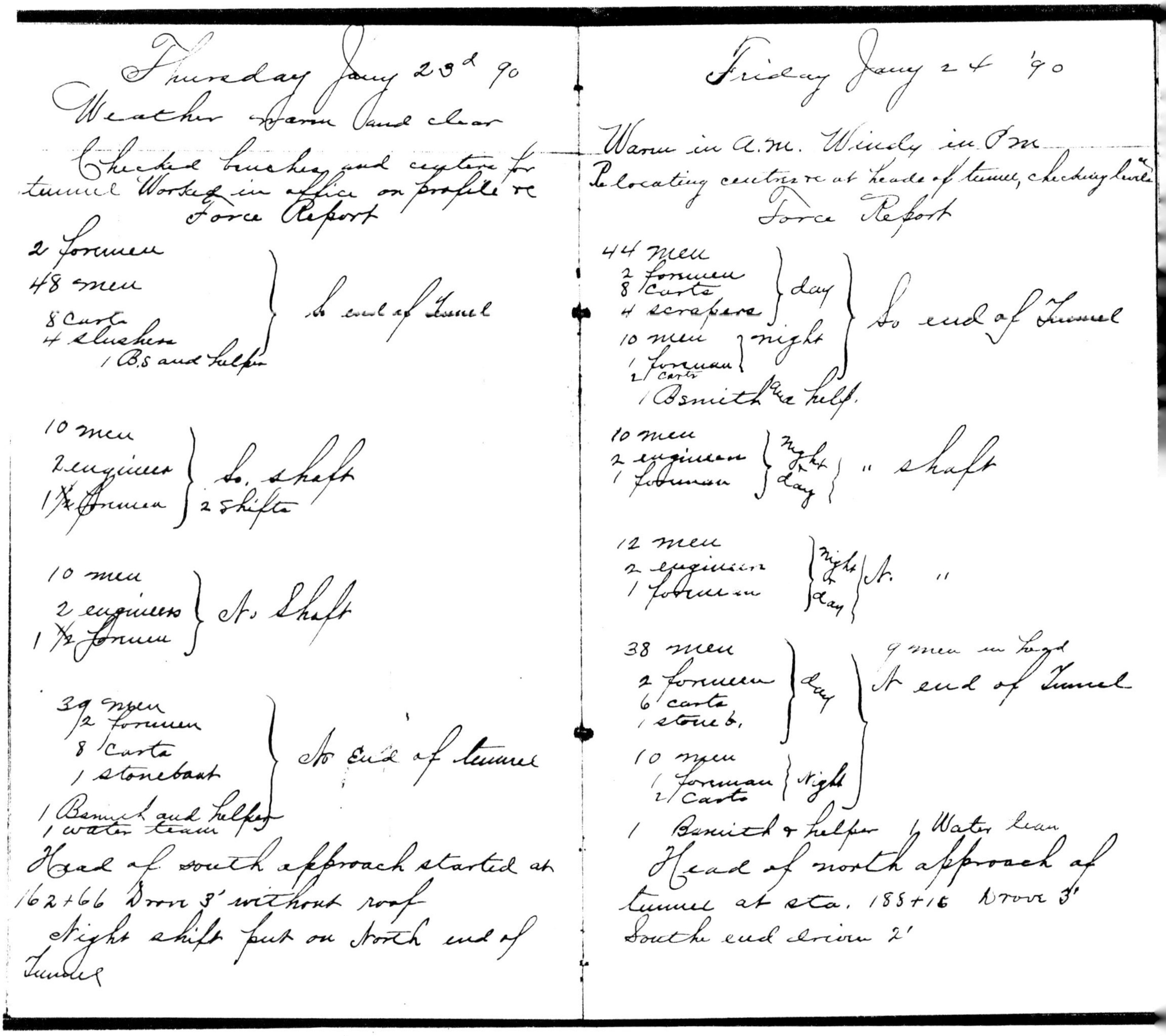

Thursday Jan'y 23d 90
Weather warm and clear
Checked benches and centers for
tunnel Worked in office on profile &c
Force Report

2 foremen
48 men
8 carts
4 slushers   } So end of Tunnel
1 B.S and helper

10 men
2 engineers   } So. shaft
1 ½ foreman   } 2 shifts

10 men
2 engineers   } No Shaft
1 ½ foreman

39 men
½ foreman
8 carts
1 stoneboat   } No End of tunnel
1 Bsmith and helper
1 water team

Head of south approach started at
162+66 Drove 3' without roof
Night shift put on North end of
Tunnel

Friday Jan'y 24 '90
Warm in A.M. Windy in Pm
Relocating centers &c at heads of tunnel, checking lines
Force Report

44 men
2 foremen
8 carts   } day
4 scrapers   } So end of Tunnel
10 men   } night
1 foreman
2 carts
1 Bsmith & helf.

10 men
2 engineers   } night   } " shaft
1 foreman   } day

12 men
2 engineers   } night   } N. "
1 foreman   } day

38 men
2 foremen   } day   } 9 men in logt
6 carts   } At end of Tunnel
1 stone b.
10 men
1 foreman   } Night
2 carts

1 Bsmith & helper } Water team
Head of north approach of
tunnel at sta. 185+16 Drove 3'
South end driven 2'

Beerbower's entries for January 1890 describe the work gangs at each location, working on two shifts in order to expedite completion of the project. Imagine night work in a Rocky Mountain winter at an elevation over 10,000 feet.

On October 29, 1890, the tunnel was completed, and the last work gang posed for its portrait inside the bore. The gentleman at the far left, holding a string to set off flash-powder, was probably the unknown photographer who took these Kodak paper "film" pictures. Sufficient ties and rails were laid on the night of October 29 so that 2-8-0 No. 246 could enter the tunnel from the southern end. During the conversion to standard gauge the right (west) rail would be moved to its proper position on the ties. (Jackson Thode collection)

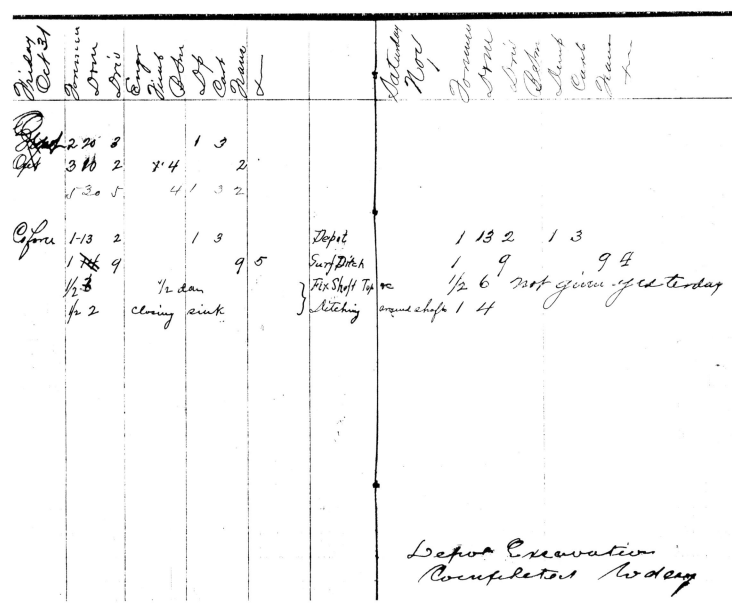

Friday Oct 31	Foremen	Drm	Drls	Engr	Pins	R.dm	Tp	Cat	Rams	
Shaft	2	20	3				1		3	
Out	3	10	2	7.4				2		
	5	30	5		4	1	3	2		
C force	1-13	2			1		3			
	1	9						9	5	
1/2 3				1/2 dm						
1/2 2	closing sink									

Saturday Nov 1	Foremen	Drm	Drls	R.dm	Sink	Cart	Rams	Tm
Depot	1	13	2			1	3	
Surf Ditch	1		9				9	4
} Fix Shaft Top &c	1/2	6	not given yesterday					
} Ditching around shaft	1	4						

Depot Excavation
Completed today

These are the final entries in the Beer-bower diary for construction of the Tennessee Pass Tunnel. On November 1, the depot site had been excavated. 4-4-0 No. 86 stands at the south portal of the tunnel on October 31, 1890. In the foreground standard gauge track has been laid, ready for the gauge widening. The roadbed of the original line over the pass can be discerned above the building at the left.

Another view of Superintendent Ridgway's two-car "extra,"
the first train to run through the tunnel. The circumstances
of this operation suggest that this could have been the final
train operated on the old line over the pass. (two photos,
Jackson Thode collection)

In 1907 the D&RG constructed a second track in Eagle River Canyon between Rex and Red Cliff. In the upper photo (opposite), a work train was backing up the new line. The lower view shows engine 1114 switching several cars of construction material to the mill at Belden being built in the fall of 1908. On this page are two scenes just north of Belden, where the new line crossed the Eagle River: in the upper photo compound 2-8-0 No. 1127, spewing steam from its cylinders, was ascending the original line. Below, a passenger train was being pulled up the new track by a 4-6-0 and one of the new heavy 2-8-0s. (all, Denver Public Library Western History Department; top left, George L. Beam photo)

In a typical 1911 scene 2-8-0 No. 1143 doubleheads
with an unidentified 4-6-0 hauling the six-car **Atlantic
Mail** up the three percent grade above Eagle Park.
(Denver Public Library Western History Department)

(Opposite) Why this head-on collision of two 500 series
2-8-0s occurred near Belden is somewhat mysterious.
Neither engine could have been moving very fast, and
there was ample visual braking distance on the long
curve. The 588 (left) appears to have been running
light downhill when it rammed into an upgrade train.
Locomotives which had been moved into a roundhouse
stall frequently crept unless a heavy chain was placed
across the rails. This "sleep walking" was due to a
leaky throttle, with the customary finale as depicted
in the photo of the 513 at Minturn about 1889. (both,
Denver Public Library Western History Department)

Snowslides and rockslides were the ususal causes of derailments in Eagle River Canyon. In the upper view, circa 1899, some catastrophe wrenched the tender's superstructure off of its underframe; in the lower scene 2-8-0 No. 561 apparently struck a rock and tumbled into the river. (Denver Public Library Western History Department)

D&RGW snowplow 043, pushed by a 2-8-0, is clearing the main tracks and wye at Tennessee Pass. (George L. Beam photos)

Although the D&RG's first 2-8+8-2 Mallets were eclipsed by much heavier locomotives, none of the later locomotives possessed larger cylinders: 40-inch diameter x 32-inch stroke. At the time of their arrival in 1913 they weighed twice as much as the railroad's biggest 2-8-0s. Here No. 1066 awaits a helper call at the Minturn depot. (C.V. Colstadt photo)

II. THE BIG STEAM ERA

Realizing that the railroad was suffering from acute inefficiency caused by a lack of adequate mainline motive power, the receivers embarked on a program which brought some of the world's most powerful and heavy locomotives to Tennessee Pass. During 1922 and 1923 thirty gigantic 4-8-2s, numbered 1501-1530, were purchased from American for both passenger and freight service between Denver and Salt Lake City, and in 1926 Baldwin delivered ten even bigger ones having three cylinders, 1600-1609. For a few years the 1511-1520 group, equipped with trailing-truck boosters, worked principally between Salida and Minturn. Then, in 1927, ten single-expansion 2-8+8-2s, the heaviest and most-powerful steam locomotives on earth, arrived from American's factory, intended for freight service between Grand Junction and Salida. These gigantic articulateds, exerting a drawbar-pull almost twice that of the 4-8-2s, cost only 50% more, and they saved $800 for each trip they made between Salida and Grand Junction. They increased freight train speeds by 50%, and reduced the cost of 1000 gross-ton-miles from 72¢ to 58¢.

In addition to this infusion of motive power, the D&RGW's management initiated a curve reduction and roadbed improvement program in 1926, with major re-alignments and reconstruction on the 30-mile stretch between Buena Vista and Malta. Almost three miles of second track were added from the western portal of the tunnel beneath the pass toward the short tunnel at Deen in 1928, and automatic block-signals were installed between Salida and Minturn. The entire northern side of Tennessee Pass was now double-tracked except for two short segments of about one mile each between the two single-track tunnels. These were such serious operating impediments that a Centralized Traffic Control system was installed to control train movements between Pando and Tennessee Pass station, where the operator was situated. It was the first such installation (1928) west of the Mississippi River and one of the first in the country. In 1929 fourteen Baldwin-built 4-8-4s arrived; they displaced the 4-8-2s on passenger trains and were operated between Denver and Salt Lake City without change at Grand Junction. One year later American delivered another ten 2-8+8-2s, which were assigned to all scheduled freight trains between Denver and Salt Lake City.

At this time just prior to the onset of the global business depression and before the Dotsero Cutoff was completed, Tennessee Pass had attained a zenith of activity. Each day four passenger trains—*Scenic Limited*, *Panoramic Special*, and two unnamed—traversed the pass in each direction. Six scheduled freight trains—two westward and four eastward—plus seasonal extra freights crawled over the divide. Sandwiched among these trains was a continuous flow of compound-expansion 2-8+8-2s—two for each freight train and one for a passenger consist—drifting back downgrade after having assisted eastward trains from Minturn to the summit. All of these helpers were turned on the wye just east of Tennessee Pass station, the 80-foot covered turntable having been removed in 1914.

Between 1901, when the D&RG was using its smallest standard gauge locomotives, and 1930, after the 4-8-4s had been delivered, the weight of both cars and trains had increased dramatically, as can be discerned in the tonnage ratings assigned for Minturn-Tennessee Pass.

Whl. Arr.	Eng. Wgt	Tract Eff.	Train Tonnage	Wheel Arr.	Eng. Wgt.	Tract Eff.	Train Tonnage
2-6-0	100,000	20,000	235	2-8-0	220,000	49,000	450
4-6-0	106,000	19,000	195	2-8-2	276,000	55,000	550
2-8-0	113,000	25,000	245	4-8-2	378,000	68,000	685
4-6-0 & 2-6-0			420	4-8-2	419,000	75,000	780
4-6-0 & 4-6-0			410	4-8-4	418,000	67,000	685
4-6-0 & 2-8-0			445	2-8+8-2	458,000	95,000	950
2-8-0 & 2-6-0			470	2-8+8-2	534,000	107,000	1100
2-8-0 & 2-8-0			500	2-8+8-2	665,000	125,000	1350

The transit times between Minturn and Tennessee Pass reflected both increased trainweights and the railroad's concern for safe operating procedures on the steep downgrade track, which had no runaway tracks. However, all locomotives were provided with water-braking equipment, and operating rules required the use of brake retainers on all freight cars, as well as a stop at Pando to allow cooling of car wheels.

		UPGRADE	DOWNGRADE
1901	Pass.	65 Min.	50 Min.
1901	Frt.	165 "	100 "
1930	Pass.	90 "	65 "
1930	Frt.	125 "	125 "

The business depression of the early 1930s cut D&RGW freight-tonnage by 50% between 1929 and 1933 and caused the financial failure of the company in 1935. Two trustees from Colorado and Utah, Henry Swan and Wilson McCarthy, then undertook the reconstruction of the railroad, and among their earliest acts was the purchase of five very powerful 4-8-4s, 1800-1804, and ten 4-6+6-4s, 3700-3709, delivered by Baldwin during 1937 and 1938. They were not a moment too early; Eagle Park was transformed in 1942 into Camp Hale, where U.S. Army mountain troops were trained; Pando—hardly more than a siding—became a passenger terminal. The ice harvesting operation, which had taken place here during the winter for many years, was transfered to a new location just west of Kremmling on the Moffat line. The new 4-8-4s worked principally between Denver and Salt Lake City, via the Dotsero Cutoff, and the high-speed articulateds hauled freight between Grand Junction and Salt Lake City, though on occasion one would handle a particularly urgent troop train as far east as Pueblo. Some 4-8-2s, relieved by the 4-6+6-4s, once again became common on Tennessee Pass, as the nation became more involved in a world-wide two-front war.

Freight traffic surged over the D&RGW in 1942 to such an extent that the railroad borrowed new Duluth Missabe & Iron Range 2-8+8-4s for a few months during the winter. Denver & Salt Lake 2-6+6-0s made round-trips out of Bond to Minturn, and Missouri Pacific 2-8-2s continued westward from Pueblo, turning around at Minturn. Five more 4-6+6-4s and two Norfolk & Western 2-6+6-2s were bought for service in Utah, releasing some of the oldest 2-8+8-2s for helper duty on the northern slope of Tennessee Pass. Again in 1943, new DM&IR Mallets worked on the D&RGW until they were needed to haul iron ore in Minnesota. Six American-built 4-6+6-4s of Union Pacific design were leased from the Federal Government, and eight compound-expansion 2-8+8-2s were acquired from the N&W for helper service in Colorado. Seven more 2-8+8-2s and four 4-8-4s were ob-

tained from the N&W during 1945, the year in which a new and larger concrete-lined tunnel was bored underneath Tennessee Pass, parallel to and several feet west of the existing one. The bottleneck was still the single-track tunnel at Deen, but because of its location, in a rocky cliff 300 feet above the valley floor, it could not be widened or by-passed without disrupting the continuous flow of traffic. A further consideration was the fact that any improvement would not be needed after the war had ended.

The final year of all-steam operations on Tennessee Pass came in 1949, culminating with the annual movement of peaches eastward from Grand Junction in September. These 56-car trains of perishable fruit charged up the hill behind a 1500-series 4-8-2 led by one of the single-expansion 2-8+8-2s which had double-headed all the way to Minturn. Two more such Mallets were spliced into the consist, at mid-train and ahead of the caboose for the slow ascent to the summit. One of those trains, motive-power included, weighed 5000 tons, and the total tractive effort exerted by its locomotives amounted to almost half-a-million pounds! Ordinary freight trains marched upgrade with three Mallets; one of the 3600s at the head was helped by two of the compound-expansion 2-8+8-2s, a 3400 or ex-N&W Mallet. Trains of iron ore, usually 28 cars, originating in Utah were escorted up the hill by a pair of 2-8+8-2s coupled fore and aft. The only passenger train was the *Royal Gorge* (the re-named *Scenic Limited*), which needed a 2-8+8-2 to assist its 1800-series 4-8-4 up the three percent grade. Helpers came back to Minturn in coupled pairs, generally just ahead of a northbound train which was obliged to descend much more slowly.

During the conflict in 1942, the first diesel-electric road-service locomotives went to work on the D&RGW, and their numbers increased every year thereafter for fifteen years. However, they were utilized on the Denver-Salt Lake City mainline until 1950, when they commenced operating over Tennessee Pass. Four General Motors Electro-Motive Division B-B units of FT, F3 or F7 models were rated at 1450, 1550, and 2050 tons up the northern side of Tennessee Pass, and they hauled freight trains as far as Salida where they were turned for a return trip. By the end of 1954 steam locomotives had made their last runs up the hill on which they had toiled over periods of 25 to 40 years. As the newer diesel-electric units—F9, GP7 and GP9 models—were delivered, the older ones were assigned to helper service, several being stationed at Minturn. Freight trains from the west arrived at Minturn behind five units, and departed with four to eight additional. On one occasion a 6000-ton train of 112 cars assaulted the grade with six units leading and nine more pushing at the rear.

Originally the narrow gauge rail laid on Tennessee Pass weighed only 30 pounds per yard; standard gauge

(continued on page 155)

These are rare photos indeed! Triple-headers were most unusual, the common arrangement of motive power on passenger trains having been a 2-8-0 helping a 4-6-0. In the upper photo, during spring 1919, one of the huge 2-10-2s is seen spliced between the smaller engines on a German prisoners special; moreover, this is the only known photo of a 2-10-2 in service between Pueblo and Grand Junction. In the lower scene a 4-6-0 (rebuilt from a compound engine) was coupled ahead of a 2-8-0, and the 2-8+8-2 Mallet followed them. The locale was Minturn in the early summer of 1919, and the train was No. 2, the **Scenic Limited**. (C.V. Colstadt photos)

*Another triple-header at Minturn in the summer of 1919 was the **Colorado, New Mexico & Utah Express**, pulled by a pair of 4-6-0s and one of the compound 2-8+8-2s. Like the 2-10-2 seen in a preceding photo, this Mallet had no jacket or lagging around its firebox and last boiler ring, for a reason which seems to have been unrecorded. (C.V. Colstadt photo)*

Taken 20 years apart at Belden, these two photos demonstrate the enormous changes in Rio Grande
motive power. In the upper scene, a small 4-6-0 was struggling uphill with a short passenger train;
in the lower scene, the 1511, a booster-equipped 4-8-2, weighing more than twice as much, was
charging up the three percent grade. (George L. Beam photos)

In 1926 at Rock Creek, George Beam photographed
the **Scenic Limited** as it descended Eagle River
Canyon. Note the almost complete absence of
brakeshoe smoke, the consequence of the engineer's
skillful application of the 1527's hydrodynamic
brake, standard equipment on Rio Grande locomotives.

rail weighed 56 pounds, and as cars and locomotives became heavier so did the rail. The 112 to 115-pound rail was worn-out after having supported the enormous traffic of World War II, and it was replaced immediately afterward by 131 to 133-pound rail, which is the present standard, to support diesel-electric units whose axle-loads equal those of the heaviest steam locomotives. The trackage configuration has changed also; instead of a double-track line, the Minturn-Tennessee Pass segment is now single-track having long sidings at Belden, Red Cliff and Pando. The original CTC installation was replaced in 1958 by one which controlled all of the track east of Grand Junction, 148 miles west from Minturn. Minturn almost vanished—roundhouse, turntable, coal chute, water tanks, most yard tracks, ice house. The quaint two-story wooden depot at Tennessee Pass was de-molished in 1960, and passenger service ended with the ultimate run of the *Royal Gorge* in December 1964. Trucks have taken the seasonal peach traffic, and Utah's iron ore is no longer needed by the blast frurnaces at Minnequa.

This report of the final regularly scheduled run of a passenger train appeared in the Rio Grande's *Green Light* employee newspaper for December 1964:

LAST RUN OF TRAIN NO. 1 WEST OF SALIDA
By William C. Jones and Ross Grenard, Members of The National Railway Historical Society

On Dec. 5, as Royal Gorge Train No. 1 headed west out of Salida, an era of railroading was drawing to a close. This was the last run of a scheduled pas-senger train over the world-famous Tennessee Pass route—ending one of the tenuous threads in a chain linking Colorado of the missle age to its heroic past.

Members of the Intermountain Chapter, National Railway Historical Society, after learning of the de-cision to discontinue service beyond Salida, ar-ranged to run their Private Car 96, former Bur-lington business car, on the rear of the last train. The original drumhead sign for the Royal Gorge was placed on the rear platform of the car.

It is late in the afternoon, Dec. 5, when we arrive in Salida to be greeted by the Chamber of Commerce and representatives of press and radio who have tickets to ride to Buena Vista on the last run.

Last orders are handed up, the last highball given and Train No. 1 rolls west of Salida. Once narrow and standard gauge rails were interlaced here, in the shadow of Mount Shavano. Miniscule passenger trains waited at Salida in years past to carry passen-gers over Marshall Pass to Gunnison and Montrose, and to towns now vanished like the rails that served them.

The last run to Buena Vista passes quickly as we talk with our visitors from Salida. The shadows are

growing long as they leave the train. By the time we have reached Malta, the station for Leadville, darkness has closed about us.

Once the center of a fierce rivalry between the "Grande," Colorado Midland and the South Park, Leadville residents today can tell of the days of H. A. W. Tabor and Molly Brown, of the people, mines and the railroads. Undoubtedly some historian will make much of the fact that the last passenger train left Denver as wreckers were finishing the demoli-tion of H. A. W.'s famed Tabor Grand Opera House at 16th and Curtis Street.

After a brief stop at Malta, we move west again, only to stop a short distance up the line when it was discovered that a young boy forgot to get off. At 5:42 p.m., Leadville is left for the last time.

As we climb Tennessee Pass we move to the grill-lounge to enjoy the steaks which have appeared on the menu for this one run. The towns slip by in the night—Red Cliff, Minturn, Eagle. As we roll west along the Colorado River, the locomotive's headlight bounces wildly on the river and the new snow. In the Glenwood Springs station we notice the train board is blank where Train No. 2 should be listed.

As we click off the last miles toward Grand Junc-tion we gather in the lounge for a final toast. The conversation turns to other last runs—The Shavano, Scenic Limitied, Mountaineer, San Juan. We move to the 96's open platform for the final miles past Palisade and Clifton. The lights of Grand Junction cause us to notice that we have made up time and will arrive almost on the advertised time. At 10:43 p.m., we draw to a stop, 13 minutes late.

A reporter rides around the wye with us. We discuss the events of this day. The story in tomor-row's paper will sadly mean little to most of the automobile-minded world of today.

A switcher nudges us onto the rear of the Prospec-tor for the overnight ride back to Denver. We slip thru the dark winter night knowing that, while a fine train is gone forever, a place is surely set aside in the annals of railroading for the memory of Train No. 1 west of Salida on the Rio Grande.

WRECKS

Despite the steepness of the track between Minturn and the summit, there were remarkably few derailments and only one known runaway train. This excellent safety record was attained by the skillful application of air brakes by expert engineers, the usage of brake retainers on freight cars, and the judicious handling of the cylinder water brake, which was standard equipment on Rio Grande locomotives. Also, the engines were equipped with an emergency steam supply to the power-reverse cylinder, which permitted its operation in case the air supply failed. That one runaway involved a 3400-series Mallet which had taken some old stock and box cars up to Pando, then turned on the wye, and coupled onto some 35 similar cars loaded with ice cut from the lake at at Pando. As the train began its descent into Eagle Canyon the engineer discovered that the train's brakes were inoperative; so, he and his fireman and head-brakeman promptly jumped off into the deep snow. Sensing impending disaster, the conductor cut off the caboose and stopped it with the hand-brakes. At Red Cliff the entire ensemble left the rails on the 12½-degree curve and piled up in the river. There was nothing to salvage excepting the locomotive, which was buried beneath the debris. So, the railroad just waited until spring, when the ice had melted, and then recovered the locomotive.

*Immediately after he had taken the photo of the **Scenic Limited** from the front (bottom, page 154), George Beam managed to photograph the train from the rear. The location is Rock Creek, and it will be interesting to compare the scene shown on page 133. Note particularly the odd rock formation in the upper-left of both photos.*

The 3600-series 2-8+8-2 at the head of this consist was about to enter the Rock Creek tunnel on the new line in lower Eagle River Canyon. One of the 3400-series 2-8+8-2s was the mid-train helper. The man sitting on the roof of the fourth car ahead of the 3400 will soon experience a suffocating exposure to moist steam and acrid smoke when that car passes through the bore. (Author's collection)

In the upper photo, taken during a snowstorm, three-cylinder 4-8-2 No. 1601 has just emerged from the tunnel and was pushing aside the drifted snow in front of the Tennessee Pass depot. In the lower scene one of the 1600s, hauling the eastbound **Scenic Limited**, had been assisted up the hill from Minturn by the 1505, an earlier 4-8-2. (George L. Beam photos)

(Opposite) In this wintry panorama just south of the pass one of the compound 2-8+8-2s was portrayed as it crawled toward the summit. Its train was composed of American Refrigerator Transit Co. cars enroute to the west coast for reloading. (George L. Beam photo)

In the upper photo the eastbound **Scenic Limited** is seen at Pando, commencing its ascent of the newer track location along the western wall of Eagle Park. In the lower view in September 1930, one of the recently delivered single expansion 2-8 + 8-2s was drifting downgrade at the upper end of Eagle River Canyon, near Red Cliff. Note the absence of brakeshoe smoke, evidence of use of the Le Chatelier water brake applied to Rio Grande locomotives. (George L. Beam photos)

The 3403 was a compound-expansion 2-8 + 8-2 displaying some mechanical modifications, employed as a helper between Minturn and the pass. The 1700 had brought the **Colorado & New Mexico Express** from Denver. This train, which was taken by a 4-6-0 on to Grand Junction, ceased running over Tennessee Pass on November 16, 1939. Missouri Pacific No. 1418 had come all the way from Pueblo in October 1941, most likely having assisted a D&RGW engine. (above, Otto Perry photos, Denver Public Library Western History Department; below, Jackson Thode photo)

A quartet of Otto Perry's classic photography from the years 1938-1941: the 3600 approaches the southern end of Minturn's yard, drifting slowly under the restraint of air brakes; the eastbound **Scenic Limited**, brought from Salt Lake City by 4-8-4 No.1802, pauses at Minturn for the addition of 2-8+8-2 helper No. 3604 (keen eyes may detect this latter engine's enclosed cab, the only such modification to this class of locomotive); at Rex the 3613 and 1707 have just commenced the steep climb to the summit of the pass, hauling the eastbound 13-car **Scenic Limited**; a most spectacular view of the 3604 and 1802, at the head of the **Scenic Limited**, emerging from the narrow twisting lower canyon of the Eagle River at Red Cliff. (Denver Public Library Western History Department)

Otto Perry found the 1527, helped by two Mallets, the 3602 and 3612, whose exhausts can be seen easily from this location at West Mitchell. (Denver Public Library Western History Department) Tennessee Pass also was a favorite location for Dick Kindig to demonstrate his photographic abilities. Close to the single track tunnel above Eagle Park, Dick photographed on October 19, 1946 an eastbound freight with the 3606 on the head end, 3557 cut into the train, and three-cylinder 1607 pushing behind the caboose. It was the last of its class to remain in operation. Earlier that year, he had encountered another such train, pulled by the 3601. The 3554, midtrain helper, was an ex-Norfolk & Western compound 2-8 + 8-2. At the rear No. 3400 pushed from its position ahead of the caboose. The original narrow gauge roadbed was located along the far edge of this almost flat valley called Eagle Park, where the Army's Camp Hale is visible. The volume of traffic during World War II was so great that this valley was frequently completely filled with smoke and steam from the locomotives.

Dick Kindig photographed this interesting sequence at the southern end of the summit tunnel on July 3, 1941. On the head end of this 50-car train was the 1517, a booster-equipped 4-8-2, and two compound Mallets, 3404 and 3414 did the helping. Note that the 3404 had been rebuilt with piston-valve low-pressure cylinders. And, hot steam had condensed on the sides of the tenders, making them appear to have been newly repainted. A rarity on Tennessee Pass was the 1203, one of the Rio Grande's 14 2-8-2s. With 20 empty troop cars, it had stopped at West Mitchell to await a train coming off the single-track segment through the Deen tunnel, March 30, 1946.

*The first section of the eastbound **Scenic Limited**, pulled by the 3404 and 1803, has just emerged from the summit tunnel and was coming to a stop so that the big helper could be uncoupled. The operator is hooping-up orders to the engine crews. The 3404 will return to Minturn, after turning on the wye; the 1803, which had brought the consist from Salt Lake City, will continue to Denver. (Otto Roach photo, Denver Public Library Western History Department)*

Above Keeldar, a short distance east of the summit tunnel, the 1800 was making 30 mph with the nine-car **Scenic Limited** on the 1.4% grade approaching the pass. Close to that same location the 3703 (4-6 + 6-4s were rarely seen east of Grand Junction) was escorting a 15-car CCC Special toward Grand Junction. (top, Richard H. Kindig; below, Otto Perry photo, Denver Public Library Western History Department)

WITH OTTO PERRY ON TENNESSEE PASS,
AUGUST 1, 1948

In the morning the 3615 charged up the 1.4% grade through Keeldar (top left), then stopped just east of the new tunnel (center left) until an eastbound freight had emerged, and finally proceeded down the hill toward Minturn (bottom left). During the mid-afternoon the 3613, displaying an uncommonly clear exhaust, roared into the great S-curve at West Mitchell (below). It was helped by the extraordinarily smoky 3401 (bottom) and the 3552 on the rear end, whose earlier trip is portrayed at the left side of the center photo on page 170. (Denver Public Library Western History Department)

Running only a few minutes ahead of the 3615 (previous pages), the 3600 lost little time traversing the su[m]
tunnel and accelerating downgrade on the single track and onto the long siding between East and West Mit[c]
(Otto Perry photos, Denver Public Library Western History Department)

Because of a rock slide on the D&RGW's Moffat Tunnel line, the westbound **California Zephyr** had detoured over the Tennessee Pass route on October 21, 1950. In the upper view it is seen passing the **Royal Gorge** and a freight train which had awaited its arrival. In the lower scene its trio of silver-painted ALCO diesels head into the new tunnel. A former roundhouse foreman at Minturn recalled the difficulty in servicing this long train with only three water hoses at that location, "We would take care of the diner, lounge and observation cars and hope they would get to Grand Junction before the rest of the train ran dry." (Colorado Historical Society)

On July 23, 1950 the Rocky Mountain Railroad Club sponsored a Rio Grande Circle Trip over the Moffat Tunnel and Tennessee Pass routes. Its road-engine, 4-8-4 No. 1705, was replaced by the 1803 at Bond, because the former had hit a rock. At Minturn the 3602 was coupled ahead of the 4-8-4 to help it take the 16-car consist up the hill (above). At Rex the articulated broke a piston ring and returned to Minturn, leaving the train stranded (below). The 3619 came to the rescue (upper right) and hauled the train up to Tennessee Pass. Two years later the trip was repeated, but with a shorter train and diesel-electric units for motive power (lower right, Joseph Schick photo; others, Otto Perry—all four from Denver Public Library Western History Department)

When the diesel-electric era arrived on the D&RGW those multipled units displaced steam locomotives as head end power, as is illustrated by these photos. Above the four-unit EMD F3 552, later assigned to the **California Zephyr** because of its high-speed gearing and steam generators in the B-units, was hauling a freight at West Mitchell in 1949. The midtrain 2-8 + 8-2 helper can be seen above the B-unit. In the lower right scene, just north of

West Mitchell, four F7s, numbered 5601-5604, growl upward with the smoky assistance of a pair of 2-8 + 8-2s. The 5484, 5483 and an F7 model unit from a three-unit set were photographed departing Minturn in July 1958 with the westbound **Royal Gorge.** At the rear were two heavyweight Pullmans in Missouri Pacific livery. (lower right, Otto Perry photo, Denver Public Library Western History Department; others, Viktor Laszlo collection)

This is not the eastbound **Royal Gorge**, but a 1962 Illini Railroad Club special train at Tennessee Pass, just east of the tunnel. The leading unit was the 5761 (Jim Ozment photo). In the lower view, taken in May 1969, a group of helpers—5721, 5734, 5754, 5902, 5653, 5664—was returning to Minturn after a trip up the hill. In February 1966 the 5611-5614 had just arrived in Minturn, where helpers would be added. At the left the 5684 and 5683 await placement in the train. (two photos, Ed Fulcomer)

"Springtime in the Rockies"—early April 1968. Five F7 models 5674, 5643, 5642, 5673, 5631 develop 7500 engine-horsepower as they climb the three-percent grade at West Mitchell (Ed Fulcomer photo). In 1962 GP30 No. 3012, GP9 5943 and another pair of those units roared out of the southern portal of the new tunnel under the pass (opposite top, Jim Ozment photo). GP30 No. 3006 leads three other units at the head of a coal train out of the new tunnel on May 22, 1971. The portal of the old tunnel can be seen to the right and the depot has vanished, having been replaced by a metal box filled with electrical equipment. (A.D. Mastrogiuseppe photo)

(upper) These six units in A-B-B-B-A-A arrangement, led by the 5764 the D&RGW's last F7 model, were the midtrain helpers for the train shown at the bottom of page 181. (lower) Having been cut out of the train at the summit, the helpers enter the tunnel on the return trip to Minturn.

(upper) *Those same helpers pass beneath the two highway bridges at Red Cliff. Note that one track has been removed. (lower) The helper set with 5741 facing west waits at the southern switch of the Minturn yard while the engineer obtains telephone instructions from the dispatcher. This series of photos was taken May 22, 1971 by A.D. Mastrogiuseppe.*

(upper) The 024 (150-tons from Salida) and the 028 (250-tons from Grand Junction) wreckers were brought to lower Eagle River Canyon on July 11, 1970 to restore operational tranquility after a derailment. (Charles Albi photo) (lower) Three Missouri Pacific SD40 C-C units and one belonging to the D&RGW produced an enormous quantity of power to haul this coal train up the grade at West Mitchell in April 1983. Five Rio Grande helpers were cut into the train and three more were pushing ahead of the caboose. (Robert R. Harmen photo)

In this photo, taken at Rex in July 1983, the 5771 had been the D&RGW's only remaining F9A unit for 15 years, following the destruction in a derailment of its last companion, the 5774. Coupled with an F9B unit, a GP40 and a GP30, this assemblage of motive power was headed for Leadville, where some of its retinue of 43 cars would be turned over to the Burlington Northern for forwarding to Climax. (Robert R. Harmen photo)

This view of Minturn, looking toward Tennessee Pass, shows the town situated between the steep hillside (right) and the Eagle River (far-left). The railroad, on the opposite bank, is not discernible. The 3-story Eagle River Hotel, sheathed in embossed metal sheets, was probably a later addition. (opposite) The D&RG's 1887 station was notable for its enormous roof. Compare this William Henry Jackson photograph with the 1958 view on page 177. (three photos, Denver Public Library Western History Department)

IV. MINTURN TO MALTA

By the end of World War I Minturn had expanded to a sizable railroad terminal. A much larger depot had been erected, and five stalls of the roundhouse had been enlarged to accommodate the long 2-8 + 8-2 helpers. The D&RG YMCA is almost obscured by the smoke. Minturn's 1945 depot (bottom) also can be seen at the far-right of the picture of the bottom of the opposite page. (This page: C.V. Colstadt photo, top; Museum collection, center; Denver Public Library Western History Department, bottom)

One of the 3600s, stationed at Minturn for helper duty, has just emerged from the roundhouse and was chuffing past the YMCA building prior to its placement on the helper track. (Robert W. Richardson photo) In the center scene, (1948) the 3400 was coming out of the roundhouse; the 3550, 3615, and 1522 had been serviced and were awaiting an eastbound freight train. (Joseph Schick photo, Denver Public Library Western History Department) The 1979 panorama shows the diesel servicing area (inside the wye), a track repair consist, and a six-unit helper in the distance. (Jim Ozment photo)

A short distance south of Rex, the new line crossed the Eagle River and followed its west bank. The location of the new Ocean to Ocean Highway between Minturn and Malta can be seen at the right of this mid-1920s view (C.V. Colstadt photo) (opposite) Perched on the cliffs above Rock Creek were the buildings of Gilman, whose access to the railroad was provided by a funicular tramway. (Denver Public Library Western History Department) A steam shovel was clearing a rock slide on the old line in the northern end of Eagle River Canyon in 1928. (George L. Beam photo)

From a spot between the two short tunnels on the new line at Belden one can see the structures of Gilman high on the canyon's rim. (George L. Beam photo, Denver Public Library Western History Department)

The Eagle Mining & Milling Co. processed ores from the Iron Mask mine in these buildings until 1915, when the New Jersey Zinc Co. acquired the property. The top view, taken during construction in December 1908, shows a rail-funicular up the mountainside; the bottom one two years later shows an aerial tramway. The center photo shows the lower end of the cable-rail funicular at Rock Creek, where the new line diverged from the old at Milepost 297, visible in the distance. (three photos, Denver Public Library Western History Department)

By 1971 a great many changes were evident in the buildings comprising Gilman (upper-right) and the ore-processing facilities at Belden, where a pair of diesel-electric units was switching some cars. (A.D. Mastrogiuseppe photo) The old highway bridge crossed the river and railroad a short distance downstream from Red Cliff. The new highway crossed the gorge over a graceful steel-arch bridge erected in 1940. (Joseph Schick photo, Denver Public Library Western History Department)

Red Cliff's second station, closed in September 1947, appears to be well supplied with kegs and barrels containing beer and whiskey in this 1915 photo. The lower panorama shows the great curve at Red Cliff and the original narrow-gauge right-of-way along the river (upper-left). The view is upgrade toward the pass. (John M. Dismant photos, Victor Laszlo collection)

The Red Cliff depot sat all by itself between the highway bridges across the Eagle River and the townsite. In this scene one of the 3600s was taking a freight train downgrade, retarding the train with its hydrodynamic brakes, whose exhausts can be seen spewing from the cylinders's cocks. (Joseph Schick photo, Denver Public Library Western History Department) Looking southward through the Pando tunnel, this stretch of single track was controlled by an operator in the Tennessee Pass depot. (Ben F. Cutler photo, Author's collection)

The original depot at Pando was closed permanently in October 1940, but the U.S. Army activities at Camp Hale required the construction of a new one, as seen in this photo, in 1943; it was closed in December 1956. Camp Hale is shown at the peak of its activity in the summer of 1944. (two photos, Colorado Historical Society) The 3600 and 3603 made their final runs in the fall of 1954, when steam power was eliminated over Tennessee Pass. Dick Kindig (right) was present on this occasion at Pando. (Robert W. Richardson photo)

(opposite) This was the original station building, erected beside the standard-gauge track in 1890. Those are not logs stacked on the platform; they are rolls of tarpaper for the depot's new roof. The venerable structure remained intact until its removal in 1960. (B.W. Richardson collection, Denver Public Library Western History Department)

A westbound freight train was just entering the southern portal of the tunnel in March 1900. (Museum collection)

This rare scene (above) shows the octagonal shed, with a corrugated-iron roof, housing the turntable. Above it can be seen the old narrow gauge right-of-way across the hillside. Note the long wooden snowshed protecting the tunnel's southern entrance. (Littleton Historical Museum)

(below) A panorama of Tennessee Pass station and facilities in 1938. The turntable had been replaced in 1910 by a wye which pointed into a gulch just beyond the station. Helpers were cut out of a train standing on the right-hand tracks; after turning on the wye, they coupled together and proceeded light back to Minturn. (H.C. Sweet, Jr. photo, Denver Public Library Western History Department)

WESTWARD					Miles from Denver (Via cut-off)		Time Table No.
THIRD CLASS		**SECOND CLASS**					
223 Local Freight		**65** Utah and California Fast Freight	**63** Color'do and California Fast Freight	**61** Utah and California Fast Freight			October 3, 1909
Leave Daily Exc. Sunday		Leave Daily	Leave Daily	Leave Daily			**STATIONS** AND SIDINGS
8.30 AM		2.15 PM	11.45 AM	4.20 AM	215.11	N	**SALIDA** 3.46
8.43		2.30	11.59 AM	4.38	218.57	T	BELLEVIEW 3.66
8.57		2.51	12.12 PM	5.03	222.23		BROWN CANON 4.98
9.17		3.16	12.33	5.20	227.21	T	ARENA 5.61
9.40		3.40	12.52	5.45	232.82	TN	NATHROP 1.20
					234.02		COLO. & SO. CROS. N 2.35
10.00		3.58	1.08	6.06	236.37		MIDWAY 3.59
10.20		4.10	1.26	6.25	239.96	N	BUENA VISTA 1.93
					241.89		WILD HORSE 2.47
10.50		4.29	1.44	6.48	244.36	T	AMERICUS 3.34
11.15		4.42	2.01	7.04	247.70	T	RIVERSIDE 4.09
11.45 AM		5.00	2.20	7.25	251.79	T	PINE CREEK 5.16
12.17 PM		5.30	2.40	7.52	256.95	N	GRANITE 2.18
12.25		5.40	2.48	8.04	259.13		WACO 3.70
12.42		6.09	3.02	8.22	262.83	T	KOBE 3.66
12.55		6.35	3.15	8.38	266.49		SNOWDEN 4.15
1.17 1.35		6.55	3.30	9.00 9.10	270.64	N	**MALTA** 2.33
					272.97		EILERS 2.49
					275.46	DT	**LEADVILLE** 3.26
1.45		7.06	3.45	9.20	278.72 273.18	□	**LEADVILLE JC** 3.73
2.00		7.16	4.07	9.47	276.91	T	KEELDAR 3.72
2.30 2.50		7.46 8.06	4.30 4.50	10.25 10.50	280.63	N	TENNESSEE PAS 2.86
3.07		8.21	5.05	11.03	283.49	□	MITCHELL 4.87
3.40 3.50		8.42 8.52	5.30 5.40	11.22 11.32	288.36	N	PANDO 5.22
s 4.35		s 9.20	s 6.10	s 11.51 AM	293.58	N	RED CLIFF 2.19
4.47		9.30	6.20	12.01 PM	295.77		BELDEN 1.87
4.57		9.38	6.35	12.08	297.64		REX 3.96
5.30 PM		9.50 PM	7.00 PM	12.20 PM	301.60	N	**MINTURN**
Arrive Daily Exc. Sunday		Arrive Daily	Arrive Daily	Arrive Daily			(86.49) Via cut-off
(9.00)		(7.35)	(7.15)	(8.00)			92.03 (Via Leadvill

Trains Nos. 1, 3, 5, 61, 63, 65 and 223 will not run via Leadville. Th
nessee Pass or Minturn without clearance. No train will leave Le
train No. 239 has arrived.

When cars are left at Mitchell they must be shoved above switch
All westward trains will stop at Tennessee Pass for inspection
Westward freight trains will stop 10 minutes at Pando to cool v
Passenger trains will not exceed schedule time between Brown
between Tennessee Pass and Minturn. Freight trains will not exce
nessee Pass and Minturn, and 25 miles per hour between other po
Trains Nos. 15 and 16 run via Leadville.

FIRST CLASS

5 Chicago- San Francis- co Express	3 Utah and California Express	1 Pacific Coast Limited	239 Stub Conn. from No. 1	237 Stub Conn. from No. 2	235 Stub Conn. from No. 5	233 Stub Conn. from Nos. 3 and 6	231 Stub Conn. from No. 4		
Leave Daily	Leave Daily	Leave Daily	Leave Daily	Leave Daily	Leave Daily	Leave Daily	Leave Daily		
5.35 PM	1.35 AM	4.15 PM							
5.42	1.43	4.22							
5.50	1.51	4.29							
6.01	2.02	4.40							
6.10	2.15	4.52							
6.19	2.25	5.02							
s 6.30	s 2.32	s 5.12							
6.41	2.43	5.22							
6.50	2.51	5.29							
6.59	3.00	5.39							
7.13	3.15	5.56							
7.20	3.21	6.03							
7.30	3.32	6.09							
7.39	3.41	6.16							
s 7.50	s 3.52	s 6.30	6.32 PM	10.02 AM	7.53 PM	3.54 AM	1.20 PM		
			6.39	10.09	8.00	4.01	1.27		
			6.47 PM	10.17 AM	8.08 PM	4.09 AM	1.35 PM		
7.57	3.59	6.38							
8.06	4.09	6.49							
8.20 8.30	4.20 4.30	7.00 7.10							
8.38	4.38	7.19							
8.52	4.52	7.34							
s 9.08	s 5.07	s 7.49							
9.15	5.13	7.55							
9.20	5.20	8.00							
9.30 PM	5.30 AM	8.10 PM							
Arrive Daily	Arrive Daily	Arrive Daily	Arrive Daily	Arrive Daily	Arrive Daily	Arrive Daily	Arrive Daily		
(3.55)	(3.55)	(3.55)	(0.15)	(0.15)	(0.15)	(0.15)	(0.15)		

ville Junction must be set and locked for Malta. No train will leave Salida, Malta, Ten-
earance except trains Nos. 16, 234, 236, and 240. Train No. 236 will wait at Leadville until

al Ovens and this switch must be set and locked for spur.
es.
train.
rop, Pine Creek and Waco, Leadville and Leadville Junction and Leadville and Malta and
our on descending grades between Leadville and Malta, 15 miles per hour between Ten-
al order.

(Museum collection)

The northern portal of the tunnel also was provided with a commemorative plate. The straight bore was 2550 feet long; the length of the older one was 2577 feet. (Ben W. Cutler photo, Author's collection) In this 1971 scene at the southern ends of the tunnels, one can see the disused overhead door frame above the new tunnel's entrance. By 1987, the mouth of the old tunnel was almost completely covered with rocky debris. (A.D. Mastrogiuseppe photo)

In 1958, as part of a CTC project extending from Kobe on the south to Avon on the north, the yard at Malta was rebuilt. Note three ex-troop sleepers and the tender from a departed 4-8-2 in the background. The station here closed in October 1966. (Jim Ozment photo)

DENVER AND RIO GRANDE RAILWAY CO.

TABLE OF DISTANCES, ELEVATIONS, GRADES, ETC.

MALTA TO ROCK CREEK.

From Denver	From Pueblo	From Leadville	Between Stations	NAMES OF STATIONS	Elevation	Avg. Grade Ascending	Avg. Grade Descending	Max. Grade Ascending	Max. Grade Descending	Maximum Curvature, Per 100 feet	Length of Side Track	Iron or Steel and Weight Per Yard	Grading and Bridging Completed	Date When Track Laid	Iron or Steel and Weight, per yard	Open For Business	REMARKS
272.3	152.9	4.9		Malta	9579.7	69.7′		72.9′		4°	870	30 lb Steel	Sept. 1, 1880	Oct. 1, 1880	30 lb Steel	Oct. 1, 1880	Junction Eagle River and Leadville lines
273.1	153.6	7.6	2.7	Ryans	9707.8	56.1′		73.9′		14°	574	"		Oct. 1, "	"	Oct. 15, "	"
274.8	155.2	11.2	3.6	Keeldar	9969.7	55.2′		84.5′		15°	968	"	Oct. 1, "	Nov. 20, "	"	Nov. 20, "	"
281.5	161.9	13.9	2.7	Crane's Park	10118.7	50.′		61.7′		8°	954	"	Nov. 1, "	Nov. 22, "	"	Nov. 22, "	"
281.7	162.1	14.1	.2	Crane's Park Y	10128.7	178.8′		211.′		15°	2,228	"	Dec. 31, "	Aug. 17, 1881	"	Aug. 23, 1881	Summit of Continental Divide.
283.4	163.8	15.8	1.7	Tennessee Pass	10452.7								Aug. 25, 1881	Aug. 25, "			
286.	166.4	18.4	2.6	Little Giant	10067.7		140.6′		158.′	15°	700	"			"		
286.7	167.1	19.1	.7	Gutchell's	9987.3		114.8′		168.′	10°	600	"			"		Bennet's Mill.
287.2	167.6	19.6	.5	Center-Mitchell Y	9945.7		88.2′		105.6′	4°	1,200	"			"		
287.5	167.9	19.9	.3	Mitchell's	9921.7		80.′		80.′	15°	2,200	"			"		
291.	171.4	22.4	3.5	Allen's	9449.7		134.8′		158.′	15°	300	"	Sept. 30, "	Sept. 10, "	"	Sept. 10, "	
294.1	174.5	26.5	3.1	Eagle Park	9229.7		71.9′		105.6′	20°	3,050	"	Oct. 31, "	Oct. 11, "	"	Oct. 11, "	
296.1	176.1	30.1	3.6	Homer	8856.7		75.′		211.′	20°	1,000	"	Nov. 1, "	Nov. 20, "	"	Nov. 20, "	
299.3	179.9	31.9	1.8	Red Cliff	8670.7		158.9′		211.′	20°	800	"			"		
300.4	180.4	32.4	.5	Red Cliff Smelter	8624.7		92.′		116.′	20°		"			"		Battle Mountain Smelting Company.
300.7	180.7	32.7	.3	Homestake	8585.7		123.3′		105.6′	10°	1,000	"	Feb. 1, 1882	Feb. 15, 1882	"		Will be completed Feb. 15. All material
302.2	182.4	34.6	1.9	Belden	8567.8		115.7′		158.′	15°	500	"			"		necessary to lay track on the ground.
302.9	182.9	35.3	.7	Rock Creek	8303.6		91.7′		175.8′	20°	500	"			"		

Total, 20.4 Miles Main Track.

Total Main and Side Track, 33.6 Miles.

Total, 16,954 Feet — 3.2 Miles Side Track.

Third Division—Leadville Dist.—Westward Trains.

J. W. WARD, Dispatcher, Buena Vista.   COLE LYDON, Superintendent, Leadville.

SECOND CLASS.			Telegraph, Water and Coaling Stations.	Time Table No. 19. July 23, 1882. STATIONS and Passing Places.	Distances from Denver	FIRST CLASS.					
No. 25. Fast Freight.	No. 23. Way Freight.	No. 21. Through Freight.				No. 1. Leadville Express.	No. 3. Gunnison Express.	No. 13. Passeng'r.	No. 34. Eagle River Accom.	No. 76. Alpine Branch.	No. 78 Alpine Branch.
			NW	Dep Denver Dep		8 15 Am	7 30 Pm				
9 00 Am	4 20 Am	6 10 Pm	NWC	Dep Salida Dep	216.5	6 55 Pm	6 03 Am	12 50 Pm			
9 35	5 00	7 07	D	" Brown's Canon "	223.6	7 12	6 23	1 09			
9 43	5 07	7 15		" Harp * "	224.8	7 15	6 26	1 13			
9 47	5 15	7 28		" Hecla "	226.1	7 20	6 30	1 16			
10 25	6 02	8 30	NW	" Nathrop "	234.4	7 42	6 52	1 38		6 57 Am	5 35 Pm
10 46	6 30	8 55		" Midway* "	239.2	7 56	7 05	1 52		7 10	5 55
			NWC	Ar Buena Vista Ar	241.9	8 05				7 20 Am	6 05 Pm
10 58	6 45	9 10	NWC	Lv Buena Vista Lv	241.9	8 10	7 13	2 00			
11 03	6 52	9 15		" Dornick* "	243.	8 12	7 17	2 03			
11 20	7 08	9 29		" Americus * "	245.7	8 19	7 24	2 10			
11 49 Am	7 35	9 50	D	" Riverside "	249.6	8 30	7 35	2 22			
12 30 Pm	8 28	10 20		" Pine Creek* "	255.4	8 48	7 50	2 37			
12 55	9 00	10 40	D	" Granite "	258.9	8 58	8 00	2 47			
1 10	9 20 Ar / 9 30 Lv	10 53		" Twin Lakes "	261.1	9 05	8 07	2 53			
1 30	10 00	11 15	D	" Haydens "	264.8	9 16	8 18	3 03			
1 58	10 40	11 48		"Crystal Lake*"	270.3	9 33	8 33	3 18			
2 10	10 53	11 59 Pm	NWC	" Malta "	272.5	9 40	8 40	3 25	4 35 Pm		
2 25	11 06	12 16 Am		" Eilers "	274.9	9 50	8 50	3 35	4 46		
2 40 Pm	11 20 Am	12 35 Am	NWC	Ar Leadville Ar	277.4	10 00 Pm	9 00 Am	3 45 Pm	5 00 Pm		
(5.40)	(7.00)	(6.25)		(60.9)		(3.05)	(2.57)	(2.55)	(.25)	(.23)	(.30)

All trains run daily. No train or engine must leave Salida without the Conductor or Engineer inquiring at the Dispatcher's office for orders.

Third Division—Eagle River Branch.

COLE LYDON, Superintendent, Leadville.

WESTWARD.		Telegraph, Water and Coaling Stations.	Distances between Stations	TIME TABLE No. 19. July 23, 1882. STATIONS and Passing Places.	Distances from Denver.	Length of Sidings—feet.	EASTWARD.	
SECOND CLASS.	FIRST CLASS.						FIRST CLASS.	SECOND CLASS.
No. 35. Freight.	No. 33. Passeng'r.						No. 34. Passeng'r.	No. 36. Freight.
	7 30 Pm			Dep Denver Ar			7 30 Am	
	9 55 Am	NWC		Dep Leadville Ar	277.4		5 00 Pm	
	10 10			" Eilers Dep	274.9		4 46	
12 01 Pm	10 20	NWC	272.5	" Malta "	272.5		4 35	10 55 Am
12 20	10 35		2.7	" Ryan's "	275.2		4 25	10 35
12 40	10 52		3.6	" Keeldar "	278.8		4 10	10 05
1 00	11 05	D	2.7	" Crane's Park "	281.5		4 00	9 45
1 25	11 15		1.9	" Tennessee Pass "	283.4		3 50	9 25
2 15	11 35	D	4.1	" Mitchell's "	287.5		3 30	8 45
3 00	12 05	D	6.6	" Eagle Park "	294.1		3 00	7 45
3 30 Pm	12 30 Pm	DWC	5.4	Ar Red Cliff Dep	299.5		2 30 Pm	7 00 Am
(3.29)	(2.35)			(22.1)			(2.30)	(3.55)

Trains run daily. No train or engine must leave Malta, Leadville or Red Cliff without the Conductor or Engineer inquiring at telegraph office for orders.

(Museum collection)

RIO GRANDE OPENS TENNESSEE PASS TUNNEL AT CEREMONIES

Million-Dollar Bore, in Highest Mainline Rail Crossing of Continental Divide, Now Is Ready For Heaviest Freight Loads.

In a typical Colorado winter setting, a huge, powerful million-pound locomotive glided thru the east portal of the new Tennessee pass tunnel of the Denver & Rio Grande Western railroad Saturday to break a tape held across the entrance by two attractive drum majorets from Grand Junction junior college. A quart of prewar champagne was broken against a bronze plaque at the tunnel's mouth as the steel monster broke the tape.

Thus, as the sun broke for an instant thru gray clouds to gleam upon the snow-garmented trees and craggy peaks, the road officially opened and dedicated the Tennessee pass bore—an improvement for the highest mainline railroad crossing of the continental divide under construction two years and on which more than a million dollars has been spent.

The dedication in a sense heralded a new era of transportation in this rugged mountain region. The locomotive which hauled the five-car special thru the steel and concrete-lined shaft which has an apex 10,242 feet above sea level, was the largest and most powerful of its type ever constructed.

HEAVIEST FREIGHT TO GO THRU BORE.

From now on, such locomotives will be hauling the largest and heaviest type of freight thru this bore, about nine miles above Leadville, on the main line of the Royal Gorge route between Pueblo and Ogden, Utah.

The scene was a far call from the days more than a half century ago when tiny narrow-gauge engines puffed over incredibly steep grades to the top of Tennessee pass.

The tunnel just completed replaces the first standard gauge line Tennessee pass tunnel completed in

1890, now an outmoded bore lined with timber, which had imposed a definite limitation on both freight and passenger traffic.

The project cuts down this mountain grade from 4 per cent to 2 per cent, and from now on trains can easily handle any size load. The bore is 2,550 feet long and has the unusually large dimensions of 23 feet in height and 16 feet in width —one of the largest in the country completely dwarfing the old tunnel some distance up the mountainside.

From the tunnel apex beneath the 10,474-foot pass, water flows eastward toward the Arkansas river and westward to the Eagle and Colorado rivers.

RAILROAD MEN FROM 42 CITIES PRESENT.

Railroad supervisors and agents from forty-two cities from San Francisco and Seattle to Boston and New York city entrained on the big special which made the dedication ceremonial trip over the picturesque route from one side of the continental divide to the other.

For most of these men, it was the first opportunity to inspect the phenomenal growth and development of the D. & R. G. W. system since prewar days, special trains of this type having been largely abandoned during the war years because of heavy traffic congestion.

VISITORS ASTONISHED AT IMPROVEMENT.

From most of the visitors came expressions of astonishment over the improvement of the railroad service thru the recent expenditure of approximately 64 million dollars on such projects as this Tennessee bore and new equipment.

The special train was in charge of F. C. Hogue of Denver, general traffic manager of the railroad. It first carried the visitors over the route to Salt Lake City and Ogden and then back thru the Royal Gorge to Tennessee pass and thence to Pueblo.

The actual dedication was under supervision of L. T. Wright, superintendent of the Grand Junction division of the railroad, including the territory in the Tennessee pass area.

It was Wright who broke the bottle of champagne against the east portal plaque when the great engine touched the tape.

A bronze plate, bearing the names of railroad and construction company officials (including Wilson McCarthy, Henry Swan and A.E. Perlman) was attached to the southern portal of the new tunnel. (A.D. Mastrogiuseppe photo taken in 1987)
The newspaper account of the opening of the tunnel on November 3, 1945, contained some inaccuracies, as one would surmise. The first train through the bore was hauled by 4-6+6-4 No. 3713, which had pulled a special train from Salt Lake City. (Museum collection)

Heralding a New Era

in freight and passenger traffic over the Royal Gorge route of the Denver & Rio Grande Western railroad was the dedication Saturday of the new Tennessee pass tunnel, about nine miles above Leadville. This new million-dollar bore, replacing an obsolete timber-lined tunnel, makes it possible to haul the heaviest loads at faster speeds. The highlight in the dedication ceremony is pictured here with the railroad's huge new-type locomotive breaking the tape at the east portal of the tunnel, as road officials and dignitaries watched.

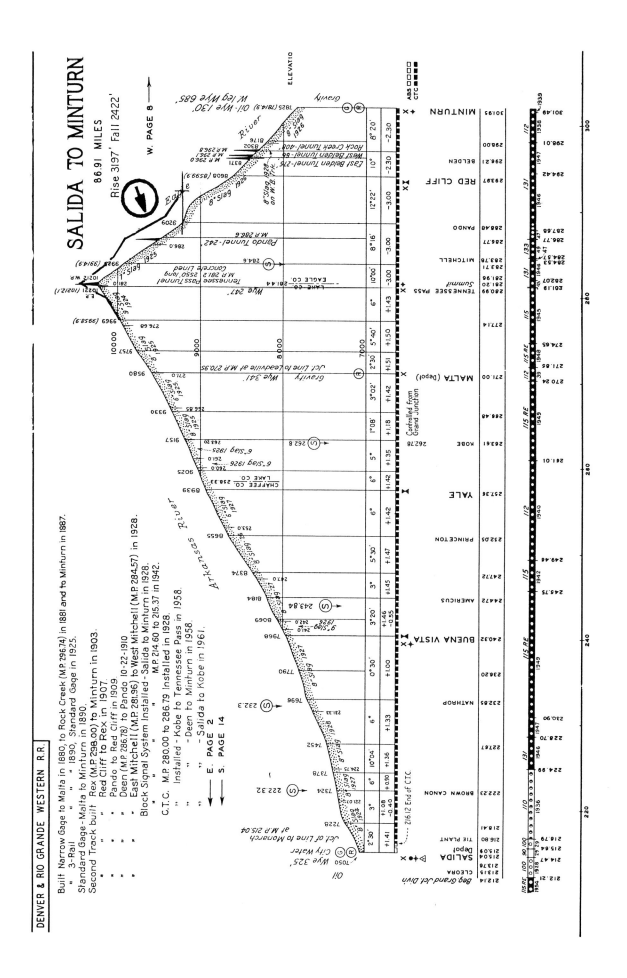

SALIDA TO MINTURN

86.91 MILES

Rise 3197' Fall 2422'

W. PAGE 8 →

DENVER & RIO GRANDE WESTERN R.R.

Built Narrow Gage to Malta in 1880, to Rock Creek (M.P. 296.74) in 1881 and to Minturn in 1887.
" 3-Rail   "   "   1890, Standard Gage in 1925.
Standard Gage - Malta to Minturn in 1890.
Second Track built Rex (M.P. 298.00) to Minturn in 1903.
   "   "   "   Red Cliff to Rex in 1907.
   "   "   "   Pando to Red Cliff in 1909.
   "   "   "   Deen (M.P. 286.78) to Pando 10-22-1910
   "   "   "   East Mitchell (M.P. 281.96) to West Mitchell (M.P. 284.57) in 1928.
Block Signal System Installed - Salida to Minturn in 1928.
                        M.P. 214.60 to 215.37 in 1942.
C.T.C. M.P. 280.00 to 286.79 Installed in 1928.
   "   Installed - Kobe to Tennessee Pass in 1958.
   "   "   - Deen to Minturn in 1958.
   "   "   - Salida to Kobe in 1961.

E. PAGE 2 →
S. PAGE 14 →

ABS ☐☐☐☐☐
CTC ■■■■■

WESTWARD — MAIN LINE — EASTWARD

SECOND CLASS 71 Fast Freight Leave Daily	SECOND CLASS 63 Fast Freight Leave Daily	SECOND CLASS 61 California Fast Freight Leave Daily	FIRST CLASS 1 Scenic Limited Leave Daily	Mile Posts	STATIONS Sub-Division 3 TIME-TABLE No. 126 MAY 13, 1945	Miles from Minturn	Capacity of Siding	FIRST CLASS 2 Scenic Limited Arrive Daily	SECOND CLASS 34 Fast Freight Arrive Daily	SECOND CLASS 36 Fast Freight Arrive Daily	SECOND CLASS 38 Fast Freight Arrive Daily
5 10 PM	9 10 AM	1 10 AM	2 30 PM	215.1	s SALIDA JBSKWFYTODN	86.9	Yard	2 05 PM	4 25 AM	12 25 PM	8 25 PM
					3.3						
5 22	9 22	1 22	2 37	218.4	BELLEVIEW	83.6	98	1 51	4 12	12 12	8 12
					3.8						
5 30	9 30	1 30	2 42	222.2	BN BROWN CANON ·D	79.8	98	1 47	4 06	12 06 PM	8 06
					5.5						
5 43	9 43	1 43	2 52	227.7	SWAN	74.3	101	1 37	3 54	11 54	7 54
					5.2						
5 53	9 53	1 53	2 59	232.9	NATHROP w	69.1	100	1 31	3 46	11 46	7 46
					3.3						
6 01	10 01	2 01	3 04	236.2	MIDWAY	65.8	99	1 27	3 40	11 40	7 40
					4.1						
6 08	10 08	2 08	s 3 14	240.3	BV BUENA VISTA WDN	61.7	89	s 1 22	3 33	11 33	7 33
					4.4						
6 18	10 18	2 18	3 21	244.7	AMERICUS	57.3	101	1 16	3 26	11 26	7 26
					3.0						
6 28	10 28	2 28	3 26	247.7	RIVERSIDE	54.3	100	1 12	3 21	11 21	7 21
					4.4						
6 45	10 45	2 45	3 36	252.1	PRINCETON	49.9	127	1 07	3 14	11 14	7 14
					5.3						
7 05 38	11 05 36	3 05 34	3 46	257.4	GA YALE WDN	44.6	124	12 59	3 05 61	11 05 63	7 05 71
					5.8						
7 17	11 17	3 17	3 55	263.2	KOBE	38.8	100	12 51	2 54	10 54	6 54
					3.3						
7 25	11 25	3 25	4 01	266.5	SNOWDEN	35.5	101	12 47	2 41	10 41	6 41
					4.5						
7 35	11 35	3 35	s 4 15	271.0	MY MALTA JWFTDN	31.0	Yard	s12 42	2 33	10 33	6 33
					6.1						
7 55	11 55	3 55	4 28	277.1	KEELDAR	24.9	100	12 26	2 22	10 22	6 22
					3.9						
8 20 PM	12 20 PM 2	4 20 AM	s 4 45 PM	281.0	PS TENNESSEE PASS YDN	21.0	1-110 2-104	s12 20 63	2 14 AM	10 14 AM	6 14 PM
Trains operate by Centralized Traffic Control between eastward ABS 2801 east end of Tennessee Pass and eastward ABS 2870 W, 2870 E, Deen.					1.0			Trains operate by Centralized Traffic Control between eastward ABS 2801 east end of Tennessee Pass and eastward ABS 2870 W, 2870 E, Deen.			
				282.0	EAST MITCHELL	20.0					
					2.6						
				284.6	WEST MITCHELL	17.4					
					2.2						
8 45 PM	12 45 PM	4 45 AM	5 02 PM	286.8	DEEN	15.2		11 59 AM			
					1.7						
9 02	1 02	5 02	s 5 08	288.5	PY PANDO WY	13.5	106	s11 55			
					5.5						
9 24	1 24	5 24	5 24	294.0	RC RED CLIFF D	8.0		11 33			
					2.1						
9 31	1 31	5 31	5 30	296.1	BELDEN	5.9		11 28			
					1.9						
9 38	1 38	5 38	5 36	298.0	REX	4.0		11 24			
					4.0						
0 35 PM	2 35 PM	6 35 AM	5 55 PM	302.0	Hd MINTURN BSKWFTDN		Yard	11 15 AM			
Arrive Daily	Arrive Daily	Arrive Daily	Arrive Daily		(86.9)			Leave Daily	Leave Daily	Leave Daily	Leave Daily
5.25 16.0	5.25 16.0	5.25 16.0	3.25 25.4		Schedule Time Average Speed per Hour			2.50 30.7	2.11 30.2	2.11 30.2	2.11 30.2

On the opposite page, the original narrow gauge line (arrow) has been added to the profile chart. (Author's collection; this page, Museum collection)

6-G. OPERATION BY CENTRALIZED TRAFFIC CONTROL IS EFFECTIVE BETWEEN TENNESSEE PASS AND DEEN

Towerman at Tennessee Pass controls all Positive Automatic Block Signals.

A green flag by day and a green light by night displayed in the West Window of Tennessee Pass Tower will be authority for Eastward trains to cut out helper engines, using crossover between main track and No. 1 track for that purpose.

A green flag by day and a green light by night displayed in the East window of Tennessee Pass Tower will be authority for helper engines to move from wye to No. 1 track.

Eastward trains having more cars than will clear between the middle crossover and the signal bridge at West end Tennessee Pass, will be authorized by towerman sounding four blasts of audible signal to make back up movement to cut out rear helper engine.

No Westward freight train with more than twenty cars will leave Tennessee Pass until the Westward signal on bridge at West end Tennessee Pass governing its movement displays a green (clear) indication.

East switches, tracks No. 1 and No. 2 at Tennessee Pass are Remote Control switches and normally operated by towerman, Tennessee Pass.

Switches at West end of Tennessee Pass are operated by carmen or trainmen under direction of the towerman, the following audible signals governing:

1 long blast—line switch No. 4 to siding No. 2.
2 long blasts—line switch No. 5 to siding No. 1.
3 long blasts—line switches for main track.

Audible annunciator is located three thousand feet west of the switch at Deen, and eastward trains will, commencing at the "Audible Annunciator" sign give the following whistle signals, using care to so space the whistle sounds as to be distinct, and so the signal will be completed by the time the engine reaches the annunciator:

Passenger trains.............1 long blast
Fruit and stock trains....2 short blasts (counting three between each blast for space)
Other freight trains.......3 short blasts (count two for space).

The following is taken from the 1935 edition of the *Denver & Rio Grande Western Freight Service and Shippers Guide*.

MINTURN
Elevation 7825', population 600, incorporated 1904.
Freight depot, three-car team track, roundhouse, shop, ice house, water and coal, 50 employees, free less-than-carload pickup and delivery within 22 miles, ten-car stockyard and scales. Eagle River Hotel, YMCA, Gem Theatre, Presbyterian and Catholic churches; weekly newspaper, *The Boomer*, crops: peas-potatoes-lettuce, professional opening: physician needed.

BELDEN
Elevation 8302', population 10.
23-car yard, mining: gold-silver-zinc-iron-copper, crops: potatoes-beans-lettuce-hay-grain *(the source of the crops at this location at the bottom of a narrow, rocky canyon is a mystery-editor)*.

REDCLIFF
Elevation 8608', population 800, incorporated 1891.
30x50-foot freight depot, five-car team track, three employees, less-than-carload pickup and delivery, station for Gilman (four miles), one grammar and one grade school, Shrine Hotel, newspaper *Holy Cross Trail*, two churches, theatre, professional opening: physician.

PANDO
Elevation 9209', population 40.
Ice house, water tank, 15-car team track, three stock pens, one school, crops: hay and timber.

MITCHELL
Elevation 10,100', population 50.
crop: timber

TENNESSEE PASS
Elevation 10,242', population 35.
12x30-foot freight depot, water tank, ten-car stockyard, Railway Express Agency, ten employees, grade school, summer stock range.

MALTA
Elevation 9580', population 28.
65-foot freight depot and platform, 20-car team track, 11-car stock yard, water and coal, seven employees, one school, crops: hay and livestock, station for Twin Lakes (12 miles).

(postal cancellations, Jim Ozment collection)

210

MAILED FROM
THE
TOP OF THE WORLD
TENNESSEE PASS,
COLO.
ELEVATION
10242 FT.
D. & R. G. W. R. R.

TENNESS—
NO—
11
193—
COLO

CHARLES T. BARTHEL
168 AMSTERDAM AVENUE
NEW YORK CITY

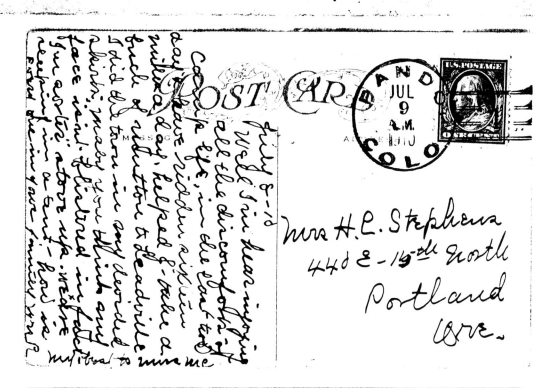

POST CARD

—AND—
JUL
9
A.M.
—COLO

Mrs H. C. Stephens
440 E - 15th North
Portland
Ore.

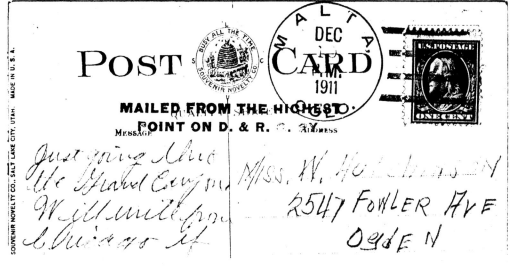

POST CARD

BUSY ALL THE TIME
SOUVENIR NOVELTY CO.

MALTA
DEC
P.M.
1911

U.S. POSTAGE
ONE CENT

MAILED FROM THE HIGHEST
POINT ON D. & R. G. RY.

SOUVENIR NOVELTY CO., SALT LAKE CITY, UTAH. MADE IN U.S.A.

MESSAGE

ADDRESS

Miss. W. Hutchinson
2547 Fowler Ave
Ogden

January 30, 1943.

SPECIAL PERMISSION REQUEST NO. 11

TO THE PUBLIC UTILITIES COMMISSION
OF THE STATE OF COLORADO,
Denver, Colorado.

The Denver and Rio Grande Western Railroad Company (Wilson McCarthy and Henry Swan, Trustees), by H. I. Scofield, its Passenger Traffic Manager, does hereby respectfully petition the Public Utilities Commission of the State of Colorado that it be permitted, under Section 16 of the Public Utilities Act, to put in force the following rates, to become effective one day after the filing thereof with the Public Utilities Commission:

Permission is desired to cancel Circular No. 20 - 1942, Colo. P.U.C. No. 1902, naming round trip coach furlough fare of $6.00 from Pando, Colorado, to Denver, Colorado, and return, routed both ways via Canon City, and issue instead Circular No. 1 - 1943, Colo. P.U.C. No. 1903, naming round trip coach furlough fare of $6.00 applying both ways via Canon City, or, both ways via Glenwood Springs and Bond, or, going via Canon City and returning via Bond and Glenwood Springs, or, the reverse. Such fares to be good in coaches only for the personnel of the United States armed forces when in uniform and traveling at their own expense from Pando to Denver and return, selling daily, to and including June 30 1943, with return limit of thirty days in addition to date of sale.

And your petitioner further bases such request upon the following facts, which present certain special circumstances and conditions justifying the request herein made:

Weekend furlough leaves from Camp Hale, Pando, Colorado, apply only from late Friday evening until midnight of the following Sunday. The only train service we have from Pando to Denver via Canon City is our train No. 2 leaving Pando at 10:06 A.M. In order to reach Pando before expiration of furlough leave, passengers must leave Denver not later than the following Sunday morning, and if the going trip is made on train No. 2, arriving Denver Saturday night, furloughees would only have Saturday night in Denver. By using our train No. 1 leaving Pando at 5:56 P.M., passengers could make the going trip to Glenwood Springs connecting with our train No. 20, arriving Denver at 6:45 A.M. Saturday morning, giving them twenty four hour period at Denver. As we desire to make this arrangement available for the next weekend, it is therefore, necessary to request special permission to publish on less than statutory notice.

THE DENVER AND RIO GRANDE WESTERN RAILROAD COMPANY
(Wilson McCarthy and Henry Swan, Trustees)

By:_____
Passenger Traffic Manager

This interesting request directed to Colorado's Public Utilities Commission enabled servicemen stationed at Camp Hale to spend a full day in Denver during a weekend furlough. Another such wartime gesture was the substitution of better dining car meals, instead of the GI-standard, without extra charge. (letter and ticket dater cancellation, Kenton Forrest collection)

212

ACKNOWLEDGMENTS

Although this account of Tennessee Pass was initiated as a story of modest dimensions, it was augmented enormously by the contributions of several other interested individuals who offered maps, photos, records and incidental data. Most of what they contributed was virtually unknown, reposing in collections or files, until this opportunity provided the catalyst for its public revelation. The author is most grateful to everyone who assisted so enthusiastically and generously to produce this brief history of the Rio Grande's first standard-gauge route across the Continental Divide. Foremost among them were Charles Albi, James Blouch, Richard Kindig, A.D. Mastrogiuseppe, James Ozment, Robert Richardson and Jackson Thode. In a broader sense, all readers are indebted to these devoted railroad historians for the remarkable and wholly unexpected photographic presentation which accompanies the text.

THE PASS TODAY

The current operating timetable is quite different from those of the steam era, showing only the schedule times at major points on the system and zone speed limits. Most of the trains do not run every day, and their composition is generally merchandise or coal. Eastbound trains add helpers at Minturn, their make-up determined by the available motive power. For a while a 10,000-ton coal train was operated eastbound over the pass. Eighteen diesel-electric units, including six six-motor units on the headend, were needed to boost that enormous tonnage up the grade to the summit. Another new aspect is the presence of motive power from other railroads—Missouri Pacific, St. Louis Southwestern, Southern Pacific, Union Pacific and, on occasion, even Santa Fe and Soo. This is due to run-through operating procedures or mileage equalization when D&RGW units run beyond their home rails.

*This special train, hauled by neatly polished 4-6-0 No. 507, named **Salida**, has stopped at Rock Creek to allow passengers to see the mining facilities. Although this photo was taken after 1890, the locomotive was still equipped with a link-and-pin coupler. (Denver Public Library Western History Department)*

Tennessee Pass Today
Photography by Ronald C. Hill

*(right) It is a cold, crisp winter day on December 23, 1985, as D&RGW freight No. 79, the Ford Train, climbs westward near the former station of Keeldar between Malta and Tennessee Pass. Rising mightily in the background is 14,431-foot Mt. Elbert, the loftiest of Colorado's 54 mountains which equal or exceed 14,000 feet in elevation. Photographer Otto C. Perry was one of the first persons to utilize this beautiful location for train photographs; his view above of Train No. 35, named **The Rocket**, behind No. 3605 was taken March 24, 1940. (Perry photos here and on the following pages, Denver Public Library Western History Department)*

(preceeding page) The Crystal Lakes near Malta afford a dramatic reflection of both D&RGW freight No. 77, and 14,431-foot Mt. Elbert on October 26, 1985. This is just one of several spectacular photo locations on the eastern side of Tennessee Pass.

(opposite) Many changes had occurred between April 17, 1938, when the 3606 was about to enter the south portal of the old tunnel and August 6, 1986 when D&RGW No. 79, the Ford Train, accelerated out of Tennessee Pass siding, after meeting coal train No. 788 which is still visible on the main line in the background.

(on this page) A caboose hop hurries westward through Tennessee Pass siding toward the tunnel under the summit of the pass on July 31, 1986, as a huge thunderhead grows larger and larger on the east side of Mosquito Pass. Leadville residents later reported that the cloud was one of the grandest ever seen in that area. At the same place on August 1, 1948, one of the ex-Norfolk & Western Mallets had just turned on the wye prior to returning to Minturn.

The west end of old Mitchell Siding has always been a superb photographic location. Otto recorded No. 3602 with First No. 36 on March 24, 1940. Richard Kindig was with him that day, and Dick's photo can be seen on page 58 of **Rio Grande West** *(Colorado Railroad Museum, 1982). GP30 No. 3007 provides a modern version of the same scene on August 14, 1976.*

After the demise of the **Rio Grande Zephyr** *in April 1983, the venerable F-units were assigned to work trains and also slag trains between Minturn and Leadville. Here, the two F9Bs are sandwiched between a GP40 and a GP30 as a slag train picks up concentrate from ASARCO in Leadville on October 2, 1983. Portions of the famous old mining town and Mosquito Pass are visible in the distance.*

Train No. 50 growls up the steep grade near the west end of old Mitchell siding on August 10, 1984. This train now transports general merchandise between Salt Lake City and Kansas City. Below, late afternoon sunlight glints off the side of coal train No. 789, powered by D&RGW SD40T-2's and MP SD40-2's, twisting through the tortuous curves of the former Mitchell siding on October 26, 1985.

The ground reverberates to the passage of an eastbound coal train laboring around the s-curve at Mitchell on June 28, 1979. Six mid-train helper units are vigorously assisting the progress of the heavy train.

The westbound Ford Train drifts around the curves at the old location of Mitchell on a wintery December 23, 1985.

(opposite) Due to a shortage of motive power, coal train 788 is doubling the hill on October 26, 1985. Here, the second half of the train crawls through Pando at a slow pace caused by the failure of one of the engines in the consist. Earlier that day the first half had been left at Kobe, the next siding east of Malta. (opposite below) On the same day storm clouds threaten train 50 as it climbs out of Eagle River Canyon and through Pando, during World War II the site of Camp Hale, the famous army mountain and winter training base.

224

The Ford Train curves through the picturesque little town of Red Cliff alongside the Eagle River on August 6, 1986.

A Rocky Mountain blizzard all but obscures coal train 788 as helper engines are cut into the huge 100-car train at Minturn on December 2, 1985. These trains regularly ran between the Roadside Mine near Grand Junction and the Mississippi Power Company in Pascagoula, Mississippi, via the D&RGW, MP and ICG until the power company cancelled the lucrative contract in October 1986. The fierce winter storm makes highway travel extremely hazardous but does not impede the progress of Train No. 50, which is assisted by three mid-train helper units on the same day.

Winter is very much in evidence on December 23, 1985, as D&RGW freight 50 roars out of the shadows of the precipitous Eagle River Canyon at Belden.

An eastbound freight takes the siding at Pando on October 6, 1973, in order to set out a piece of earthmoving equipment on the house track. Autumn storm clouds are gathering, and another winter is about to begin on Tennessee pass.

On a pleasant winter afternoon in January 1951 Fort Collins' original Birney car pauses in City Park under a tree that was planted in pioneer days. Over three decades later both Car 21 and Vern's are still Fort Collins institutions. (Ane Clint photo, Museum collection)

LAST OF THE BIRNEYS

by Ernest S. Peyton
and
Al Kilminster

College Avenues and Linden Street

OB51'N

The caption on the back of the postcard reproduced above reads: "The intersection of College and Mountain Avenues is the 42nd and Broadway of Fort Collins. It is the heart of the business district, the crossroads of the town, where all streetcars meet and all highways converge." (Charles Albi collection)The photo below from which the card was made reveals the artifice which color artists of the 1930s used to enhance postcard views. (Miller photo, Museum collection)

This line up occurred during the Fort Collins Municipal Railway's only recorded fantrip, May 30, 1951, as described later in the text by E.J. Haley. (Ane Clint photo, Museum collection)

The heydey of the trolley car may be over, but who doesn't remember the singing sound of the trolley wire, the rumble of traction motors, the cheerful voice of the motorman as he calls the stops, and the clang-clang of the bell? For each of us, the streetcar will remain a cherished part of our American heritage.

Fort Collins was by no means the first city of the state of Colorado to have a street railway line, but it has gone down in the annals of Colorado history as the last. In its enduring days, the Fort Collins Municipal Railway was one of the most fascinating and unique street railway systems in the United States. Its dinky Birney type trolleys, all dressed in silver and red livery, bobbed along the tree-lined streets of this agricultural and college center. Aficionados, electric railway historians and photographers armed with more than one camera flocked into Fort Collins from all corners of the nation. The story of this remarkable little railway is full of civic struggle and accomplishment.

A youthful conductor awaits passengers on the step of Car M-103 at Lindenmeier Lake in the early days of the system. The roofline of the pavilion and dancehall is just visible above the horse drawn rig behind the car. (Museum collection)

234

I. DENVER AND INTERURBAN

In 1906, the city council of Fort Collins granted a franchise to the Denver & Interurban Railroad, a subsidiary of the Colorado & Southern Railway, for the construction and operation of streetcar lines on certain streets within the city. The C&S was at this time an important unit in the transportation system of Colorado, especially the northern part of the state. Contrary to the policy of most steam operated railroads, the C&S was interested in local transportation systems of towns served by its steam lines. Under its subsidiary company the Denver & Interurban, the C&S owned a half interest in the electric division of the Colorado Springs & Cripple Creek District Railway. This line served the mines of the fabulous gold camps of Cripple Creek and Victor. A proposed electric railway connecting Denver, Boulder, Longmont, Loveland and Fort Collins was on the drawing boards. Though its various electric properties were widely separated, they were connected by the steam railroad lines of the parent company. If the automobile had not changed the American transporation picture in such haste, this system might well have reached from Cripple Creek to Cheyenne, Wyoming. There was some speculation at the time that an extension to the great steel mills of Pueblo was in the offing.

The first step in the construction of the D&I was the development of a city system in Fort Collins. The *Fort Collins Express* noted that "Work on the street railway will begin in earnest on next Tuesday (July 9, 1907)." On that day a large steam traction engine began plowing up West Mountain Avenue in preparation for the actual work

of laying track. Enough rails and ties were on hand for about four blocks of track. Second-hand steel from the C&S mainline was obtained. A new carbarn and power house were under construction at the corner of Howes and Cherry Streets. Newspapers expressed some concern that College Avenue would be "spoiled by the construction of a street car line on its much driven surface." In spite of high wages ($1.65 a day) labor was scarce. Workmen were recruited in Denver, and the line progressed rapidly into the winter months.

One of the events of the year was the annual Race Meet and Stock Show, held during August. In 1907 local advertisements appeared in the papers saying: "Everyone should attend the Race Meet and Stock Show, August 28, 29, and 30. Street Car Service all the way." This, in spite of the fact that the power plant had not been completed, track work had barely been started and not a single car had been purchased. In order to carry out this promise, the C&S built a temporary transfer track across the Court House lawn to the D&I track on West Mountain Avenue. Track was completed to the fairgrounds at Prospect Park and a small steam locomotive No. 203, an 0-6-0 type, and four ancient open platform wooden coaches were used to carry passengers to the Race Meet.

Clyde Brown of the Fort Collins Pioneer Museum, remembers riding this train. The *Fort Collins Express* of August 29, 1907, gave the following account of the operation:

By far the greatest portion of the people were taken to the grounds by means of the steam cars which were

On August 28, 1907 Colorado & Southern 203 steams down West Mountain Avenue with the Race Meet and Stock Show shuttle train. (Denver Public Library Western History Department)

On a late fall day in 1907, a trio of fashionably dressed young men poses in the vestibule of the M-102 which has just arrived from Denver's Woeber Car Works on a C&S freight train. This car later met with an untimely fate. (R.H. Kindig collection)

run by the C&S in lieu of street cars which it was impossible to secure electricity for at the present time. When the first train pulled out to the fair grounds in the morning a great deal of interest was shown by all concerned. Officials of the road and citizens of the city packed the train with passengers. Conductor William Hill had control of the train, Engineer Walter Hayes and Fireman E. Kirkpatrick were in the cab, and B.L. Collins and C.A. Wilfong collected the nickels. The engine, Number 203, had just been brought from Denver where it had received a thorough rejuvenation.

The train ran west on Mountain Avenue to the fairgrounds, then backed up to the starting point. It ran the three days of the fair. Although there was some disappointment at the use of a steam train, the papers noted that: "The use of the heavier train had a tendency to help settle the track." This train operated every half hour, and business was good. The fare, as provided by the street railway franchise, was five cents. After the fair closed the train was returned to the C&S and the transfer track removed.

By early December 1907, the Fort Collins City Lines of the D&I were about ready for use. The *Express* stated that: "Power has been turned on at the new power house of the Denver & Interurban Railway, and the machines are running every day. The machines will have 400 horsepower each. All the trolley wires are in place and are ready for use and little remains to complete the system. An official of the road said Thursday that some cars will be run out on the track, most any day now, but that the road could not omit put in operation before two weeks,

and the schedule would not be in force before January 1st."

Several trips were made to instruct motormen and, prior to Christmas 1907, the company issued a statement to the papers outlining details governing operations and schedules that were to be in effect following a dedication trip on December 29, 1907.

OPERATIONS OF CARS AND SCHEDULES
Cars will leave the intersection of College and Mountain Avenues at 5:30 A.M., returning to the C&S depot at 6:10 to give passengers for the early morning train time to purchase tickets and check baggage before departure. Beginning at 6:20 cars will depart every twenty minutes, that is, at 6:20, 6:40, 7:00, 7:20, 7:40, and 8:00, keeping up this schedule until 11:20 P.M. Cars will stop to receive and discharge passengers at the further side of street crossings. College Avenue cars and Mountain Avenue cars will run over the loop, that is, they will continue down College Avenue to Jefferson Street, around Jefferson to Linden Street, back on Linden to the intersection of Mountain and College Avenues. Transfers will be issued at the intersection of College and Mountain Avenues to passengers wishing to continue on either line. Passengers should ask for these transfers when paying their fares to the conductor. Children under six years of age, when accompanied by a paying passenger, will be carried free of charge. Children over six years of age and under twelve years of age will be carried at half fare. Conductors will be provided with half-fare tickets at the rate of ten for twenty-five cents.

This pair of builder's photos shows the M-104 when new at Woeber. The rattan seats are identical to those used in Denver's cars of the same era. (R.H. Kindig collection)

Denver & Interurban Railroad

1908-1918

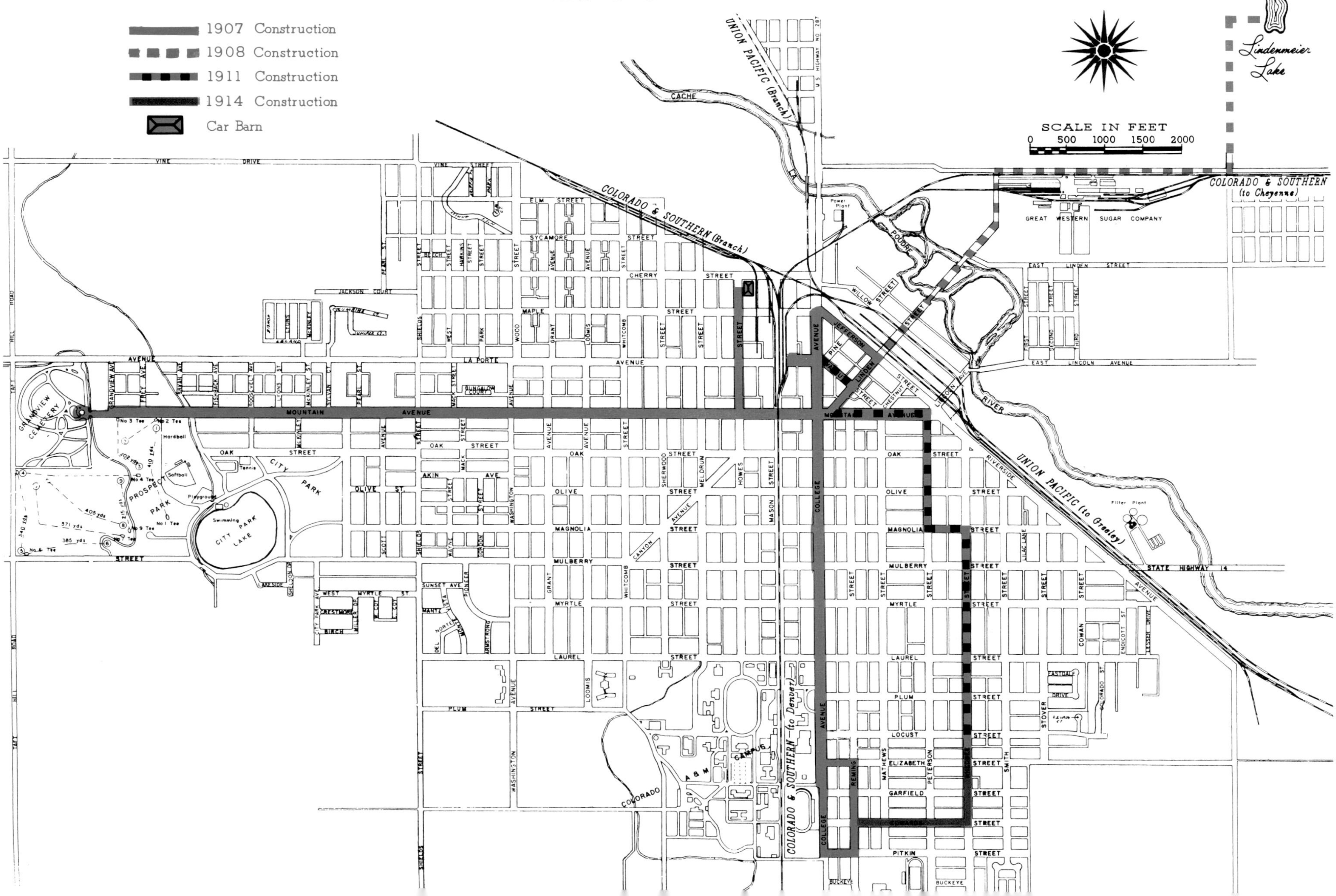

1907 Construction
1908 Construction
1911 Construction
1914 Construction

Car Barn

N

SCALE IN FEET

0   500   1000   1500   2000

Lindenmeier Lake

COLORADO & SOUTHERN (to Cheyenne)

GREAT WESTERN SUGAR COMPANY

UNION PACIFIC (to Bradley)

Filter Plant

State Highway 14

UNION PACIFIC (Branch)

COLORADO & SOUTHERN (Branch)

COLORADO & SOUTHERN (to Denver)

U.S. HIGHWAY NO 287

CACHE LA POUDRE RIVER

Power Plant

CITY PARK

CITY PARK LAKE

PROSPECT PARK

GRANDVIEW CEMETERY

Street names: LINDEN STREET, MASON STREET, COLLEGE AVENUE, REMINGTON STREET, MATHEWS, PETERSON, WHEDBEE, SMITH, STOVER, LESSER, COWAN, LILAC LANE, RIVERSIDE AVENUE, OAK, OLIVE, MAGNOLIA, MULBERRY, MYRTLE, LAUREL, PLUM, LOCUST, ELIZABETH, GARFIELD, PITKIN, EDWARDS, BUCKEYE, PINE STREET, JEFFERSON STREET, WILLOW STREET, MOUNTAIN AVENUE, WHITCOMB STREET, LOOMIS, GRANT, SHERWOOD, MELDRUM, HOWES, MACK, AKIN, WAYNE, SUNSET, WASHINGTON, ARMSTRONG, PIONEER, SHIELDS, TAFT, MULBERRY, MCKINLEY, LYONS, MACK, BIRCH, WEST, CRESTMORE, MYRTLE, CITY PARK AVENUE, OAK STREET, MCKINLEY AVE, LIONS, MCKINLEY ST, JACKSON COURT, PEARL ST, VINE, ELM STREET, SYCAMORE, MAPLE, WOOD, CHERRY STREET, PARK AVENUE, HANNA STREET, PEARL STREET

Fort Collins Municipal Railway

1918-1951

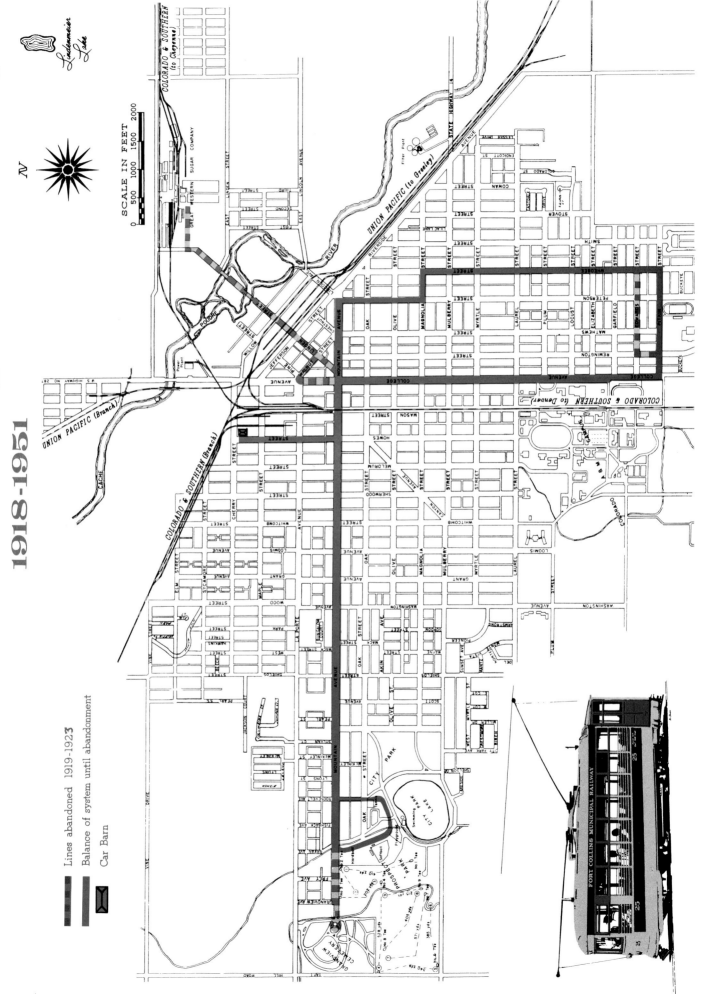

Lines abandoned 1919-1923

Balance of system until abandonment

Car Barn

IV

Lindenmeier Lake

SCALE IN FEET
0   500   1000   1500   2000

FORT COLLINS MUNICIPAL RAILWAY

COLORADO & SOUTHERN (to Cheyenne)

UNION PACIFIC (to Greeley)

UNION PACIFIC (Branch)

U.S. HIGHWAY NO. 287

COLORADO & SOUTHERN (Branch)

COLORADO & SOUTHERN (to Denver)

STATE HIGHWAY 14

GREAT WESTERN SUGAR COMPANY

Filter Plant

Power Plant

Swimming Pool

CITY PARK

GRANDVIEW CEMETERY

Two lines were placed in operation, and two cars operated the base service. Additional cars were added when needed.

The College Avenue line ran south on College Avenue past Colorado A&M College to Pitkin Street, east on Pitkin to Remington (one block) and then north on Remington to Elizabeth Street (three blocks), then back to College Avenue. The Mountain Avenue line ran straight west on Mountain Avenue for 20 blocks to the cemetery where there was small loop and a shelter for passengers.

The *Express* gave an interesting account of the dedication of the new road. "The cars are of a modern type superior in many respects to those in use in Denver. They are new, clean and comfortable. The equipment at the power plant is adequate. All the citizens who enjoyed the dedication ride were pleased with what they saw, and pronounced everything to their liking. Mr. Parker (Vice-President of the C&S) was delighted and showed his pleasure like a boy of 16 years."

The motor cars were built by the Woeber Carriage Works of Denver, Colorado, car builder for the Denver Tramway Corporation. They were double-truck, double-end, monitor deck wooden cars with open platforms and equipped with air brakes. Capacity was 44 passengers and each car weighed 40,000 pounds. The trolleys were painted Brewster green with gold lettering and striping.

Scheduled operations began December 29, 1907, and Fort Collins became a "Streetcar Town." In 1908 a line was built to Lindenmeier Lake, a resort some two and one-half miles from the city. A pavilion and boat landings were already built there and the lake became well-known as a summer recreation spot. Trolley service made it easy for the people of Fort Collins to spend an evening dancing or a pleasant Sunday afternoon boating on the lake. The Lindenmeier Lake line was combined with the College Avenue line, two cars being used in base service, and they passed each other on the downtown loop. Since the Lindenmeier Lake car was often late, a hand-operated semaphore was installed at the corner of Jefferson and Linden Streets, governing the outbund car. Inbound cars came straight down Linden Street to the intersection of College and Mountain Avenues, while outbound cars went north on College Avenue to Jefferson Street, and then east to Linden Street, then north toward the lake. Some fast running was necessary on the Lindenmeier Lake line as cars made the round trip in 20 minutes. On holidays and weekends trolleys were packed on this line and extras were often run.

There was some agitation on the part of the directors of a country club located a mile north of Lindenmeier Lake to have the line extended to the club's grounds. This the company was willing to do provided the club would bear part of the expense of building the extension, and if the club would guarantee a certain percentage of business. Since a bridge was necessary over a large irrigation ditch, and the cost of the extension would be around $20,000, the club was either unwilling or unable to assure responsibility for the project and the idea "died a 'borning."

In summer of 1909, streetcar No. 106 struck and completely cut in half a large Russian Wolfhound. The *Express* noted editorially; "The death of the dog itself is unimportant in comparison to the lesson it teaches in regard to the danger of the cars equipped as they are with ineffective fenders for the protection of life. — WHAT WOULD HAPPEN TO THE CHILDREN?" The paper also stated: "The fenders in use were some eight or nine inches above the rail, but when cars were heavily loaded they sometimes touched the rails." Conductor Beeler stated in 1957 that he believed this to be inaccurate. The only place he recalled fenders or pilots touching the rails was at the C&S steam railroad crossing on West Mountain Avenue. Here the track was not always well maintained and often rough.

Another operating problem was corrected by the company, as described in the following story in the February 11, 1910 *Fort Collins Review*:

SPEED REDUCED IN BUSINESS DISTRICTS

In accordance with an order issued the first of the week from the Denver office of the Denver and Interurban, the street cars of this city are now moving at a more leisurely schedule in the business portion of the city, the maximum rate of speed now allowed by the company being 6 miles an hour in the district extending for three blocks along each line from the intersection of the lines at the corner of College and Mountain. The issuance of the order accounts for well high snail-like gait which cars have been travelling for the past two days.

The order was brought about partially through complaints registered by members of the city council to P.S. McMurray, attorney for the road who was in the city a week ago, and partially, it is said, because the road wished to do away with the motormen on some of the lines for resting too long at the terminals. More stringent orders governing the running speed on all lines have also been issued and the company will endeavor to bring its cars to a more accurate conformity with the schedule at all points along the line.

For the most part, the people of Fort Collins were satisfied with their trolley system and considerable local pride was shown in the numerous articles appearing in local newspapers. The *Fort Collins Courier* published a semi-centennial edition in 1914 which carried this article:

FORT COLLINS STREET CAR SYSTEM
EQUAL TO METROPOLITAN IN
EQUIPMENT AND SERVICE

The Fort Collins street car system is equal in every respect to the best metropolitan street railroad and is always the cause of comment by visitors to the city. There are between six and seven miles

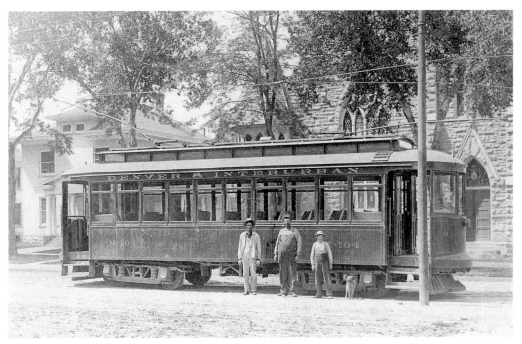

Car M-104 is at the west intersection of Mountain Avenue and Howes Street. The positions of the car's seats and trolley pole and the garb of the men indicate that this is the carbarn crew ready to move the M-104 three blocks up Howes to the barn. A young boy and his dog are on hand to observe the proceedings.

A street railway was an important and vital public service of the era, and its equipment and employees reflected that fact. Conductor J.O. Beeler and Motorman Bill Williams, with Jewett-built M-106 at Lindenmeier Lake, are as well dressed as the crew of any comparable car in New York, Chicago or San Francisco. Both pictures date from about 1910. When the author originally researched this history in the early 1950s, Mr. Beeler gave him invaluable help. (both, R.H. Kindig collection)

Exactly one-half of the D&I car roster is at the downtown intersection of Mountain and College Avenues. In the foreground a Lindenmeier Lake car turns east onto Mountain, with a southbound College car at the left, while two more cars await departure for City Park to the west.

of track covering the business and residence sections of the city and extending to points of interest in the outskirts of the town. The cars are of the most modern type, comfortably heated in winter and cool in the summer. So good is the system and service maintained in fact, that the system has never really been a paying proposition and is continued in order to hold the franchise against the time when the city will have grown to such proportions as to make the system a paying one. The system is operated by the Denver & Interurban Company, a subsidiary to the Colorado & Southern Ry. Co. Twenty men find steady employment in the service of the company and its payroll amounts to $16,000 annually. The policy of employing only Fort Collins men as pursued by the Railway Company is followed by the Street Car Company, thus giving the City twenty substantial citizens, some owning their own homes and rearing their families.

In a history of Larimer County published in 1911, an account of the company presents the following favorable comments:

Built by the Denver & Interurban. City council granted franchise in 1906. Construction started in summer of 1907 and began operating over five miles of track December 29, 1907. College Avenue; Jefferson to Pitkin to Remington to Elizabeth, to College Avenue. Mountain Avenue; Mountain Avenue to Grand View Cemetery. Jefferson; from College Ave. to Mountain Ave. at Peterson. (This is incorrect for the line ran down Jefferson Street only to Linden St. The Mountain Avenue line had been

extended along Whedbee Street in 1909). In 1908 lines extended past the Great Western Sugar factory to Lindenmeier Lake. The Company gives twenty minute service on all these lines, and the people of Fort Collins find the street cars a great convenience. The tracks and equipment are first class in all respects, and the Company is well managed.

In the years that followed, the Denver & Interurban was just another small town trolley line, somewhat better than the average. People were proud of their streetcar system and patronized it. Yet there was always criticism of the Lindenmeier Lake line. Business was good on weekends and holidays, but base weekday traffic was light. As business fell off on this line, schedules were reduced.

The rapid decline in patronage on some scheduled runs became a nationwide street railway problem. The average number of passengers carried per car mile during 1912 for most of the smaller traction properties was between four and five. This was also true for the Denver & Interurban. This meant that a car had to travel one-fourth mile for each fare collected. On many trips the crew outnumbered the passengers. On a few runs there were no passengers at all. Small wonder the street railway operators began to question the need for two men on each trolley. One-man operation was a quick solution. This would cut platform expense in half, and one man could keep reasonably busy yet offering efficient service to the rider.

Conversion to one-man operation was simple. The company closed up the back end of the car, and installed a fare box in the front end under the eye of the motorman.

One of the Woeber-built cars on the route to the lake rumbles past the Elk's Lodge on Linden Street. Below, North College Avenue represents a 1910-era American main street—trolley, horse-drawn vehicles, bicycles and pedestrians—but not a single automobile. Note the double track on College and the wye leading to the track going one block to the right down West La Porte to the C&S railway station. (three photos, Museum collection)

Here is conductor Beeler again, this time posing with the M-103 on the Lindenmeier Lake line along the Colorado & Southern main track. His run downtown will proceed as soon as the C&S switch engine is in the clear. This trip required some fast running to maintain the schedule. In the rare view below, an inbound car races past the Great Western Sugar Factory.

Stops were then changed to the near side of the cross streets for easier loading. The public believed this a sensible thing to introduce rather than cut service to effect an economy. Management stated, "A single-man car equipped with folding doors and steps, if operated properly, is practically as safe as when operated by two men, and the number of accidents and the amount of damage therefrom does not exceed to any perceptible degree than those with two-man operation." The one-man car very often enabled the company to give streetcar service in thinly populated districts.

The D&I owned six motor cars and two trailers. As wages began to climb with other operating costs, the company began to consider other economies. The ends of the Whedbee Street and the College Avenue lines were connected, thus forming a loop. It was possible to eliminate one car and improve service at the same time. The Whedbee Street line was extended south from Elizabeth Street to Edwards Street, west on Edwards to Remington Street, where it joined the old line.

The conversion to one-man operation caused some dissatisfaction with the public. The company had hinted without actually promising that new cars would be used when one-man oepration became a reality. At this time the track was removed from Edwards Street north to Elizabeth Street, and west one block on Elizabeth to College Avenue, being replaced by the new loop.

Safety was the watchword on the D&I. Crewmen were instructed that the greatest danger to the company and their job was that of accidents and resulting law suits. The only serious accident on record was a collision between Car No. 102 and a steam shovel at the sugar factory in which William Vanderwark was seriously injured. The streetcar was so badly damaged that it was junked. Trucks, controllers and mechanical parts were used to convert trailer No. 107 to a motor car. The accident happened when Vanderwark heard a passenger shout a warning and thinking he had forgotten to pick up a passenger, looked to the rear of the car. The collision followed immediately. Vanderwark was seriously injured and not expected to live. He rallied, and served many more years with both the D&I and the Fort Collins Municipal Railway.

Probably the main factor in the downfall of the Denver & Interurban was the seizure and operation of the Colorado & Southern, along with all other railroads in the

The hazard of the C&S crossing at grade ultimately resulted in the almost total destruction of car M-102 one day in 1915. From the damage to the car, seen at the barn after the wreck, it is amazing that more serious injuries did not happen. (three photos, Museum collection)

Along with all other mainline and street railways in Colorado, the December 1913 blizzard hindered D&I operations in Fort Collins. Car M-105 was stranded at the corner of Pitkin and Remington streets. Horseless carriages, like the one chugging past car M-103 near Lindenmeier Lake, were a factor more effective than snow in ultimately disrupting streetcar operations everywhere. Near the end of service, a revised paint scheme was applied to M-103, with "Fort Collins Street Ry." replacing "Denver & Interurban" on the letterboard, "D&I RR" applied below the sash on the car side and the end-numbers centered below the headlight (right, R.H. Kindig collection; others, Museum collection)

nation, by the United States Railroad Administration in 1917. Since the federal government was interested only in essential transportation units, the D&I was not taken over. It was left to its own fate as a small and comparatively unimportant company.

The interurban line from Denver to Boulder was separated physically from the Fort Collins city lines, a situation not conducive to efficient management. Wages were high and labor was scarce. Operating expenses were up and some items which were necessary to the proper operation of a street railway were impossible to get. The company was not on a profitable basis, especially the Fort Collins line. There were no surplus funds to meet soaring expenses. The old five-cent fare was still in effect. Public sentiment was not too favorable and complaints began to roll in. Many trolley riders became prosperous enough during the war to be able to own one of those new-fangled automobiles.

Finally in 1918 the D&I was unable to pay interest on its bonds. The company was immediately thrown into receivership by the Guaranty Trust Company of New York City representing the bondholders. W.H. Edmunds, general manager, was appointed receiver and there was some talk of abandoning the entire system, including the Denver to Boulder interurban line. Edmunds was a very quiet, unassuming man, but a highly efficient manager. The receivership was soon terminated.

Attempts were made in court to have the D&I declared a part of the Colorado & Southern, making the parent company responsible for the obligations of the city line. The courts ruled that the C&S was completely separate from the D&I, and no longer responsible for the financial problems of the struggling company and the D&I was left to its own resources.

Abandonment was not immediate, but business was rapidly declining. Owners of Lindenmeier Lake claimed that their business had been ruined by poor service. Edmunds asked permission to junk the entire system, pleading war necessity.

On the night of July 10, 1918, without warning, employees were told not to report for work the next day as service was being annulled. Fort Collins awoke the following morning without any form of public transportation. Attempts were made by a private party to operate a bus line, using a 16-passenger Stanley Steamer bus and charging a ten-cent fare. This was of short duration. The city officials began to study the possibility of local operation. In the meantime the White Motor Company proposed operating a gasoline car and equipped an open sight seeing bus with flanged steel wheels for rail operation. This car was put on a 30-day trial service. Gasoline cars had been tried in other parts of the country, but had met with little success. This gasoline streetcar was not popular. It was rough riding, noisy and smoky. Frequent derailments damaged the steel wheels, causing excessive maintenance. The White Motor Company pointed out that this car was built for trial purposes only, and that they could build an adequate car. The gasoline

car was discontinued and again Fort Collins was without service.

Suggestions were made that the city buy and operate the streetcar lines. Proposals and counterproposals were made. In the meantime as one newspaper said: "Fort Collins will continue to hoof it."

Today, with a car in every garage, it is difficult to realize the extent to which people of a small city could become dependent upon a streetcar line. Buses had not yet reached the point where they were dependable, and the automobile of that time was expensive and temperamental. Real estate values in outlying areas were affected, and business at some of the downtown stores sagged.

At long last Edmunds agreed to accept $75,000 for the physical plant. This was some $20,000 less than junk value. It was agreed that the company would be turned over to anyone paying a $5,000 deposit, and that service could be resumed. J.O. Beeler, stated that "cars and track of the D&I were well-maintained and were in fairly good condition, considering the fact that the company had been losing money for some years." However, the D&I cars were heavy and consumed a high quantity of electric power. To make matters worse, the nearby community of Greeley, Colorado, had just received a new shipment of one-man streetcars to revamp its local lines. The citizens of Fort Collins were envious of their neighbor city. Civic and community groups got together and put pressure on city officials to do something.

The White Motor railcar enroute to Nevada for a trial run on the famed Virginia & Truckee paused for a 30-day run in Fort Collins. One look at this photograph demonstrates the unsuitability of this type of vehicle in street railway service. (White Motor Company, Author's collection)

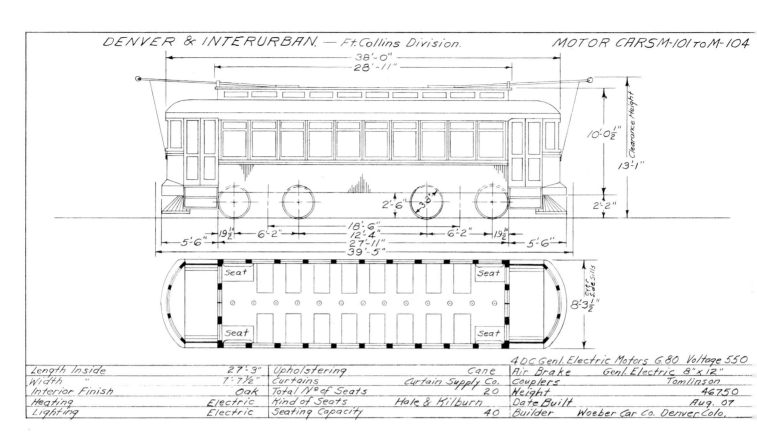

4 DC Genl. Electric Motors G.80 Voltage 550

Length Inside	27'-3"	Upholstering	Cane	Air Brake	Genl. Electric 8"x12"
Width "	7'-7½"	Curtains	Curtain Supply Co.	Couplers	Tomlinson
Interior Finish	Oak	Total Nº of Seats	20	Weight	46750
Heating	Electric	Kind of Seats	Hale & Kilburn	Date Built	Aug. 07
Lighting	Electric	Seating Capacity	40	Builder	Woeber Car Co. Denver Colo.

(Drawings by F. Hol Wagner, Jr.)

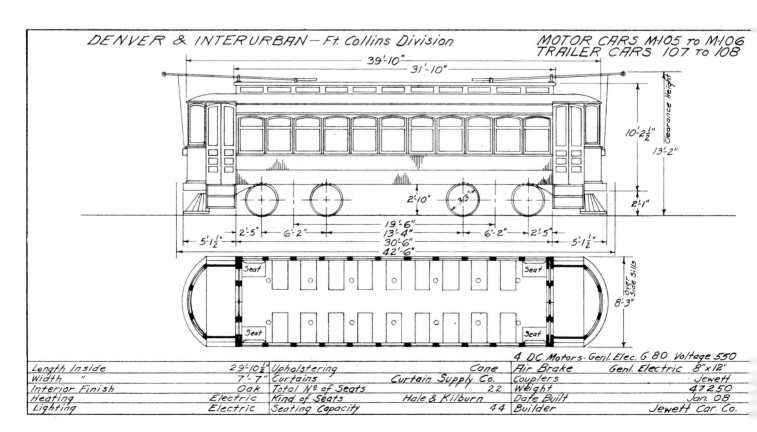

4 DC Motors - Genl. Elec. G 80 Voltage 550

Length Inside	29'-10½"	Upholstering	Cane	Air Brake	Genl. Electric 8"x12"
Width "	7'-7"	Curtains	Curtain Supply Co.	Couplers	Jewett
Interior Finish	Oak	Total Nº of Seats	22	Weight	47250
Heating	Electric	Kind of Seats	Hale & Kilburn	Date Built	Jan. 08
Lighting	Electric	Seating Capacity	44	Builder	Jewett Car. Co.

DENVER and INTERURBAN

Fort Collins Division

Number	Builder	Date	Remarks
1	Michigan Car	1905	Line car converted from Colorado & Southern flat car 843 in November 1909.
M-101—M-104	Woeber Car Co.	1907	Double truck, wood streetcar, 39'5" with 4 GE 80 motors of 40hp 500V, 2 controllers K-28, 2 trolleys, seating capacity 40. Motor 102 was destroyed in wreck with steam shovel in 1915. All cars were converted to one man operation in 1914.
M-105, M-106	Jewett Car Co.	1908	Double truck, wood streetcar, 42'6" with 4 GE 80 motors of 40hp 500V, 2 controllers K-28, 2 trolleys, seating capacity 44. When conversion was made to Birney cars, equipment sold to Oklahoma Railways as 94-95.
M-107	Jewett Car Co.	1908	Built as double truck, wood trailer. Converted to motor car in 1915 when M-102 wrecked by steam shovel. Sold to Oklahoma Railways as 96.
108	Jewett Car Co.	1908	Double truck, wood trailer. Same construction as M-105—M-107 less motor equipment.

A gathering of pioneers in a new mode of transportation, on Mountain Avenue near Linden, overwhelms a College Avenue car crossing in the background. (Museum collection)

The beautiful old trees along South College Avenue were at the peak of their autumn color on the afternoon of October 24, 1937, when the motorman of immaculately maintained Birney 22 had his portrait taken at the corner of Myrtle Street. The longtime employees of the railway seemed to grow old gracefully along with the cars, and this gentleman's posture still reflects a pride in his occupation. (Ernest Simmerman photo, Museum collection)

II. FORT COLLINS MUNICIPAL RAILWAY

According to local newspapers, it was claimed that it would cost more than the old cars were worth to restore them to proper running order. The track and overhead required complete rebuilding. It was recommended that: "Cars on hand be disposed of as soon as possible," and that new lightweight cars and lighter power equipment be installed.

An estimate of operating costs was published:

Maintenance of way & structures	$ 4,500
Maintenance of equipment	2,500
Power	6,000
Motormen a $.29 per hour	6,520
Supervision	2,500
TOTAL	$21,750

The Lindenmeier Lake line was to be abandoned and sold. It was estimated that new equipment and faster schedules should increase revenue by about one-third. The following editorial appeared in the *Fort Collins Express:*

BUY THE STREET CAR SYSTEM

If the city can buy the street car system for a reasonable sum and can operate it at no great annual deficit, it would be a good business proposition to close the deal and take the system over. Fort Collins needs a rapid transit system of some kind. There can be no doubt about that, and it would seem a good business proposition to accept the receiver's offer to sell the system for $75,000. The original cost of the Fort Collins Street Car System was about $315,000, and it is worth today many thousands more as junk than the receiver asked for it. The city will therefore lose nothing on the deal, but on the other hand, stands to reap a good profit on the transaction.

On January 7, 1919, an election was held. There was little opposition either to the purchase of the new system or the bond issue of $100,000 to pay for it. Publicity was freely given by the newspapers. Typical headlines:

"NOW OR NEVER FOR THE STREET CARS!"
"YOU MUST SAY TODAY WHAT YOU WANT"
"EITHER A CITY OR AN OLD FASHIONED
  TOWN"
"LOSS OF STREET CAR SYSTEM WILL
  CRIPPLE CITY FOREVER"

The election carried eight to one for the purchase of the lines and five to one for the bond issue necessary to foot the bill. All of the bonds were sold locally, and one of the papers stated that $500,000 worth could have been sold just as easily.

It was announced that service would not be resumed with the old equipment and before delivery of the new cars, track work would be necessary. An editorial said:

We are proud of Fort Collins, proud that it is composed of people who not only went over the top in every patriotic war issue, but on a progressive peace issue also responded in a whole souled manner.

On a quiet morning earlier in the 1930s Car 21 waits downtown for its departure time. The opposing car is just visible across the intersection. Farmers Lunch competed for the ice cream soda trade with the City Drug Store next to the F.W. Woolworth 5, 10 & 15 cent store. (Miller photo, Museum collection)

At some time in the mid-1930s the "bowtie" paint scheme was applied to the Birneys to make them more visible to motorists. The safety-stop buttons installed at the downtown intersection of the tracks provided a modicum of protection for passengers waiting to board.

It was stated that four new streetcars had been ordered for the municipal system and each car would cost approximately $6,000. Delivery was promised in 40 to 60 days from the time the order reached the factory. The new cars were of the one-man Birney type, named after its designer, C. O. Birney who was employed by the Stone & Webster syndicate. Prior to Birney's revolutionary design, streetcars were built to suit an individual system. Birney felt that streetcars should be designed to meet the average needs of traction companies and produced on a semi-mass production basis. The result was the Birney Standard Safety Car. The first of these was built by the American Car Company of St. Louis, Missouri. They were single-truck, double-end, light weight steel construction, and equipped with full safety equipment (deadman control which was a button on the controller that would automatically stop the car in case the motorman died or was stricken).

The Western Light & Power Company was awarded the contract to supply power for the line and the overhead line was put in good condition. Track and structures were checked, and where necessary rails were replaced. The whole system was put in first class condition awaiting the new trolleys.

On May 2, 1919, word was received the cars had been shipped from St. Louis and were in transit. By May 24, the cars arrived on several flat cars and preparations were made for the unloading. A trial run of Car No. 21 was made to establish a schedule. It had been planned to run on a 15-minute headway, but the trials showed that "although the motorman put on some extra speed, the trip took between 17 and 18 minutes." As a result, the old 20-minute schedule was resumed. (Incidently, Car

No. 21 which made the trial run remained on the property until 1953 when it was towed through the streets by a truck to the Pioneer Museum.)

Richard S. Baker, assistant city manager of Fort Collins, in an article published in 1950, while the system was still in operation, presented in detail the story of the modernization of the old D&I and the creation of the Fort Collins Municipal Railway. He says:

Early in 1919 at an election the citizens voted 940 to 132 in favor of buying the system. At the same time a $100,000 bond issue was approved. About the 24th of May, 1919, four Birney Standard Safety Cars were unloaded and put in service. These cars were numbered 20, 21, 22, and 23. In June the city began to dismantle the track and overhead between Andersonville and Lindenmeier Lake, a distance of one mile, about 1,000 feet of steel and wire were taken to Roosevelt Street and used in construction of the City Park Spur. In December 1919, two 75 kw., 600 volt, 125 amp., 1,160 r.p.m. motor generator sets were installed in the carbarns to replace the 500 kw., 550 volt, 750 r.p.m. rotary converter. The generator sets made a saving of about 33⅓ percent in power. On Labor Day, 1920, a new car was put in service that had been purchased from the National Car Company at a cost of $6,500 plus freight. This was No. 24.

The annual report of the city engineer made available through the courtesy of Baker gives a good picture of the situation shortly after modernization.

On February 12, 1920, work on the track on South College Avenue was taken up and completed about March 22. On April 13, 1920, dismantling track and

TIME SCHEDULE
FORT COLLINS MUNICIPAL RAILWAY
LEAVING TIMES

OUTGOING		INCOMING	
Junction College and Mountain	Whedbee and Laurel / College and Laurel / Mountain and Mack	City Park / Whedbee and Edwards	Whedbee and Laurel / College and Laurel / Mountain and Mack
6:25	6:30	6:35	6:40
6:45	6:50	6:55	7:00
7:05	7:10	7:15	7:20

And thereafter each 20 minutes as above.

DAILY—2 Cars Regular 6:25 A. M. to 10:25 P. M.
1 Car Whedbee Street 6:45 A. M. to 8:25 A. M.
10:45 A. M. to 6:25 P. M.
SUNDAYS—2 Cars Only—8:05 A. M. to 9:45 P. M.

A perusal of the schedule shows how two cars provided 20-minute headways with an additional car to give ten minute service in clockwise direction on the Whedbee Street line. The sign over the former Denver & Interurban carbarn at Howes and Cherry Streets shows the year ownership was assumed by the city. (both pages, Museum collection)

Its bright paint scheme notwithstanding, the driver of this black Ford sedan underestimated the speed of eastbound No. 22 at Mountain and Whitcomb one day in March 1942, resulting in $150 damage to his auto. Virginia Transit 1530 arrived in October 1946 (right) to become second No. 24. It is seen below in the barn with second 25, which had been No. 1520 in the Old Dominion. Both cars were painted in the new silver, green and red paint adopted sometime between late 1944 and early 1946. (below, Museum collection; others, Author's photos)

overhead from Anderson Corner and the sugar factory was begun, using about 900 feet of material for a spur to the sugar factory time office, on the east side of the Colorado & Southern main line, and the balance hauled up to the barns and stored with other material. By making this change we did away with two railroad crossings that were badly worn and would have to be renewed and maintained at a cost greater than moving the track.

On May 1, 1920, work was begun on rebuilding and ballasting track on Mountain Avenue from Howes Street to Shields Street, putting in crushed rock ballast and a four-inch drain tile at each intersection. This work was completed about August 15.

The system has more than proved its need to the public. It has held up the standards of our city far above that of a country village and in addition has offered continous service to its patrons. The utility has operated during periods when other railroads were snowbound. It has paid all operating and maintenance costs and for a new car since the beginning of the system. Service to the public by the street railway was greatly improved in December 1922, by providing a new ten-minute schedule which seems to be working satisfactorily.

In early 1920, Superintendent W. C. Johnson proposed the following track extension, but his plan was never acted upon:

The proposed Mulberry-Mountain Avenue loop would extend from intersection of Mountain and College Avenues, across bridge at Haymaker's barn, thence around loop to present terminus of Roosevelt Avenue Line, around east border of lake to Mulberry Street, down Mulberry Street to Whitcomb, south on Whitcomb to Laurel Street, east on Laurel to College Avenue, north on College Avenue to place of beginning. Distance of Mountain Avenue line to Haymaker's barn is 8,000 feet, from Haymaker's barn to south end of present Roosevelt Avenue line is 1450 feet and from that point around east side of lake to Mulberry Street is 1,100 feet. From last named point to Whitcomb, south on Whitcomb to Laurel, east on Laurel to College Ave. 8,100 feet and north on College to place of beginning 3,150 feet. Total round trip distance is 21,800 feet or 4.13 miles.

10 minute service would require 4 cars for this loop with passing sidings on Laurel, Mulberry near lake and present sidings on West Mountain Avenue. Number cars required on Whedbee and College loop for 10 minute service would be 2. One car for sugar factory making total of seven cars active and one inactive. Grand total eight cars or double the present number.

The ten-minute schedule first attempted in 1922 was not satisfactory. Several schedule changes were made and the ten-minute service was discontinued at various times. Finally a new plan was tried out in 1925. Two cars were purchased from the Cheyenne, Wyoming,

street railway system, and the following notice appeared in the *Express Courier*, May 4, 1925:

(Monday) Two way service on the College Avenue and the Whedbee Street line will be inaugurated sometime Tuesday or Wednesday. Regular cars leave the junction (College and Mountain Ave.) at five, 25, and 45 minutes past the hour from 6:25 A.M. to 11:05 P.M. except on Saturdays when cars run until 12:05 A.M. In addition to regular service, split-shift cars will operate on Mountain Avenue and College Avenue lines only, leaving the junction at 15, 35, and 55 minutes past the hour during the busy periods of the day, making the downtown loop in reverse direction.

Ten minute service 6:25 to 8:55 A.M.
Twenty minute service 8:55 to 11:55 A.M.
Ten minute service 11:55 A.M. to 7:35 P.M.
Twenty minute service 7:35 P.M. on.

Even this service did not work out too well, increased revenue not being sufficient to cover additional expenses. During the year 1924, for example, the report of the city commissioners showed that:

City cars carried 478,848 passengers during 1924. The greatest number in one month, December — 56,674. Lowest number of passengers, April — 35,352.

RECEIPTS

Advertising	$ 1,006.25
Fares	6,452.85
Tickets	17,604.09
Operating maintenance	625.84
TOTAL	$25,689.03

EXPENSES

Operating labor	$13,337.60
Maintenance labor	4,166.86
Operating materials	5,714.79
Maintenance materials	5,024.54
Rebates	46.53
Improvements	1,819.13
TOTAL	$30,109.18

This would indicate a deficit of $4,420.15. However, in defense of this the commissioners reminded the public that two cars had been purchased from the Cheyenne line. The two Cheyenne cars were shown on the roster of the Fort Collins Municipal Railway as Nos. 25 and 26.

The city engineer's report for 1925 included the following information about the railway:

During the year 1925, considerable work was done to put the railway service on a still more efficient and systematic basis. A passing track was contructed on South College Avenue between Plum and Locust Streets to permit ten minute service on the College Avenue line. When Pitkin Street was paved the line was shifted to the center of the roadway and extended to Whedbee Street; and by the installation of wyes at Remington and Pitkin and at Edwards and Whedbee Streets, a loop was formed with the existing system. This loop is a necessary factor in

(continued on page 259)

The downtown intersection of College and Mountain Avenues was the Fort Collins equivalent of a grand union, those double-track street railway crossings in large cities where lines converged from four directions with connecting switches between all of them. On Saturday afternoon, June 25, 1949, the First National Bank clock on the southeast corner shows exactly 5:25 PM and, as it occurred every 20 minutes, the three cars have moved forward simultaneously. 21 is southbound on the

College-Whedbee route; 26 has completed this counter-clockwise run and is headed west on Mountain; 24 is the clockwise car on the Whedbee-College loop only. Visiting railfans who might tire of this routine could walk down the street to the Lyric Theater and see Joel McCrea and Dorothy Malone in the premiere of "Colorado Territory." (Museum collection)

On this and the following pages we will take a composite photographic tour of the system, starting at the meeting point where cars 26, 25 and 20 are commencing their runs on June 26, 1948. (Below) No. 26 has left the business district and traversed the first block of the grass median on South College to Magnolia in August 1949. This car and first 25 had removable headlights.

Seven blocks farther along the 20 has reached the end of the median at Garfield and is about to enter two blocks of side-of-the-street private right of way along the east side of the Colorado A&M College football field. (center, Tom Gray photo; all from Museum collection)

maintaining regular, efficient service on all the lines, as it eliminates the obvious delays and unsatisfactory schedules incident to changing ends for return trips. The railway area down Pitkin Street is nine feet in width, wood ties being used throughout. These were set on six inches of crushed rock ballast and filled in with concrete flush with the pavement level. A special rail joint was used on the work, which is in accordance with the most modern practice. Steel plates were used on each side of the rail web and also under the rail base beneath the joint, these plates being spot welded to the rail to make a tight rigid joint with a view towards eliminating objectionable vibration and breakage at the joints. The trolley wire was carried on a span from poles on each curb line, creosoted wooden poles being used at much lower cost than similar steel poles would have entailed. The cost of the Pitkin Street loop, including the passing track on College Avenue was $10,254.05.

With these improvements, utilizing the seven cars which are now the property of the Municipal Railway, very satisfactory service is being maintained, even under the worst weather condition. A unique service feature was introduced in the fall of 1925 when it was decided to allow students of the public schools, including the High School, to ride for a fare of two cents, and many now take advantage of this opportunity. There was 29,233 school fares during the months of September, October, November and December of 1925, and 29,670 during January, February and March of 1926.

There were 36,043 more passengers carried during the year 1925 than 1924. The total passengers carried for the year 1925 was 514,891. The total receipts for year 1925 were $24,857.87.

The Fort Collins Municipal Railway remained without any significant change for over 25 years. Service was equal to that anywhere and superior to that found in many larger cities. Cars were clean, well maintained even down to the changing paint schemes. The city of Fort Collins was unique, being the smallest city in the United States having an electric municipal railway system.

During the disintegration of the Denver Tramway, Greeley Electric Railway and Colorado Springs & Interurban Railway, many comparisons were made with the fine operation of the Fort Collins system. In all of these cases, the Greeley line came out decidedly second best and it was not too long before the company abandoned. As was often the case with small properties having inadequate shop equipment and limited financial resources, maintenance was neglected. Cars were unpainted, and operating speed was reduced because the track was in poor shape. Before long the public found another way to travel. The limited amount of nickels dropped in the fare register hardly covered wages, power bills and taxes. That is, when they were paid!

Fort Collins had new cars, track and overhead were in good condition, service was every ten minutes, and further improvements were planned. In 1925 one could not find a more modern street railway operating in the United States than the Fort Collins Municipal Railway. The population of Fort Collins increased from 8,000 to nearly 15,000 by 1950 and without a further extension of the street railway. All was not roses, for the family automobile became increasingly popular as a means of travel within town. Streetcar patronage declined throughout Colorado, while costs rose without an increase in fare.

There were a few accidents, of course, most not serious because of the modest operating speeds. As might be expected, the cars occasionally tangled with careless motorists, and at least one such incident resulted in a derailment, with the trolley having to be taken out of service for two days.

The grade crossing with the Colorado & Southern mainline at West Mountain Avenue and Mason Street was a potential operating hazard, with at least one serious collison happening as described in the report to Commissioner of Works Frank P. Goeder:

On November 6, 1925, at 6:05 P.M., Streetcar #24 in charge of Motorman J.A. Inman, collided with Engine #800, Colorado & Southern freight train, at the intersection of Mountain Ave. and Mason St., which resulted in the wrecking of the streetcar to a damage of from $1500 to $2000, and injuring the motorman and several passengers.

As near as can be ascertained from the passengers and witnesses seeing the collision, the motorman made his stop at the junction on the west side of College Ave., taking on some passengers, and then starting west, making his usual stop for the railroad crossing on the east side of Mason St. C. & S. freight train Engine 800 coming north on Mason St., at approximately 15 miles or over per hour, entered the intersection at about the same time the streetcar did, the two coming together.

John E. Kimmons, a passenger on Car 24, gave this account of the accident:

I was a passenger on the street car involved in the accident in question. I had boarded this car at the corner of College and Mountain Avenues, or one block east of point of accident, and was seated in next to rear seat on north side of this car. As car came to Mason Street car was stopped at the usual place to receive or discharge passengers, but no passengers were received or discharged at that time. I distinctly remember that car was stopped, and just about the time motorman started car towards railroad tracks, I saw the headlight of the freight train when it was about at the south curb of Mountain Avenue. I saw this headlight before any one in car did any yelling. I did not yell, but grabbed on to a seat to hold on and try and avoid injury. I could not estimate speed of train as collision happened very quickly after I first saw headlight of train. After collision, car was turned in exactly the opposite direc-

The meet at the south end of the system was rarely photographed. Clockwise Whedbee street Car 25 has pulled into the Remington Street stub track as Car 26, this time with headlight in place, has come one block east from College on Pitkin. (John Horan photo)

On May 30, 1951, the day of the Rocky Mountain Railroad Club fantrip, Dick Kindig found Car 22 stopping on its regular run north on Whedbee to board several passengers. Below, No. 23 nears Mountain Avenue on Peterson. (Museum collection)

Dick returned on June 23, one week before the end of service, and got this unusual shot of only one car at the usually busy downtown junction, the westbound 21. Several years earlier 21 was nearing the outer end of its Mountain Avenue trip. Observe the different paint scheme on the anti-climber and around the windows here and on No. 23 on the previous page. (Museum collection)

tion in which it had been going, and was a few feet north of north rail of street car track, in front of Skaggs grocery, but had not been turned over. Motorman had curtains at his rear and right side down, and I could not see any of his actions just prior to accident. I had a few minor abrasions about the legs and bruises and shaken up, but did not see a doctor, and as far as I know now my injuries have all cleared up. When I got out of car, motorman was lying on pavement about 5 feet from both railroad and street car tracks—about an equal distance from both tracks. The only whistle of the train I heard was just about the time I saw the headlight, and I did not hear its bell ring at any time.

Litigation with a woman who was a passenger on the trolley and suffered a head injury continued for over a year. In an interesting contrast with today's legal climate, her claim amounted to only $200.

On school days a pair of cars would run about a block apart, with the second car handling the overflow when the first car filled up. One time, not long after second cars 24 and 25 had been received, the 25 was running as the second section on the evening school run. The city had hired a motorman who had previously run the large electric cars of the Pacific Electric in Los Angeles. He ran the poor old Birney wide open, and, with the tracks covered with wet autumn leaves, slid right into the rear of the first car as it was discharging passengers.

No serious damage was done, and it was an unusual happening. The old time motormen—such as Beeler, Thompson, McLaughlin, Undem and Vanderwark—treated their cars like the old friends which they were.

Traction companies throughout the United States began to consolidate, or cut service. Still the citizens of Fort Collins remained strongly pro-trolley. At four different times, elections were held to determine the fate of the streetcars. In each case the voters decided in favor of the trolleys. As a matter of fact the streetcars were not legally voted out of Fort Collins until November 1952, over one year after service had ended. Why would a town hang on to its own streetcar system? There were several reasons, but the prime point was that many feared, and rightly so, that a privately-owned bus line might not last, leaving the city without any public trans-

261

The ride over the system was a pleasant one, especially the portion through City Park. No. 20 glides along under a graceful corridor of trees adjacent to the picnic pavilion, and No. 21 crosses a small canal before turning east onto Mountain near Bryan Street. Commencing in late 1984, this second bridge reverberated again to the passage of a reborn Car 21, its location being a short distance east of the new carbarn. (top, Museum collection; others, R.H. Kindig)

portation. Besides, the city received much local and national publicity because of its city-owned trolley operation.

The *Saturday Evening Post* published in 1947 an article entitled, "Some of My Best Friends Are Street Cars." If we may quote directly, "For truly fancy performance in the field of transit, no place on earth can beat Fort Collins, Colorado." The article goes on to describe in detail operations of the system, noting that three cars operate on two loops and a long connecting line running in two directions. At no time do cars pass on sidings although there are two passing tracks on the line, switching operations being carried out on a wye and a spur. At one point three cars pass simultaneously on a wye, located at the corner of Mountain and College Avenue, "truly a sight to behold." In concluding, the following statement is made: "The municipally-owned Fort Collins system holds two impressive records. It has the lowest trolley fares in the nation, five cents a ride, six tokens for a quarter, and a dollar for an unlimited monthly pass—and it makes money." This was true at the time the article was written.

It became impossible to get repair parts for the ancient Birney cars. Many parts had to be made by hand in local machine shops. In an effort to relieve the situation, the city bought two more Birneys at scrap prices plus freight from the Virginia Transit Authority at Norfolk, Virginia. One was to be dismantled to provide spare parts. Upon arrival both cars were in such bad condition that it seemed their purchase had been a mistake. After rebuilding, the new second-hand cars were given Nos. 24 and 25. The author remembers riding both cars at various times. No. 25 remained in service for some time; however No. 24 was removed from service shortly after purchase and used for parts to keep the others running.

Former conductor-motorman Beeler stated that, "The Birneys were well kept and in good condition. They were in much better condition than most people supposed." A large number of new ties were placed in the track during the last few years of operation but were not properly tamped. This caused the track to settle in places, resulting in low joints with high centers. This gave the

passengers a peculiar sensation as the trolley glided down the track. The big problem was the track was not properly built from the start. It is common railroad parctice to stagger the rail joints thus giving a more even ride. The Denver & Interurban placed the rail joints directly across from each other when the line was built. There is no reason obtainable as to why this was done, as this practice was not carried out on any of their other operations.

Operating statistics for the last two full years of operation are of interest:

	1949	1950
Number of Cars	7	5
Track Miles	7.5	7.5
Employees	11	9
Total Fares	469,793	359,445
Passenger Miles	171,923	171,709
Deficit	$6,445	$13,013

Although the total fares in 1949 were only 9,000 fewer than collected in 1924, the operating deficit had risen over eight-fold from just $1,519 in 1946.

By the late 1940s, the Bussard Bus Company of Englewood, Colorado, was granted a franchise to serve outlying parts of the city. In some cases Bussard offered direct competition to the city-owned trolley lines. Early in 1951, the Birneys began to fall apart one by one. They were replaced as they became unfit for service by a bus. Transfers were honored between the two systems. The city council decided to substitute buses entirely on a six months trial period. The physical plant was to remain intact until the end of the experiment.

E. J. Haley, perhaps the dean of Colorado electric railway enthusiasts, gives this account of the only recorded railfan trip over the line, which occured in the last month of operation:

On Memorial Day, Wednesday, May 30, 1951, the Rocky Mountain Railroad Club ran a five-car excursion train from Denver to Fort Collins, leaving the Union Depot at 7:00 A.M. At Fort Collins, Colorado and Southern locomotive No. 647 was backed up to the open end observation car on the train and, with C&S No. 374 (the locomotive that had brought

(continued on page 266)

1	2	3	4	5	6	7	8	9	10	11	12	13	14	15	16
17	18	19	20	21	22	23	24	25	26	27	28	29	30	31	

FORT COLLINS MUNICIPAL RAILWAY
Fort Collins, Colorado

No. 95701

Not Transferable. Good only for one continuous trip from line punched, when presented by person to whom issued at permitted transfer point of the respective lines indicated hereon and before the expiration of time canceled. **Passenger** is required to see that this transfer is properly punched as to time and line before accepting same. **Motorman** will register and cancel this ticket.

Form 1001

City of Fort Collins, Colo.

Whedbee St. Mountain Ave. College Ave.

Good for Transfer to any except line punched above

1926	1927	1928	1929	Half Fare	A. M.	1	2	3	4	5	6	7	8	9	10	11	12
Jan. Feb. Mar.	April May June	July Aug. Sept.	Oct. Nov. Dec.	●		10	10	10	10	10	10	10	10	10	10	10	10
						20	20	20	20	20	20	20	20	20	20	20	20
						30	30	30	30	30	30	30	30	30	30	30	30
						40	40	40	40	40	40	40	40	40	40	40	40
						50	50	50	50	50	50	50	50	50	50	50	50

Never-on-Time Toonervilles Win Citizens' Hearts

Trolleys Run in Red; Ft. Collins Loves It

Special to The Rocky Mountain News

FORT COLLINS, April 6.—The four streetcars clattering up and down Fort Collins' College and Mountain aves. were dubbed "desire" today—nostalgically so.

The 35-year-old streetcar system got a reprieve on life by Fort Collins voters in Tuesday's election by a wide 2-to-1 berth. And in so doing the eight-mile line and its four cars and its 14 folksy employes became heroic city institutions.

Most of Fort Collins' 18,000 residents have their lives entwined in the figure-eight trackage of the nation's smallest municipal tramway. Its Toonerville cars, its wide gauge, its sound and fury have created a panoply which makes the city and the system memorable.

* * *

TRUE, IN THE 29 years which the city has owned and operated the line, the system seldom has shown any black in its books. But strangely enough, the little white-elephant line and its deficit operation have endeared it to the hearts of the townfolk.

The city's mayor, Dr. Robert W. Hays, put his popularity on the block when he came out forcefully against continuance of the line. The voters who gave him big majorities turned their backs on his advice and the tramway still lives, stronger than before.

Last year it carried a half million persons and ended up $7400 in the hole.

"Shucks," an oldtimer said after casting his ballot. "I'm for the cars because I like to stand out on the back porch in the evening and watch them rattle past. I guess I can afford a dollar a year just to see them run."

BACK IN THE WAR YEARS when gasoline was short the four cars ran chock full from Colorado A&M campus to the residential area near Lindenmeier Lake.

To encourage use of the cars, City Manager Guy Palmes whittled down the fare to a $1 ticket which gave residents the right to ride a whole month as often as they liked.

When revenues started to drop with the return of gasoline, the fare jumped. Today it costs residents $3 a month for the always-good ticket.

Most generally the line is used by school and college students and by the city's oldsters. Visitors in automobiles are surprised to see the little cars stop anywhere along the street to pick up women with children, old gentlemen with canes, ladies with groceries. The conductors get down off the cars to help load the groceries as well as the passengers.

Fort Collins' picturesque streetcar system turns on a figure-eight course in the downtown district. From this point it moves four miles in either direction carrying approximately 35,000 passengers a month for a $3-a-month ticket.
—Colorado A&M College Photos.

"The line is supposed to have a 20-minute service from 6:25 a. m. to 11 p. m.," one businessman observed, "but I doubt if it ever is on time and I don't believe anyone cares too much."

* * *

J. M. HOWELL, city finance commissioner, pointed out that the road was built by the Colorado & Southern Railway before World War I as a traffic sideline. After a few years of profitless operation, the railroad sold the line to the city.

The purchase was made by bond issue and the townspeople still are paying interest and principal on the bonds. They point out that they have only $25,000 more to pay and that the debt will be liquidated in 10 years.

Before election, one of the strong arguments used by the streetcar lovers was that the city should guard against making the "mistake Denver made when it blew down the Grant Smelter stack."

"You never know how much an institution means to the people until it is gone," one of the streetcar faction argued.

Conductor Charles J. O'Laughlin, a veteran of the Fort Collins streetcar service, sits at the controls of one of the line's four cars. The stove at his feet is used in winter and on chilly spring mornings and evenings.

The little Birney cars received much publicity during their last years such as this Denver newspaper story. (left) Motorman Charles O'Laughlin demonstrates the use of his switch iron for a photographer. Below are examples of the obverse and reverse sides of one of the types of tokens used and a monthly pass which had a time schedule printed on its back side. (this page, Museum collection; opposite, Fort Collins Municipal Railway Society)

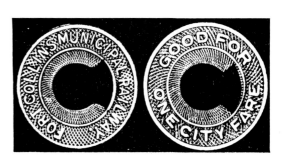

MUNICIPAL RAILWAY
FORT COLLINS, COLORADO

VOID IF TRANSFERRED   No. 6980

ISSUED TO

GOOD FOR PASSAGE DURING MONTH OF

_____ 19_____   PRICE $1.25

SIGNATURE

COUNTERSIGNED

Miles F. House
CITY CLERK

7 6 5 4 3 2 1

RULES AND REGULATIONS OF FORT COLLINS MUNICIPAL RAILWAY

Instructions to Motormen

1. Motormen, in handling the controller, must at all times use care so as not to overheat the resistance; also be careful to give car time to accelerate in order that the full series point does not give the car a sudden jerk. The heating of the resistance is due to using series points between first and full position. It is always well to cross the first points in series as rapidly as possible to prevent heating of the resistance, but in doing this the Motorman must use good judgment and be governed by acceleration of the car in going from one point to the other, and not give the car a jerky motion during acceleration.

2. Motormen must also use care in shutting off from first point, that is, if the controller is given first point and it is necessary to stop immediately, the controller must be shut off quickly to avoid arcing of the fingers.

3. Motormen must not take car from barn without properly testing the air to know that it is in working order. You will be held strictly responsible for this and you must not move car at any place, even though a motorman who has been handling the car has just stepped off, until you have made an application of air, and know that you have the same in perfect order.

4. Motormen must watch closely that the heaters in cars are not used, only when necessary.

5. Motormen must not pass over any railroad tracks without bringing his car to a full stop at least twenty (20) feet back from railroad track, and be sure that there are no trains or switch engines approaching.

6. Motormen must know that all switches are clean and in safe condition to pass over, have his car under full control when approaching the same, and must not take it for granted that a switch is safe to enter into simply because they passed through it a few minutes previous.

7. Motormen must at all times have the car under control on approaching all street intersections, expecting to find automobiles approaching the tracks, and sound gong twice before entering each and every street intersection.

8. When a car has been brought to a stop at switches or otherwise, or to discharge or take on passengers, the Motorman must sound gong twice before starting car. A car must not back up without sounding gong three times before starting car backward. Also, sound gong when approaching track men when they are near or repairing tracks.

9. Motormen in charge of car must not leave the car standing at any time without removing the reverse handle.

10. Motormen must report for their respective runs fifteen minutes before leaving time of cars at car barns.

11. Cars should leave car barn not later than five minutes before leaving time of cars at intersection of Mountain and College Avenues.

12. Car-barn Foreman is instructed that in case any motorman has not reported, as herein specified, he will call another man to take the place of the one who has failed to report, and the tardy man will lose his shift.

13. Should a motorman at any time notice the power off the line, he will at once proceed to the nearest telephone and call up the car barn, notifying the engineer of the same. The number of car barn telephone is 500.

14. Motormen must be properly uniformed, neat and clean in appearance.

15. Near side stop will be made at all streets unless otherwise designated.

16. Avoid stopping car in center of blocks to take on or discharge passengers, especially on West Mountain Avenue and College Avenue. In case you cannot make near side or regularly designated stops and it is necessary to cross street to far side, do not stop car until you have cleared crosswalk on far side of street. Do not block crosswalks at junction.

17. Not more than one car will be allowed to enter the intersection of square at Mountain Avenue and College Avenue at one time. The car having the right-of-way must pass through and be on the straight track before other can can proceed.

18. Under no circumstances will motorman be allowed to run his car above series position in the downtown district. This includes 100 and 200 blocks on East Mountain Avenue, 100 and 200 blocks on South College Avenue, 100 block on West Mountain Avenue, Linden Street, Walnut Street and North College Avenue loop. Cars going north on South College Avenue, east on West Mountain Avenue, south on North College Avenue and east on East Mountain Avenue in the above blocks must not exceed a speed limit of five miles per hour.

19. **Dangerous places that must not be overlooked.** Slow down both east and west bound cars at West Mountain Avenue and Shields Street; both north and south bound at Laurel Street and South College Avenue; both ways at corner of East Magnolia and Whedbee Streets; north bound at gate by College Athletic Field; depot at City Park; and both north and south bound on Howes Street at Laporte Avenue. Car must be brought to a full stop both north and south at Elizabeth and Whedbee Streets. Under no circumstances will motorman run car across any street intersection with controller on full running parallel position.

20. When two or more cars are run in sections while in service or going to or from car barns, they must not be run closer than 200 feet or two pole lengths apart.

21. Lights must be turned on cars at sunset. Headlights must not be allowed to burn on rear end of cars. Lights must be left turned on in the mornings until sunup.

22. Bicycles will not be allowed on cars.

23. Baby buggies that fold up and two-wheel baby carts may be carried.

24. Dogs may be carried on cars when accompanied by owner and upon receipt of full fare for dog in addition to owner's fare, providing owner of dog has a chain on it or carries it in arms.

25. Motormen are strictly forbidden smoking while on duty.

26. Motormen are required to pass a medical examination before being employed, the examination fee of $1.00 to be paid to the regular railway physician by motorman.

27. A fee known as Hospital Fee of fifty cents (50c) will be deducted from motorman's monthly wages.

28. Motormen must not hold unnecessary conversation with passengers. Do not allow passengers to stand in front end of car when there is room or unoccupied seats elsewhere.

29. Motormen are hereby cautioned to avoid any unnecessary arguments with passengers. Be courteous at all times. Run safe. Give the best you have for Service. Keep schedule as near as possible.

30. The above instructions supplement all previous instructions relating to handling and operation equipment to date.

Passed and adopted at a regular meeting of the City Council, held Saturday, November 20, 1926.

Reprinted, 1985 by FCMRS Inc.

The two cars from Virginia offered riders the comfort of high-backed individual leather upholstered seats as well as hand holds for standees. Note the switch iron placed to the left of the farebox. (Museum collection)

the train up from Denver) still on the head end our train headed west on the Owl Canyon Branch. Company officials told us it was the first passenger train ever to operate on this line up to the stone quarry at Rex. On the way back a short stop was made at Ted's Place near Bellevue so passengers could buy sandwiches, pop and beer. Arriving back at Fort Collins at 1:30 P.M. we were met by three of the Fort Collins Municipal Railway's small Birney cars—the 25, 21 and 20—on Mountain Avenue at Mason (the street the C&S mainline is on). Each passenger was given a special ticket for a tour of all the street railway's remaining lines. A stop was made at the Pioneer Museum on Whedbee Street. Our tour ended at the spot where it had begun, we boarded our special and were taken east to Windsor where Great Western No. 90 with the company's only piece of passenger equipment, ancient combination car No. 100 (now at the Colorado Railroad Museum) were waiting. Running south out of Windsor through Officer Junction we came to Johnstown and from here toured both the Welty and Elm Branches. From Johnstown the No. 90 hauled us to Longmont where it was uncoupled, turned on the wye, picked up car No. 100 and headed back to Loveland. No. 374 was waiting and pulled us back to Denver where we arrived about dusk. It was a long and wonderful day spent riding over little-known trackage with a

ride on Colorado's last remaining city trolley system—all for the huge sum of $7.50. No wonder I look back and long for what we are wont to call "the good old days." They were very good.

On June 30, 1951, Car No. 22 clattered through the streets of Fort Collins for the last time, closing the curtain on a colorful past performance. This was to be the last scheduled Birney car operation on the North American continent, and the last streetcar to operate commercially in the state of Colorado. It was a black day for the citizens of Fort Collins and for electric railway enthusiasts.

During 1953, No. 21 was given to the Pioneer Museum of Fort Collins. With the overhead power turned-off, the old car was pulled from the carbarn and then towed disgracefully to the museum site by a tractor. It was later placed on a short section of track alongside the museum. The bowed little trolley resting on its pedestal could be viewed by following generations who might one day ask: "What is a trolley car?"

It would be interesting to gaze into the crystal ball and speculate on a few things. What would have happened if the city of Fort Collins had authorized a small amount of money and leveled up the track, extended the lines to the newly developed areas of the city, and purchased three or four of the streamlined PCC type streetcars which could have been secured at scrap prices? For many years the old timers wished they had their little old dinkey cars back.

For all that they were beloved by Fort Collins residents and traction enthusiasts, the little Birneys saw no crowds or ceremonies at their demise. On the night of June 30, 1951 the last revenue passenger dropped her nickel in the farebox, and at 10:45 PM No. 22 clattered through the deserted intersection for the last time and disappeared down West Mountain Avenue. Upon returning to the carbarn on Howes Street, Charlie O'Laughlin paused for a final picture before stepping into retirement. Behind the car in the next bay, a gasoline bus is ready for service the following morning. (David Clint photos, Museum collection)

Two years after abandonment one more Birney found itself at the familiar downtown crossing. On February 24, 1953, enough track remained in place to allow this movement of No. 21 from storage in the old barn to public display next to the Pioneer Museum in Lincoln Park. City employees Roland Young, William Long and Harold Griffen acted as "pall bearers." Most of the rail was then removed and by June 1958 the car was already decayed and neglected. (both, Museum collection)

Upon arrival in Detroit for preservation in the Henry Ford Museum, No. 26 made several runs on that city's Department of Street Railways. This one was on August 6, 1953. For a brief time in the early 1920s Detroit had a fleet of 250 of these cars. (Museum collection)

Of the Fort Collins cars remaining on the property at the time of abandonment only 23 and second 24 escaped preservation. The carbody of the former was disintegrating in a vacant lot in April 1957. In the 1980s the former carbarn, still with its "Fort Collins Municipal Railway 1919" sign, remains in use as a city shop. (center, Al Moorman; left; James Kunkle—both photos, Museum collection)

FORT COLLINS MUNICIPAL RAILWAY

Number	Builder	Date	Length	Remarks
20-23	American Car	1919	27'9"	Cars 20-23 were purchased new. Each car had a seating capacity of 28. 20 sold to Pioneer Village, Minden, Nebraska, when line abandoned. 21 to display, Pioneer Museum, Fort Collins. 22 purchased by Rocky Mountain Railroad Club, displayed at Colorado Railroad Museum, Golden. 23 abandoned at Fort Collins, scrapped by 1957.
24	Cincinnati Car	1920	27'9"	Car proved unsatisfactory and was retired soon after purchase. Scrapped 1930.
2nd 24	Brill	1922	31'	Built as Virginia Railway & Power Co. 1530. Purchased in 1946 from Virginia Transit Co. Car seldom used, supplied parts for 2nd 25.
25	American Car	1922	28'½"	Built as Cheyenne Electric Railway Co. 6. Purchased in 1924. Scrapping date unknown.
2nd 25	Brill	1922	31'	Built as Virginia Railway & Power Co. 1520. Purchased 1946 from Virginia Transit Co. Sold to James Stitzel 1953.
26	American Car	1922	28'½"	Built as Cheyenne Electric Railway Co. 7. Purchased in 1924. To Henry Ford Museum, Dearborn, Michigan in 1953.

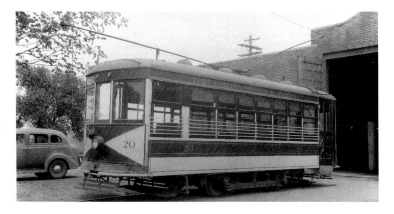
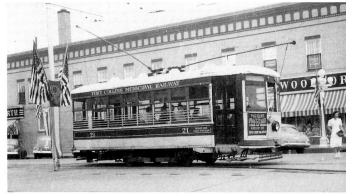

Here is an almost complete photo roster of the Birney fleet. No picture of first Car 25 has come to light. Cars 21 and second 24 display the original version of the green, silver and red paint scheme, while the 20 was recorded in the prior green and cream colors. (above right and right, Dick Rumbolz)

The dash sign on No. 23 warned prospective skaters about conditions at City Park Lake. (W.C. Whittaker photo, Museum collection) The rare view of First 24, dating from the 1920s, clearly shows the original version of the first color scheme with rectangular striping on the car ends. (Fort Collins Municipal Railway Society) On June 23, 1951 the carbarn foreman lined up 22, 20 and 25 on Howes Street for their portraits by Dick Kindig. This hospitable gesture was typical of the railway. These cars had the final version of the second paint scheme—solid silver ends. Gordon Lloyd found 26 sans headlight resting in front of the barn on a day in 1941. (Museum collection)

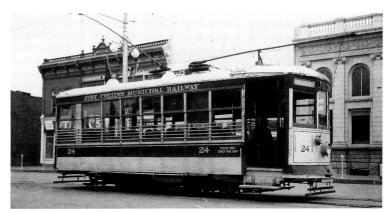

Fort Collins
Municipal Railway
SOCIETY

After almost a quarter century of sitting in the park, the venerable 21, Fort Collins' original Birney, is loaded for a return trip to the carbarn and eventual resumption of operation. (Fort Collins Municipal Railway Society)

III. FORT COLLINS MUNICIPAL RAILWAY SOCIETY

BY AL KILMINSTER

For nearly 50 years the principal means of transportation in Fort Collins was its streetcar system. For a little over 30 of these years it was the beloved fleet of Birney cars. Of the nine cars purchased over the years, five have survived the rigors of time and found good homes where people would take care of them. Car 21, unfortunately, was destined to decay in Fort Collins Library Park, eventually being enclosed in chain link fence to ward off further destruction.

The rebirth of car 21 started in 1976 when the Fort Collins Junior Women's Club won $500 in a "Business for Beauty" contest. The club, under Carol Turner's urging, agreed to put money into fixing up the car to be displayed in downtown as an information booth for the Chamber of Commerce. When Carol first saw the car in 1977 it was in deplorable condition. The wooden roof was rotted through and sagged around the trolley bases from the constant spring tension over the years. The ends of the car were several inches lower than the middle from years of stress. The bottom of the sheet metal sides near the wheels was rusted through, many windows were broken and their frames rotted. What appeared at first to be a cosmetic fixing up, now took on the proportions of a more extensive restoration.

Enter Roger Smith, a skilled woodworker by avocation, who volunteered to start replacing the rotten wood. But first the car needed to be moved under cover, so the city donated limited space in the semi-heated old car barn in amongst the dump trucks and front-end loaders. The contractor building the new library offered to move the streetcar by trailer to the old barn, but in the process of lifting he failed to use spreader bars on the cables, thereby squeezing the car two inches narrower at the roof than at the bottom.

As rotted wood was removed more rotted wood was discovered and more underneath that, until one end was entirely removed. As windows were removed they fell apart. Then the Breakfast Optimists Club donated its services and carefully disassembled the roof board by board, numbering each end piece for later identification and duplication. Fred Lewis welded angle iron under the vestibule to stop the sag and installed three-inch wide plates along the bottom of the sides, where rust was bulging through. At this point the project was still considered to be a cosmetic restoration.

In 1978 the Junior Women's Club won $1000 in another "Business for Beauty" contest which was added to the pot along with $250 from the Red Garter Bar and $100 from the Calico Questers, a local history group. In August Al Kilminster joined the project after hearing Carol Turner present a slide program to the local historical society. by this time all interior wood had been removed and carefully labeled as to location on the car, one end

was being reassembled and new cherry windows had been fabricated.

As work progressed, Fred Lewis planted the seed of an idea to run the restored car down Mountain Avenue; after all car 21 had run on the last day of service 30 years before, and essentially all the parts were still there. If the Minneapolis Transportation Museum could restore the Como-Harriet line, why couldn't Fort Collins restore part of its trolley system? Discussion among members centered on the logistics of trying such a project, never considering the fact that they had zero background in streetcar operation. Al Dunton made many phone calls to steetcar museums all over the United States to determine the unknowns of such an undertaking.

On April 1, 1980 city council gave approval of the idea to operate the car on Mountain Avenue, and at this point the Fort Collins Municipal Railway Society was formed. The Junior Women's Club continued to provide financial support for car restoration, but any cost that involved operating, such as new air lines, electrical wiring and motor rebuilding was borne by the society or through donations. Subsequent to the council's approval, meetings were organized to familiarize the public with the project. Any concerns were addressed, and some suggestions were incorporated in our construction agreement. On March 17, 1981 after a year of negotiations, a contract was signed between the city and the society. The main features were that no funding would be provided by the city and that the project would be finished by December 31, 1985. How naive we were!

While the politicians were having their way, the restoration took on new dimensions. Seats were removed, rotted floor boards ripped up, wiring harness carefully labeled and removed. With Dan Gornstein's encouragement, air lines were taken out, after first being photographed to show location. The car was placed on cribbing and the truck frame, with motors attached, was eased out from underneath; the motors along with the air compressor were sent to Denver Electric Motor for rebuilding. Axles also were carted off to Denver to have new ends fabricated and turned. As all this was occuring, Roger Smith was on sabbatical leave in Australia. Carol Turner was in a state of shock for fear that the car would never be reassembled correctly.

Gallons of paint stripper were consumed over the next year in removing layer upon layer of paint from window guards, truck frame, miscellaneous metal parts and any reusable cherry wood. Every weekend two roof boards were steam-bent and allowed to cool in a special jig, until all 80 were done.

Planning for the car barn and loading area in the park started in the fall of 1981 and had to be approved by numerous city departments. On weekends Al Dunton

The thoroughness of the car's restoration is clearly evident in this picture and the one at the top of the next page which were taken at the Howes Street barn. (Fort Collins Municipal Railway Society)

was heading up a crew removing 2500 feet of rail, ties and hardware from a defunct railroad at Central City, Colorado. All this had to be hauled back to Fort Collins in borrowed trucks and trailers.

Car 21 was again resembling a streetcar by the spring of 1982. The new maple floor donated by Reed Mill and Lumber was finished, both ends rebuilt, new air lines installed, truck frame reassembled, part of the roof installed, interior wiring strung and motors with axles returned from Denver. Plans for the barn were being finalized and material appropriated for construction. The ground breaking ceremony for the barn, dedicated to the late Chet Watts, the society's first president, took place August 7, 1982.

Tom Dougherty, a local builder, acted as supervising contractor for the barn. He shepherded the volunteers along and aimed people in the right direction for free materials or supplies at cost. Claylite of Denver donated the concrete blocks for the walls, while the Larimer County Voc-Tec masonry students erected the building as a class project under the guidance of Paul Halseide.

According to the original construction schedule signed in 1981, the barn was to be finished and 500 feet of track built by September 1982. It was now March 1983, the barn was not finished and no track had been laid. A new city council had just taken office and some new people moved onto Mountain Avenue. A well-organized and

vocal attack on the trolley project began. Through the use of massive amounts of misinformation delivered door to door the opposition, known as Parkway Preservation Society, was able to get 60% of the Mountain Avenue residents to sign a petition against the project. Canvassing by FCM Ry. Society members showed 25% of the residents against the project. The Parkway Preservation Society, or P.P. as it was known, was to dog the project until completion in August 1986.

A grand parade and celebration on August 21, 1983 marked the transfer of car 21 to the new trolley barn. The car was sufficiently finished and presentable to be rolled onto a trailer and carried down Mountain Avenue. With the new barn we gained much needed space and security. The barn site became the construction area for track panels and was also used for storage of ballast and topsoil.

Then-President Mark Bassett supervised construction during a period when the society was learning track building techniques. According to city contract no more than one intersection (90 feet) or one median (400 feet) could be excavated at any one time. The median was excavated by Virgil Dowell with a backhoe, to about 11 feet wide and 16 inches deep. Next several loads of pea gravel were dumped into the trench and leveled by tractor. A 30-foot track panel, fabricated at the barn, was loaded on two handcars and rolled to end of track, at which

A large crowd turned out on August 21, 1983 to witness No. 21's journey down Mountain Avenue to the new City Park carbarn where the project was to be completed. (Kenneth Jessen photo, Denver Public Library Western History Department)

There should be no doubt in anyone's mind that building railroad track is hard, sweaty, back-straining labor. This group at work on the west end of Mountain Avenue in November 1983 illustrates the dedication and effort of all those people who devoted their free time over many months to see the job brought to a successful conclusion.

point the panel was jacked up and hand cars removed. The panel was then pried to the end of track, into the ditch and bolted to the previous panel. More gravel was added, and the panel was lined, leveled and tamped. Part of the previously removed dirt was spread on top of the ties and sod laid even with the tops of the rails. The first 400 feet of track was built by this method—no wonder the society was behind schedule.

The construction season of 1984 started with the spanning of the Bryant Street irrigation ditch using "I" beams from the original streetcar bridge on the City Park loop. It had been converted to a foot bridge after abandonment in 1951. One afternoon a man strolled into the car barn and asked how he could help. Chuck Hoffman is a jack of all trades; he painted the streetcar, hauled gravel and dirt with his dump trucks, did cement finishing, loaned equipment of all kinds and had many helpful contacts. One of these was with Duane and Darlene Jessen, owners of a front end loader and flat bed trailer. All three individuals did yeoman service loading and hauling track panels, gravel, ties and rails for the duration of the project.

Spring 1984 also brought the opposition out of hibernation to try stopping the project again. Their claim was that the society was in default of the contract since it was

behind schedule. The city council, under pressure, required the society to have the car operational into City Park by December 31, 1984. By this time only 800 of the required 2100 feet of track was finished, no overhead was up, every other bracket arm pole needed to be set, a switch had to be made, the loading area in the park landscaped, rectifier assembled and the car finished. All this would be impossible to do by the end of the year.

Reid Burton was contacted and, either for donation or at reduced rates, heavy equipment appeared on the site. Cement finishers showed up to do intersections, Machaud Electric sent out Jeff Reynolds to hang the overhead and Empire Labs donated the service of Ernie Schmidt with an auger truck to drill holes and set poles. Car restoration crews, some from the Rocky Mountain Railroad Club, worked all weekends plus weekday evenings. Even Thanksgiving and Christmas saw progress in the work. Thank goodness for the warm fall weather.

On Friday, December 28, 1984, at 12:30 PM, after much checking and double checking, Roger Smith powered the car down the track a few feet. For the first time everything worked!

The car operated the next day for two hours providing rides for the city council, the press and members of the society, during which time only two minor problems

Friday, December 29, 1984 was a memorable day for the City of Fort Collins and the Municipal Railway Society. At 12:30 PM, for the first time in 33½ years, an electric trolley was moving under its own power in the streets of a Colorado city. By coincidence it was 77 years to the day since the dedication run of the Denver & Interurban line in Fort Collins. (both; Kenneth Jessen photos, Denver Public Library Western History Department)

arose—a hot journal box bearing and an improperly placed overhead frog. The council was impressed and relieved that the deadline had been met, but the opposition was upset. Therefore, the Parkway Preservationists convinced the council to set a new deadline, August 31, 1986, for the completion of the entire project.

June 2, 1985 saw the beginning of regular streetcar service on that portion of track already built. Passengers boarded at the park, traveled to the barn and back to the park. By the end of the operating season, 9,500 delighted riders had made the short trip. Meanwhile the track department proceeded eastward building 900 feet of track per month. Track panels now were carried four per load on Jessen's flat bed trailer. All ballast was donated by Sterling Gravel and Colorado Lien Company. As the winter of 1985-86 set in, the track department had finished one third of what was needed to complete the project. Poles had been set along the same distance. The opposition, to keep the pressure on, filed suit against the city in another move to halt the project. After a week-long hearing in February, the judge ruled in favor of the project. The next weekend, he and his family rode the streetcar!

March saw the resumption of construction, with overhead getting priority to permit car operation on the new track section. The last 30 of 60 trees were moved in April, while previously moved trees leafed out nicely in their second year. A revision of contruction techniques was made and to be able to finish on schedule, each median needed to be completed in two weeks, or half the previous time. Two track workers were hired full time to work with volunteers Ed Hanson and Jim Stitzel.

Construction progressed smoothly all summer with only one minor interuption when an overlooked irrigation line was ruptured by the front-end loaders, and within a half hour a lake eleven feet wide by 400 feet long formed. The final section of overhead wire was strung on August 17, with dedication ceremonies scheduled on Fort Collins birthday, August 20, 1986. Some past and present city officials were present to take part in the ceremonies, along with police officers looking for possible trouble from the Parkway Preservationists.

The future holds more problems to be resolved. The seven or so people who spent every weekend since 1978 working on the project are taking a breather, trying to put family lives back together, catching up on other hobbies or just leaving town occasionally on vacations. The end of track is 500 feet short of the original goal, blocked by two large power poles which were to be removed several years ago. The society refuses at this time to pay the high price to have them relocated. There is talk by downtown merchants of extending the line 1000 feet to the center of town; however, this would entail crossing the Burlington Northern Railroad mainline which would be very expensive. This contruction would be in concrete streets, also an expensive proposition. A second car may become a necessity to handle the increasing ridership and as a spare. If an accident occurs with car 21 being extensively damaged, the society will lose it only means of earning revenue.

July 4, 1987 saw the little Birney carrying its 30,000th passenger. Watching it travel down the median loaded with happy people gives me a great deal of satisfaction, but would I do it all over again? Probably not, under today's political conditions. To quote Mark Bassett, "Nobody said this was going to be easy."

ACKNOWLEDGMENTS

At the time this history was originally written in the 1950s, the author received help from several individuals. The late R.A. Moorman assisted with interviews and research and provided materials from his collection. Dick Baker, then assistant city manager of Fort Collins, spent many hours going through old records, reading the finished article and offering helpful comments and encouragement.

The late W.H. Edmunds, one-time receiver of the D&I, supplied valuable information. J.O. Beeler, longtime conductor and motorman for the D&I and F.C.M. Ry., gave the writer a wealth of valuable information in several interviews and through his efforts many errors were corrected. Several other employees of the City of Fort Collins were also interviewed.

Clyde Brown, at that time curator of the Pioneer Museum, shared his vast knowledge of the area, being an old resident of the city. Donald Duke, without whose advice and ideas this article could not have been written, gave the writer the idea for the subject matter.

In updating and revising the story for publication in the Colorado Rail Annual, E.J. Haley and F. Hol Wagner, Jr. provided essential material. Al Kilminster supplied valuable bits of information and wrote Chapter III. He was assisted in this task by A.H. Dunton, Roger Smith, Dr. James Stitzel and Wayne Sundberg.

Eight years of effort culminated with the completion of the track, and dedication ceremonies were held at the east end of the line on August 20, 1986. Dr. James Stitzel, one of the many volunteers, presided over the brief speeches and a history of the project. The mayor drove the final spike. It was stressed in the program that the society was giving the city a $2.5 million gift on the 122nd anniversary of the city's founding, an operating electric railway over one-and-a-half miles long, at no cost to the municipal or county governments. A sizeable crowd watched and listened, no detractors made an appearance and it was obvious that most of the city approved whole heartedly of the project.—Robert W. Richardson

ABOUT THE AUTHORS

Michael C. Doty, a native of Colorado Springs, became interested in railroads at an early age. At five he had his first train ride on the *Rocky Mountain Rocket*, to Omaha, thus beginning a long affinity with the Rock Island. He is a director of the Colorado Midland Chaper of the National Railway Historical Society and a member of the Rock Island Technical Society. He also spends much of his spare time working as a volunteer on the Cadillac and Lake City Railway and is editor of a bi-monthly newsletter "The Trackside Report." He and his wife Cheryl often can be found working on one of the C&LC's special excursions.

Edward M. "Mel" McFarland, also is a Colorado Springs native and remembers the *Rocket* as the first train which he rode. Growing up near the Midland Terminal, and later the Rock Island's Roswell Yard, his interest in these railroads continues. The CRI&P played a key role in the stories of through rail traffic at Colorado Springs, included in his previous books, *The Midland Route* and *Cripple Creek Road*. A teacher and artist in addition to being an author, Mel is secretary of the Colorado Midland Chapter of the National Railway Historical Society, director of photographic collections at the Ute Pass Trail Museum and a member of the Rock Island Technical Society and the Pikes Peak Posse of Westerners International.

A native of New Jersey, **Robert A. Le Massena** displayed an early interest in railroads at the age of four. While attending high school, he spent many afternoons riding on Erie engines and learning about steam locomotives from their crews. His senior thesis at Stevens Institute of Technology concerned the calculation of locomotive performance on the Lackawanna Railroad. At Bell Telephone Labs his career was devoted to U.S. Navy radar equipment; meanwhile, he traveled extensively by rail, covering 200 different railroads and some 200,000 miles of trackage. After five railfan vacations in Colorado. Bob moved to Denver in 1948, where he worked for Heiland Research and Minneapolis-Honeywell. During that period he commenced the background work which resulted in ten books and nearly 100 magazine articles about steam locomotives and Colorado's railroad history. His first photography was done with a 6x9 cm camera using cut film; later it was supplemented with 35mm cameras.

Ernest S. Peyton was born in Bronxville, New York, but his family moved to Fort Collins when he was five months old, and he grew up and graduated from high school there in 1947. His career included employment with the U.S. Post Office and on the Colorado & Southern, Union Pacific, Rio Grande, Great Western and Stockton Terminal & Eastern Railroads. He later spent 17 years in sales and then as a vice-president of van line operations. Presently residing in Tempe, Arizona, he is a dealer in postal history and old stock and bond certificates. Ernie's hobby is collecting old railroad annual passes, and he is contemplating a move back to Colorado. Railroading runs in the family; his daughter Anne is art director of *On Track* magazine and grandson Danny has started HO modeling.

Al Kilminster was born in New Jersey along the route of the Delaware Lackawanna & Western. He moved to Colorado in 1957 in order to attend Colorado State University. While in college he discovered narrow gauge steam and has been addicted to it ever since. He worked for eight years on the restoration of Car 21 and is presently employed as a medical photographer at CSU. His hobbies include mountain climbing, skiing, traditional jazz and "poking around southwestern Colorado."